Dutch
Tiles

C. H. de Jonge

Dutch Tiles

translated by P. S. Falla

Praeger Publishers

New York • Washington • London

Published in the United States of America in 1971

Praeger Publishers Inc.
111 Fourth Avenue, New York
N.Y. 10003, U.S.A.
5 Cromwell Place, London SW7, England

Originally published as *Nederlandse Tegels*
© 1971 by Uitgeverij J. H. De Bussy N.V., Amsterdam
Translation © 1971 by Pall Mall Press Limited, London

Library of Congress Catalog Card Number: 70-150699

Printed in the Netherlands

Contents

Preface

I am very glad to have been invited to write this book by Messrs J. H. de Bussy of Amsterdam.

A separate book on Dutch tiles may properly be regarded as a complementary study to my publications *Oud-Nederlandsche Majolica en Delftsch Aardewerk* (Amsterdam, 1947) and *Delfts Aardewerk* (Rotterdam and The Hague, 1965) translated as *Delft Ceramics* (Pall Mall Press, London, 1970).

The tile industry is a popular Dutch art that spread over the whole country without losing its simplicity as regards materials and style. It was not confined to Delft, though the fact that tiles were made there in close connection with ornamental Delftware no doubt gave rise to the misleading but ineradicable habit of referring to 'Delft tiles' as if there were no other kind. The products of Delft were chiefly works of art and objects of practical use; relatively few tiles were made, and those that were, belong to the 'work of art' category. The revival of interest in Delftware in the 1880s contributed to the fact that attention was once more devoted to Dutch tiles in general, not only as a commercial product but for their historical importance. It can but be a source of satisfaction that this interest continues and that it is increasingly lively beyond the frontiers of our country.

The primary object of this study, based on systematic research into a pre-eminently Dutch form of applied art, is to furnish connoisseurs and collectors with a reliable guide. In this connection I should not fail to mention my especial debt to the late Arthur Lane, former Keeper of the Department of Ceramics in the Victoria and Albert Museum, London, for the scientific treatment of the subject which formed the basis of his catalogues and writings ever since the first edition of his *Guide to the Collection of Tiles* at the Museum was published in 1939.

For readers who wish to study the subject further I have provided in Chapter xiv a brief review of the standard literature and a list of tile collections. These include, besides the Rijksmuseum and some foreign collections, almost all the municipal and provincial museums in the Netherlands which have tiles among their exhibits, thus illustrating the special features of local productions.

I owe especial thanks to P. J. Tichelaar of Makkum for providing an account of the technique of manufacturing tiles and placing at my disposal a vast number of unpublished photographs.

I am also most grateful to M. C. van der Hoop, former Director of the Royal Delft pottery De Porceleyne Fles, and to his successor G. J. Geluk, for helpful discussions and advice.

New blue Delft tiles are no longer manufactured at Delft but at Utrecht, in the factory known as the Westraven Faience and Tile-works, formerly Ravesteijn Brothers, and C. de Jong, the director of this establishment, was kind enough to give me full information on the revival of this ancient Utrecht industry. I am also indebted to Mrs A. G. Cazemier-Kammer of Delft and Miss C. A. M. Vlasveld of Voorburg for the secretarial and administrative work that the compilation of such a work requires. I should also certainly have been unable to complete it without the editorial help of Miss L. H. Stegeman and B. F. Heesen. Finally I acknowledge with much gratitude the personal co-operation of the publishers, Messrs J. H. de Bussy, who spared no trouble in assisting me throughout the preparation of the book.

Thanks to the invaluable help of colleagues and friends, enabling me to travel over almost the whole country, I have gained a basic familiarity with the various regional styles, and lively discussion of the material has done much to improve my understanding of the diversity of this typically Dutch art form.

It goes without saying that Professor F. W. Hudig's masterpiece of 1926 and 1933 remains, after nearly forty years, the essential basis of any attempt to give a fresh picture of the tile industry and, above all, the art of tile production in the Netherlands. This is an art of greater significance than can hitherto have been realized, and even now the last word on its range, both at home and abroad, has not yet been spoken.

September 1970   C. H. DE JONGE

I *The tile industry in its relation to Dutch history and culture*

The appearance of an international edition of this book on the Dutch tile industry makes it desirable to recall some facts and events from our national history which made it possible for the art of tile manufacture to reach such a high level in this small country and to expand to a world-wide trade during nearly four centuries.

In the years shortly before 1600, when the tile industry first made its appearance, a distinction was made between the Southern and the Northern Netherlands: on the one hand the Catholic South, governed by the Spanish Habsburgs, on the other the Northern provinces, which for the most part leant towards Protestantism and acknowledged Prince William of Orange as their leader. The breach between North and South took place during the period of hostilities known in history as the Eighty Years' War (1568–1648) and was terminated by the Treaty of Münster. With the help of the Dutch merchant aristocracy, the Union of Utrecht (29 January 1579) laid the foundation for the independent Republic of the United Provinces.

In the preceding years William of Orange had created a solid basis for independence, which was further strengthened by the military talents of his sons, Prince Maurice and Prince Frederick Henry. The economic foundations of the new Republic were laid by the Princes of Orange and the Grand Pensionary Johan van Oldenbarnevelt. In 1609 the Twelve-Year Truce was concluded, in which Spain recognized the independence of the Northern Netherlands. These developments did much to foster the prosperity, self-reliance and distinctive character of the Northern region.

The fall of Antwerp in 1585, followed by the closing of the Scheldt which was by then under Dutch control, is generally regarded as marking the period in which trade and industry began to be diverted from Bruges and Antwerp to Middelburg, Rotterdam, Delft and further inland. Among the Flemish refugees who settled in the Northern Netherlands at this time were innumerable potters and tile-manufacturers, who thus created the beginnings of the Dutch tile industry.

1

In the early Middle Ages earthenware had been produced in the Northern Netherlands, but this bore no resemblance to the polychrome majolica now imported by the Flemings. Before 1600 one can scarcely speak of Dutch ceramics as an independent art, though the transition from decorated floor-tiles to wall-tiles took place at this time. The Flemish polychrome tiles met with an enthusiastic reception and soon took on a distinctive style and decoration. When blue tiles came into use some years later, infinite possibilities were opened up for the production of tiles with portraits, landscapes, Biblical scenes, ships, flowers and ornament of all kinds.

By the end of the sixteenth century the Flemish art of tile manufacture had reached a high standard as the result of many years of development and the influence of Spain and Italy, especially the former; both countries were of course familiar with the ceramic art of the other Mediterranean countries. According to tradition their products were exported to the Southern Netherlands via Majorca, and this is said to be the origin of the term 'majolica'. The tiled floor of the abbey of Herckenrode near Liège (1532) bears witness to co-operation between the Mediterranean lands and Flanders, as does the name of Guido da Savino from Castel Durante.

Although records show that there was contact at an early period between Brussels and Haarlem, it would seem that Rotterdam was the centre from which the spread of the Flemish tile industry was organized. Next to Delft—which occupies a special place owing to the superior quality of 'Delftware' and the artistic imitation of Chinese and Japanese porcelain—Gouda and Utrecht were probably the first cities into which the new industry was introduced. Haarlem passed on the art to Amsterdam, whence in later years it spread widely in the Zaan district of the province of North Holland. Thanks to the personal contacts of Delft and Utrecht tile-makers with Friesland, centres of manufacture sprang up in the northern part of the Netherlands at Bolsward, Harlingen and Makkum, whence the trade routes ran by sea to the northernmost part of North Holland, the West Frisian Islands and Groningen—not to mention, at this stage, foreign export and foreign settlements. Thus from 1650 onwards the industry was established throughout the Netherlands.

The technical achievement of manufacture in the Netherlands was not yet perfected at this time, but the glories of Dutch art provided the model for an infinite variety of subjects and ideas. One has only to think of the importance for tile-decoration of the flowers painted from nature or from botanical works, and the lavish flower-arrangements in Chinese vases.

As the tile-makers became more skilled in their art they were able to depict historical events, sea battles, views of cities and panoramas, some of which rivalled the highly developed standard of contemporary Dutch engraving. One may say, in fact, that the tile-making industry became an art in Holland thanks to Dutch art in other fields. It is not surprising that Dutch tiles became famous throughout the world and were much prized not only in Spain and Portugal but also in Scandinavia, Finland, Poland and Russia, throughout the period from 1650 to 1800.

The revived interest in Dutch tiles was so strong that at the beginning of the twentieth century attempts were made in Holland to build and decorate houses in the style of our forefathers. This, as might have been foreseen, was not a success, for reasons of scale. It is no use trying to repeat the past in the present; one needs to stand back from it in order to see it properly.

Nevertheless a later generation saw the opportunity of reviving the art of blue Dutch tiles by means of an improved and modernized technique, so that they are now widely used in houses, kitchens and public buildings and, with their traditional style of ornament, recall the spirit of past ages without giving the impression of imitation.

One reason for the renewed popularity of this rather naive form of folk art is no doubt that the present century has seen a gradual increase of interest in all forms of applied art, and particularly furniture and ceramics. It was necessary, however, to advance by the successive revival of the Gothic, Renaissance and all the 'Louis' styles, until the *Art Nouveau* or *Jugendstil* put a sharp end to this process around 1900.

The popularity of Dutch tiles at the present time is perhaps also to be explained as representing a search for tranquillity, a reaction against the complications of modern art. The contemplation of contrasts is one way of rediscovering oneself.

Just as the traveller likes to bring back souvenirs of popular art, made by simple craftsmen in earlier ages, so the blue and purple Dutch tiles, among other products, are a reminder of bygone days—and the discerning collector may still have the good fortune to take original specimens home with him. None the less, it is to be regretted that as a result of this trade, thousands of tiles have been removed and sold from country farmsteads and the cellars and kitchens of town mansions.

II From flagstones and flooring-tiles to wall-tiles, c. 1350 to 1600

The North Netherlands majolica, which in the second half of the sixteenth century was influenced by the finer product of the Southern Netherlands, had developed from an indigenous earthenware industry which was not without artistic significance. The excavations carried out since the foundation in 1947 of the State Institute for Archaeological Research at Amersfoort have given us a clear idea of the metal and earthenware objects used from the earliest times by the inhabitants of the Low Countries, both in their religious ceremonies and in their daily life. We thus know much more than we did of the culture of bygone ages. Much importance attaches in this connection to the exhibitions *In kannen en kruiken* (1963), *Symposion Rotterdam* (1966) and the article 'Drie eeuwen drinkgerei'.[1]

Apart from numerous articles that must have been produced throughout the country, we now know for certain that by the fourteenth century there were three established native potteries. The craftsmen of South Limburg exported their wares via England to northern and western Europe. Other centres were at Aardenburg in Dutch Flanders and further east in the Meuse valley at Andenne, so that the North Netherlands were provided with earthenware from three regions.

At this time square flooring-tiles were already in use, both decorated and undecorated. The latter were of red-firing clay, measuring from about 10×10 to 22×22 cm. Others are also found, some of them very small tiles 6 cm. square, in yellow, green, black and brown, covered with a lead glaze. The decorated tiles, which show remarkable progress in the potter's art, came gradually under French influence to be adorned with lines and figures in Gothic style.

Both types of tile are found in great numbers in the capitular churches and their surrounding monastic buildings at Utrecht. The Central Museum in that town contains a room in Gothic style in which may be seen portions of a tiled floor from one such house belonging to the church of St. John. These give a good idea of the elaborate composition of the pattern: besides

4

bands of continuous geometric design there are sections of tiles decorated with fleurs-de-lis, animal figures including dragons, stags and eagles, and a six-pointed rosette, white on a green ground with a black outline.[2]

A fragment of equal importance belongs to a floor laid in Utrecht Cathedral in the middle of the fourteenth century. The fragment measures 78.5 cm. square and was assembled at the time of the restoration of the Cathedral in 1924: it was found under the level of the present floor just before the entrance to the choir.[3] The nine central tiles are the most important. Besides lions rampant, a dragon and lozenges with a quatrefoil pattern, we notice in particular the head of a man wearing a hood and that of a woman with her hair bound in a net in the French fashion (ill. 1a). The colours were painted within the outlines before the lead glaze was applied, so that we have here the earliest example of under-glaze decoration. It has also been technically shown that very light tints were used and the tile of red-firing clay was finished with a thin layer of white-burning clay—the so-called slip technique.

A similar female portrait, but in much better condition, with the same type of hair-net and headband has been found in the tiled floor of the refectory of St. Paul's abbey (ill. 1b).

A more recent excavation in 1956 of the Cistercian convent of Mariendaal at Utrecht produced specimens of fourteenth- and fifteenth-century floor-tiles and fragments, and also of arabesques in early Renaissance style. Dr. J. Renaud has devoted a study to these fragments in which he concludes, from the composition of the material and other evidence, that they form a class apart. He thinks it possible that the tiles may have been manufactured on the spot by travelling craftsmen. Among the most important of the late group is a large tile, 20 cm. square, portraying a monk who, it is thought, may be either St. Bernard, the founder of the Cistercian order, or Theodoric 'known as Kovelwaet', the canon of Oud-Munster and founder of Mariendaal in about 1245 (ill. 1c).[4]

French stylistic influence is shown by a group of early floor-tiles, which became common in the Northern Netherlands in the course of the fourteenth and fifteenth centuries. These are tiles of red-firing clay into which a relief pattern was impressed: this was filled with white slip, levelled and finished off with a lead glaze, giving the decoration a light yellow tint. Netherlands specimens have a double circle or diamond in the centre with the Burgundian flint-and-steel device, or medieval maxims such as *Alle dinc heeft synen tyt* (There is a time for all things) or *Die Tyt is cort—Die doot is snel—Wacht U van Sonden—So doe di wel* (Time is short, death is soon; beware of sin and act righteously.) (ill. 2a).

Floor-tiles inscribed with the date 1556 (ill. 2b) show how long-lived this tradition was, while a set of four tiles—the so-called *viertje*—shows an arrangement of diagonals with sprays of flowers in Renaissance style, bordered by crosses with a leaf pattern which recalls the Gothic type (ill. 2c).

As many examples and fragments of this kind of tile have been found at Gouda, where they are now housed in the De Moriaen Municipal Museum of Pipes and Pottery, it can be assumed that they were manufactured there. Meanwhile the majolica tiles of the Southern Netherlands, made chiefly at Antwerp and Bruges, had become famous. We need only refer in this connection to the specimens found in the floor of Herckenrode abbey near Liège (1532) or the Hampshire mansion The Vyne (1520), which probably come from the same workshop. Square tiles with portraits, clothed in the fashions of 1520, varied with octagonal tiles depicting flower-sprays, combine to form a rich and colourful pattern in light tints of blue, green, orange-brown and yellow.[5]

The surface of medieval floors, whether of flagstones or majolica tiles, has suffered a great deal from wear, and in the case of the tiles particularly, this rapidly destroys their brilliance and design. We may infer that the period of polychrome floor-tiles did not last long and that such tiles soon came to be used instead to decorate walls, especially as the use of brick for building increased steadily.

Polychrome wall-tiles with an interlace pattern of blue, yellow and white originated in Antwerp and were first imitated in Rotterdam about 1600. These motifs are generally referred to as the Hispano-Moresque style, but they rather suggest an Oriental origin under Persian influence, with a style of decoration found in the countries of the Mediterranean seaboard.

Shortly after 1600 a new period began with the appearance of a large quantity of polychrome tiles with varied decoration, initially under the strong influence of south European majolica, then in great vogue. Later these displayed portraits, people and animals in a landscape, pomegranates, fruit and flowers as the main elements of the decoration, while the Hispano-Moresque elements were relegated to the corners. These were executed in dark blue on a white ground, in what are known as 'reserves', a type of decoration brought northwards by Flemish craftsmen at the end of the sixteenth century, when first Haarlem and then Rotterdam became the principal centre of the Dutch tile industry and whence in a few decades it spread to the west and north of the country.

6

Notes

1 *In kannen en kruiken* (In jugs and jars), Boymans-van Beuningen Museum, Rotterdam, with introductory article by A. Bruijn, 'De middeleeuwse potten-bakkerijen van Zuid-Limburg' (The medieval potteries of South Limburg).

The *Symposion Rotterdam* was held simultaneously in the following five museums: the Historical Museum in Rotterdam (*Verborgen Verleden*, The hidden past); the Prins Hendrik Maritime Museum in Rotterdam (*Gekeerd Getij*, Time turned back); the Boymans-van Beuningen Museum ('t Gheduldich Huysraet, Enduring furniture); the Gemeente Archief (*Kastelen in en om Rotterdam*, Castles in and round Rotterdam); and the Schiedam Municipal Museum (*In kannen en kruiken*, II).

The article 'Drie eeuwen drinkgerei' (Drinking vessels through three centuries), also by A. Bruijn, appeared in *Vrienden van de Nederlandse Ceramiek, Mededelingenblad* 36 (September 1964).

2 Utrecht, Central Museum, catalogue of the Historisch Museum der Stad (1928), No. 483. Another portion of this floor is in the Rijksmuseum in Amsterdam. See Hudig, *Altholländische Fliesen*, Part II (1933), Pl. 1b. As the chapter-house of the deanery of St. John's Church was used for a time in 1378 as the episcopal palace it may be, as Hudig thinks, that the tiled floor dates from this period.

3 Nine separate fragments of this floor are preserved in the storeroom of the Central Museum. Together they measure 3 meters long by 1.36 meters wide. See Dr. E. J. Haslinghuis and C. J. A. C. Peeters, 'De Dom van Utrecht' in the series *Nederlandse Monumenten van Geschiedenis en Kunst*, part II: Province of Utrecht, 1st edition; municipality of Utrecht, 2 (1965).

4 Dr. J. Renaud, 'Middeleeuwse vloertegels', in *Vrienden van de Nederlandse Ceramiek*, 12 (July 1958). In the Central Museum catalogue *Keuze uit tien jaar nieuwe aanwinsten, 1951 en 1961* this portrait is incorrectly described under No. 384, ill. 115 as a 'floor-tile representing a horseman in armour, half-length . . . fourteenth century'.

5 Specimens in the Boymans-van Beuningen Museum were acquired by way of exchange, those in the Frisian Museum at Leeuwarden come from the Anjum monastery in North-Eastern Friesland.

7

III *The manufacture of Dutch tiles*

While it is clear from archaeological fragments that tiles, plain or decorated, have for centuries held a firm place in the culture of 'developed' peoples, historians do not tell us much about how they were manufactured. When one hears of any development in the art of tile-making through the ages, it has as a rule no connection with the choice, preparation and treatment of materials, but is nearly always concerned with the decoration of the surface. It is noteworthy that since the majolica technique was described by Abulqasim in 1301 with reference to the making of Persian pottery,[1] the same methods seem in principle to have survived to this day for the manufacture of painted tiles and earthenware.

Previous descriptions of the technique of making the Dutch majolica or faience tiles with which this book is concerned have leant heavily on Paape.[2] It has, however, usually not been observed that when he wrote his account tiles had ceased to be manufactured at Delft, so that he was probably quite ignorant of the specific techniques involved. The word 'tile', in fact, does not even occur in his description.

The reason why he is nevertheless so often quoted is that the 'Delft porcelain' described by him was made by the same majolica or faience technique as our tiles, and often in the same workshops—if not in Delft, probably in Rotterdam and certainly in Friesland. This may be seen at a glance from the tile picture of 1737 (Plate 1) showing a cross-section of the Bolsward factory. But Paape's account cannot be taken as a direct description of the Bolsward picture, which he probably never saw.

In this chapter an attempt is made to describe the making of Dutch painted tiles on the basis of our knowledge, derived from records, recipes and tradition, of the methods of Frisian manufacturers, which accounted for more than half the total Dutch tile production. In cases where methods elsewhere are known to have differed from those used in Friesland, the fact is mentioned. A more detailed description will be found in the work

by Anne Berendsen and others, *Tiles: a general history*,[3] or in the booklet by Tichelaar.[4]

When the majolica technique was introduced into the Northern Netherlands by immigrants from the south at the end of the sixteenth century, the country already possessed a flourishing ceramic industry using the lead glaze technique.

Since the late Middle Ages, makers of red pottery and glazed earthenware—the floor-tiles known as *plavuizen* or *estriken*—had prepared their dried products for firing with a pulp-like mixture of lead-ore and clay. A transparent lead glaze formed in the kiln at 950°, and this could be coloured by the addition of metal oxides.

If a light colour was desired, the product formed from red-firing clay was again treated, after a first firing before the addition of the lead-ore slip, with a slip of yellow or white-firing clay.

It was also possible to use this light-firing slip to make patterns on the red-firing clay, and afterwards apply the transparent lead oxyde glaze.

We may deduce from the volume of their output that these Dutch potters possessed efficient kilns and considerable empirical skill. Given their experience and equipment it cannot have been insuperably difficult for them to adopt the twice-fired, tin enamel majolica process, although doubtless not every attempt was successful. The existence of this ceramic tradition serves to explain the rapid spread of majolica technique in the northern Netherlands in the first half of the seventeenth century.

Since the majolica or faience technique involves two firing processes, a description of the method falls naturally into two parts or phases, each being completed in the kiln:

I	II
Extraction of raw materials	glazing, trimming
preparation of clay mass	splashing
shaping (making, rolling, cutting)	pouncing
drying	painting
first firing	final firing

MATERIALS

The tile factory or *gleibakkerij* was generally located near the place where the clay was found, i.e. the principal ingredient of the required 'mass'. Of the sixty or so factories and workshops engaged in majolica or faience production in the Netherlands, we know that all were situated either west of the line Antwerp—Dordrecht—Gouda—Amsterdam—Staveren—Leeuwarden—Dokkum, or in regions watered by the main rivers. Thus the basic material used was generally alluvial sea or river-clay. This was extracted by hand from the fields or foreshore and transported to the factory by water.

PREPARING THE MASS

In the case of seventeenth-century tiles with a thickness of 1 cm. or more, we know that the colour of the body is red or reddish. Frequently it contained foreign bodies such as coarse sand, or bits of shell, and sometimes streaks of other types of clay that fired yellow instead of red. This points to the fact that the mass from which the tile was made was not washed but merely kneaded before use. We may suppose that such kneading, with or without the addition of water, was the only process to which the clay was subjected to give it plasticity and to ensure the even distribution of moisture. We do not know whether craftsmen at this time used the pug-mills shown in the bottom right-hand corner of the Bolsward picture, but Ottema tells us that this invention was patented and used by the associated Frisian brick-makers. It is noteworthy that Paape knows of no mechanical contrivance for the purpose of kneading, which according to him is done by the 'earth-treader'.

About 1660 there was an important innovation made in preparing the mass, in that local clay was mixed with marl, known from its place of origin as 'Tournai earth', which had a lime content of 30-50 per cent. The purpose of adding marl was to make the product less liable to crack. Apart from this, it had the effect of making the material fire yellow instead of red. Another consequence was the introduction of the process known as 'clay-washing', whereby the raw materials were stirred together in water to form a slurry. This was then sieved and excess water drained into a trough. As the mass still had to be kneaded before use, the pug-mill (or, in Delft, the earth-treader) still had a function to perform.

SHAPING AND DRYING

As the lumps of clay left the pug-mill they were taken to the 'brick-maker's attic' on the second floor (cf. the Bolsward picture). Here they were again thoroughly kneaded and beaten by hand into oblong slabs. These were cut into smaller pieces about 12 cm. square which were placed in the tile-frame. To the right of the picture, on the second level, we see the craftsman with the H-shaped frame, made of wood or iron, in his right hand; with

10

his left he scatters sand on the work-bench to prevent the tile from sticking to it. He then lays the frame on the bench, presses the clay into it and with his right hand takes a levelling stick from a small bucket of water by his side. With this he smooths the clay and removes superfluous pieces so that it exactly fills the frame—the tile is now 'made'.

The frame is then lifted up so that the tile falls out of it. Twelve tiles prepared in this way are laid on a board, and placed on a stand to dry. Between twelve and twenty-four hours later, when they are partially dry, they are arranged in stacks of about thirty and 'put in the corner'. The second man to the right of the kiln is engaged in this operation.

After a suitable interval, perhaps as much as a week, the tiles are rolled. Ten of them are arranged along a lead-covered plank between two long parallel laths, 15 cm. apart. A heavy roller sheathed with copper is run several times backwards and forwards over the laths so that the tiles are brought to the same height as the latter, while losing their previous neatness of shape. The tiles are once again stacked and put in the corner, after which they are cut. For this purpose they are laid separately on the bench and covered with a square board, a chopper being used on each side in turn to cut away any protrusion. To prevent the board from slipping one or more tiny nails are fixed in its corners, and these leave an indentation in the tile. The importance of the tiny holes in dating a tile is generally exaggerated, though they may at times serve to prove the identity of origin of two tiles that appear different.

In the Bolsward picture we may suppose that the man on the left in the second register is rolling tiles, while the man behind him is cutting.

During the days that pass before cutting, the tiles have been gradually losing moisture. After cutting they are stacked for the last time and placed, not in the corner but somewhere in the workroom, and later against the kiln itself, so as to dry out thoroughly.

FIRST FIRING

Tiles that are to be fired for the first time are stacked on the floor of the furnace, while glazed and painted tiles are placed above them. The entire furnace part of the kiln is about two meters wide by four meters long—in some cases it may have been square—with walls about one meter thick. While the furnace is being stoked and cooled, the door to it is walled in with stones and sealed with clay. The floor and vault of the furnace are respectively about 1.50 and 3.50 meters above the factory floor. Vent holes measuring 10 cm. square lead from the vault into the chimney, while slits in the floor provide a draught from the fireplace below.

11

The furnace is stoked for thirty to forty hours to a temperature of about 1000° Centigrade, while cooling takes about three days.

In the middle of the picture we see the kiln as a structure within a building. To the left, at the bottom, a stoker is standing before the stoke-hole; two boys are bringing kindling-wood, and at the top another boy sees to it that the fire is evenly distributed over the vent-holes.

GLAZING

After the tiles are fired they are sorted by ringing and then glazed. Before the actual glazing, dust and loose sand is wiped off and the tiles are then partially saturated with water in the so-called 'baptizing' process.

The 'glazing' consists of covering one side of the tile with liquid glaze so that the moisture sinks into the tile and the solids remain on the surface. In order to apply the liquid, the tile is held over the basin with the front edge pointing obliquely downwards and the glaze is thrown against it twice from a smaller vessel. The glazing soon dries, so that the tiles can once more be stacked in twos.

The solid part of the glaze consists of glass prepared in the potter's workshop; it is fused with tin oxyde and is thus white and almost opaque. After fusion the glaze-mass is broken, crushed to a fine powder and stirred in water to a semi-liquid state. The glaze conceals the coloured body and serves as a white background for the decoration. The use of this coating of white tin-glaze is essential to the majolica or faience technique. The sides of the glazed tiles are then scraped clean with a knife.

PAINTING

The first process performed by the painter is called *pouncing* (from pumice, the powder used). The pouncing pattern is a piece of paper, the size of a tile, in which the outline of the desired figure has been pricked with a needle. The paper is laid on the tile and struck with a small bag containing powdered pumice or charcoal, so that the outline is transferred to the tile (ill. 3a–d). It is then painted over with a fine brush using the pigment known as *trekverf*, outline paint, after which the tints or colours are added.

The pigments, like the glazing, are made of frit which is prepared in the workshop from its ordinary constituents plus colouring metallic oxides; again the resulting substance is ground to powder and applied in a semi-liquid state.

The painters may be seen in the picture (bottom left), in a separate room; it is not clear how many of them there are.

12

After the tile is painted it is fired for a second time at about 1000° C., so that the glaze and pigments are fused together to form a surface. The pigment penetrates the glaze layer to some extent, so that the original sharp line of the brushwork is softened: this feature is characteristic of majolica or faience. Occasionally—and, so far as we know, only in Delft— tiles were fired a third time, at a temperature between 600°–800° C. The object of this firing in the muffle-kiln was to give full effect to colours such as golden and red, which could not stand the higher temperature.

As the tin enamel has a high coefficient of expansion and therefore shrinks considerably on cooling, it is important for the tile to have a similar coefficient. Otherwise crazing will occur in the glaze shortly after firing, and will sooner or later become evident as a result of damp and dirt.

Another cause of cracking is the expansion of the clay due to mineralogical changes caused by moisture. Thus the appearance of cracks in tiles is not simply a result of their age but may be due to various factors.

Modern processes of manufacture have almost driven the majolica tile from the market as far as general use is concerned. It is gratifying, however, that for less everyday purposes these tiles, manufactured by an almost archaic process, have sufficient charm to captivate a small circle of devotees.

PIETER JAN TICHELAAR, MAKKUM

Notes

1 H. Ritter, J. Ruska, F. Sarre and R. Winderlich, 'Orientalische Steinbücher und persische Fayencetechnik', in *Istanbuler Mitteilungen des Archäologischen Instituts des Deutschen Reiches* (1935). German translation of a commentary on a chapter on faience technique written by Abulqasim at Kashan, 1301.
2 Gerrit Paape, *De plateelbakker of Delftsch Aardewerkmaaker* (Dordrecht, 1794).
3 Anne Berendsen and others, *Tiles, a general history* (London, 1967).
4 N.V. Tichelaar, *Makkumer aardewerk* (Makkum, 1961).

IV *Polychrome tiles from before 1600 to c. 1650*

From 1550 onwards Southern Netherlands majolica became increasingly well known in the Northern provinces, and the latter's cruder workmanship was influenced for the better by the quality of Flemish pottery with its elaborate and colourful decoration. Not only trade relations but also historical events—religious strife and above all the sack of Antwerp by the Spaniards in 1585—led to a wholesale migration of Flemish potters to the North Netherlands. After 1600 the production of majolica in Antwerp and Bruges virtually ceased, while, in the North, Flemish influence can be traced far into the seventeenth century.

The study of archives has brought to light the names of numerous craftsmen who settled in the Netherlands during this period and were of importance as tile-makers. We shall discuss them in the context of the towns in which they worked (Rotterdam, Haarlem, Delft, Gouda and Hoorn). Towards 1600 these tile-works began to develop rapidly, both as part of the majolica industry and separately from it. Access to the ports was easy, and from there the goods were transported by river. Rotterdam, in particular, was destined to be in the forefront of the development of the tile industry.

To realize the importance of this it will be desirable first of all to describe the art of tile-making in all its rich variety. We may then discuss the characteristics of different regions and towns and discover what we can about their mutual influences and co-operation.

There are several types of tile decoration; in this field Antwerp was initially predominant. To begin with there are the tiles with Hispano-Moresque motifs, which clearly show the influence of the Far East. They have ornamental compositions of interlacing lines with regular colour-schemes of blue or blue-green, orange-brown and bright yellow: for technical reasons little variation was possible here. White plays an equally important part in the range of colours (the 'reserve technique'). The composition includes lines and circles and also diagonal subdivisions with stylized leaf

14

and flower motifs in octagonal and star patterns. Such tiles may have been manufactured in Rotterdam by Flemish or Antwerp craftsmen.

A pattern of this sort was painted on a single tile in such a way that when four tiles were laid together the corners formed a further pattern (ills. 4, 5a and b, 6a and b). It is the great artistic and architectural merit of this form of wall decoration that any area can be filled with a continuous pattern. In regular arrangements of four or sixteen, the tiles become an integral part of the whole.

Later the Dutch form of the reserve technique emerged, in which flower and leaf patterns, and scalloped borders become the main feature of the composition, while the lines rapidly become more flexible and less severe. Tiles of this kind may have been made in Rotterdam even before 1600. There are patterns with two diagonals crossing on a single tile with the whole decoration in blue, yellow and white (ill. 7a), and also tiles each containing a quarter of the motif, four being needed to complete the pattern. In this type, continuity is still possible from the point of view of wall decoration (ill. 7b and c). The latter of these, with a dark-blue leaf motif and a bright yellow background (ill. 7c), was discovered during the excavations in Rotterdam in 1941 and therefore probably belongs to one of the earliest North Netherlands types.

The reserve technique continued to be used until well into the seventeenth century, though by then it was confined to the corner patterns. A new period thus begins: that of the Dutch style of tilemaking, introduced from Flanders and influenced by the majolica ware of the Mediterranean. A technical difference between Flemish and Dutch tiles at this period is noticeable in the colours and tints, especially orange-brown, which is generally heavier in Flemish tiles.

Italian ceramics had attained a high degree of perfection a century earlier, especially in Florence, Siena, Castel Durante, Urbino, Faenza and Venice. Venice ware is characterized by its deep-blue *foglie* decoration. The French name for majolica, *faïence*, is derived from Faenza, where the art was popularized. For all this Italian influence, Dutch tiles took on a character of their own as regards painting, composition and colouring. Among the oldest polychrome specimens, manufactured before or about 1600 and gradually developing additional variations, we find portraits, human and animal figures in a meadow indicated by a few blades of grass and perhaps a fence, soldiers—Dutch or Saracen—in action, pomegranate or orange motifs, bunches of grapes, bowls of fruit, flowers in Renaissance vases, at a later date exotic flowers, and abstract patterns of all kinds. It is quite impossible to classify all the subjects, such is their variety and infinite range of imaginative composition.

15

For the corners certain motifs remain in use, such as three small white petals or buds reserved on a dark blue ground which can form a simple flower when four tiles are placed together, or more complicated Oriental motifs in so far as they can be fitted round the circle, medallion or scallop, the square or lozenge in the centre of the tile. Such motifs are carefully copied from earlier specimens. In the seventeenth century the reserve technique gradually went out of use, a natural consequence of the introduction of blue tiles. Instead we find a much greater variety of blue corner-patterns, which are completely detached from the main composition (see Chapter VI, below, and the illustrations of the principal corner-patterns on p. 38).

PORTRAIT TILES

Continuing an Italo-Flemish tradition, North Netherlands portrait tiles form an early group and are very rare. Bolognese floor-tiles with portraits have survived, and there are also many portraits on the *albarelli* (apothecaries' jars) which, in their traditional form, found their way northward in the sixteenth century, as did portraits on ornamental dishes.

The link between Italy and the Southern Netherlands is illustrated by a tiled floor commissioned in 1532 by the abbess of Herckenrode, and displaying busts, mostly in profile, in a blue and yellow circle, sometimes surrounded by a cable in the Faenza style. The persons depicted are figures of classical antiquity, Oriental rulers, mythological and historical personages—this, at least, is usually the case in Italian tiles, but the Antwerp craftsmen, as the Herckenrode example shows, came by degrees to specialize in portraits of contemporaries, a tradition adopted by the Northern Netherlands.

Some portraits in Italo-Flemish style may have been executed by an Antwerp pottery-painter at Rotterdam: the style of their costume with the man's small cap and woman's head-cloth preceded the late sixteenth-century fashion with the heavy broad-brimmed hat, doublet and Spanish ruff. Men's portraits in lozenge-shaped frames, with reserve patterns in the corners, may also be dated by their costume. Apart from the large linen ruffs, a high-crowned toque was in fashion from 1585 to the beginning of the next century, after which the Dutch style was characterized by a large low-crowned hat with a soft brim, and the Italian, by a dashing broad-brimmed style (ill. 8a–f).

In 1968 polychrome portrait tiles of this kind were discovered in a cellar near the Nieuwe Kerk in Delft: it remains an open question whether they were manufactured there or whether we should assume that the potteries

16

traded with one another. One gets the impression that women's portraits on Dutch tiles were more common than men's, but this may be due to chance survival. We may definitely assign to this period a particular type of female portrait, usually in profile but somewhat later, in three-quarter face, in a plain medallion with white rosettes in the corners. The costume precisely portrays the fashion of just before 1600: a long cloak with shoulder-rolls over the bodice and skirt, of which little is seen, and a huge linen ruff. The most important feature, however, is the hair-style. Towards 1600 the hair was puffed at the sides and combed back, and the plain head-dress replaced by an arched cap trimmed with lace, more in the style of a diadem. This type of portrait is thought to represent the usual North Netherlands style of dress prior, for example, to the portraits of Amsterdam merchant princes, which as early as 1587 had a stiffer and more severe, Spanish look (ill. 9a,b,c).[1]

Finally there is a group of portraits in quite a different style, derived from models that have not come to light but which presumably were Italian. These are profiles of men, facing either right or left, the younger of whom look as if they were wearing wigs. The portrait is finished by a carelessly painted piece of drapery at the neck (ill. 10a). Two tiles exist which show, in a similar setting, winged cherubim seen full-face. All the tiles of this series have a scalloped border and a fretted corner-design in which, as in the medallion, we are struck by the motif carried out in loose linear fashion, blue on white. All this suggests an imitation of Chinese models (cf. the similarly-framed bird and flower-vase tiles, ills. 14c and 20b). The series is thought to date from about the mid-seventeenth century; there must have been earlier examples in the same manner, as is shown by a tile in the Frisian Museum at Leeuwarden, with medallion and a corner-design of white flowers.

Special mention should be made of certain tiles belonging to a series of thirty small portraits, 9.5 cm. square, which came to light in an English sale in 1962. Some of them are now in the Tile Museum at Otterlo or in private collections. Their origin and date is not yet known for certain, nor is the identity of the persons concerned, although the studies of A. Dorgelo and J. van Loo have thrown much light on the question.[2]

Dorgelo called attention in his article to similar small portrait tiles whose subjects he identified as Queen Elizabeth I of England, the Regent Margaret of Parma and the Sultan Suleiman; in a postscript he mentioned the resemblance to the tiles in the advertised English sale. Later, in 1965, Van Loo devoted a study to this collection with interesting results. The English collection comprised two types of tile: the subjects were represented in a three-coloured circle or cable medallion with reserved corner-patterns or with orange-yellow vertical stripes with dark-blue dots in the middle.

The last of these arrangements, which occur in no fixed order, bears a vague resemblance to the Herckenrode floor-tiles of 1532. Apart from this the tiles of the first group show delicate wisps of blue cloud, while the others suggest a landscape with some vegetation. Both types display the usual majolica colour-range: only one tile is entirely blue. As Dorgelo rightly observed, there is no reason to suppose a Flemish or Antwerp origin, in view of the war situation and the Dutch-English alliance. Van Loo discovered that some of these portrait busts were taken from a book published in Amsterdam in 1608 and entitled *Historische Beschrijvinghe ende Afbeeldinghe der Voornaamste Hooft Ketteren so vande Catholijcke ende Christelicke Kercke gelijck als Swermers ende dwaelgeesten verbannen ende verworpen sijn, haer leer, leven, begin ende eynde int cort beschreven* (An historical description, with portraits, of the principal arch-heretics who have been banned and cast out from the Catholic and Christian Church as fanatical spirits and instigators of error: their teachings, lives, beginning and end set forth in a short compass): this was published by Christoffel van Sichem, the engraver, at his establishment *Inde Seylende Windt-Waghen*. It depicts seventeen persons in half or three-quarter length, together with full biographies. The engravings may be by either Christoffel van Sichem senior (1546–1625) or his son of the same name (1581–1658), as they signed in the same fashion.

Among the Dutch Anabaptists, portraits are now known of Johan Mathys van Haerlem (ill. 10b), Jan Beuckelsz. van Leyden (ill. 10c) and others. Altogether the above-mentioned article covers eight portraits out of the seventeen identified figures. In the Van Loo collection the framing and corner-design is different and the portraits face left. The tiles may be copied from Van Sichem's book, but separate engravings are also found, including some of Mohammed and the Turkish Sultan. In any case the tiles must have been produced about 1608, probably in a North Netherlands workshop.[3]

Besides the English collection some specimens have been found in Amsterdam, among other places in the IJ river, the Vijzelstraat and near the Waterlooplein.

After a decade or so the circle and medallion tiles were regularly made in Holland, lending themselves equally well to the portrayal of full-length figures, soldiers and huntsmen. By degrees less attention was paid to the setting, but the same themes persisted.

PEOPLE AND ANIMALS

Tiles depicting people and animals became very popular; they were often shown in a lozenge with reserved corner-patterns. They are generally classed as Rotterdam tiles, but as the tile industry spread throughout the country by about 1635 it is safe to suppose that they were also made elsewhere, for example at Harlingen which was in close contact with Delft (ill. 12a,b). There is a well-preserved set of 25 tiles depicting a variety of subjects. This set is of exceptional quality, especially in the carefully stylized leaf ornamentation in the corners, and is indeed one of the finest specimens of the Dutch tile-maker's art (ill. 11).

Books on exotic fauna must have served as examples for the animal tiles. In medallions with white flowers in the corners we find eagles, camels, elephants, monkeys, sea-monsters and dogs, as well as swans sailing proudly through reedy waters (ill. 12c–f). A varied blue and white corner motif bears witness to the painter's imagination but may indicate a somewhat later date, as in the case of the rabbit in the ornamented medallion with leafy sprigs around it (ill. 13d). There seems to have been a pronounced liking for elephants, both in blue and in polychrome (ill. 13b,c). Another tile of great artistic value represents a peacock standing on a fence and displaying its tail (ill. 13a).

Special mention should be made of tiles depicting birds with varied plumage, butterflies and insects (ill. 14a,b). To some extent we have detailed information concerning their origin. Again Rotterdam was first in the field, but records show that a factory was founded from Rotterdam at Gouda, which remained celebrated until after 1725 owing to the work of Willem van der Swaen (d. 1659) and his family. It was noted for birds, vases of flowers and copies of the stained-glass windows in St. John's church at Gouda, as well as tiles advertising the factory itself. The birds shown here (ill. 14c) appear from their workmanship to have been made at Makkum, according to Tichelaar, in which case they must date from after 1650 (see Chapter VII below).

FRUIT AND FLOWERS

Pomegranates, grapes and tulips. A new group, perhaps in imitation of Italian models, is characterized by the pomegranate motif. These fruits are referred to in a Rotterdam inventory of 1603 as 'orange apples', perhaps a symbolic reference to the leadership of the House of Orange in the war against Spain.

In this case the design probably began with the single tile: a simple diagonal arrangement of two bunches of grapes and two bursting pomegranates, radiating out from an eight-petalled flower in the centre (ill. 16a). A somewhat richer design shows an eight-pointed star with four pomegranates around it and tulips pointing into each of the corners, surrounded by grapes (ill. 16b). The splendid effect of this arrangement is shown by a set of tiles in similar style in the Rijksmuseum, which completely fulfils its architectural role as a wall decoration (ill. 15).

An intermediate style is found in a set of four tiles forming a quadrilobe in which pomegranates alternate with marigolds and the corners of the pattern are still in reserve technique (ill. 16c). The continued use of Hispano-Moresque motifs is also clearly seen in the upper half of an especially fine set of four tiles with similar ornamentation (ill. 17a).

Finally, in the old tradition, a single burst pomegranate, yellow or orange, appears as a still life on a green leaf within a circle, with white flowers reserved in the corners of the design (ill. 16e,f). Another imaginative composition shows a bunch of grapes placed diagonally and pointing to a burst pomegranate, with leaves to either side of it (ill. 16d).

An especially novel and characteristic design shows three pomegranates on a single stem within a quatrefoil, with delicate sprays of foliage in the corners: a later version of this dates from 1650 or later (ill. 17b).

BOWLS OF FRUIT

It is fairly obvious that the polychrome sets of tiles depicting fruit-bowls arose from an arrangement of pomegranates and bunches of grapes, but the Renaissance style of the bowls is a new feature, both in table-ware and on tiles (ill. 18a,b). As a self-contained picture is thus formed, the corners lose their complementary function and cease to have any connection with the principal motif. They are replaced by independent motifs in blue such as the fleur-de-lis, the 'ox-head' and the 'spider', or a variety of leaf and flower designs (see the table of corner designs in Chapter VI, below.) This evolution became complete at the time when polychrome flower and 'flower-vase' tiles were fashionable.

FLOWER-VASES AND FLOWERS

Flower-tiles play a predominant part in the development of Dutch polychrome tile-painting to its full perfection after 1600. In ten years or so this branch of the art developed with extraordinary variety, and its predominance continued for many decades. It falls into two phases: the first, deriving from the Italian Renaissance, is followed by a completely new approach rooted firmly in native Dutch culture.

In the first form the flowers are generally displayed in a ribbed vase with two handles: old inventories refer to this type as 'flower-pot' tiles, which is not in fact correct. The flowers are marigolds and marsh-mallows, sometimes enclosed in a quadrilobe; in groups of four tiles the corners form a star-like flower motif in a circular border, but the vase of flowers remains the chief feature (ill. 19a,b).

A show-piece of this type, consisting of twelve tiles surrounded by a pattern of flower-tendrils, is the sign of the Three Flower-vases which belonged to a seedsman in Gorinchem. This tile picture, now in the Victoria and Albert Museum in London, shows three Renaissance vases containing different flowers, and above them to either side the arms of Gorinchem and the van Arkel family. It is probably the work of the potter Anthoni de Hooch, who had an interest in the *porceleynhuis* established in Rotterdam by Lambert de Hooch in 1614, where the glass-painter Claes Jansz. Wijtmans also learnt the potter's art. Anthoni de Hooch bought the pottery in 1616 and transferred it to Wijtmans in 1619. The latter's son Jacob afterwards settled in Gorinchem and was a master-potter there in 1633. The coats of arms help to date the picture: Jonkheer Roelof van Arkel was high bailiff and dike-reeve of Gorinchem from 1605 to 1616, Gorinchem being the capital of his sovereign territory, the 'land van Arkel'. It is thus possible that Anthoni de Hooch made the sign, or commissioned it, in the year he became the owner of the pottery there.

Inventories of 1611 and 1620 describing Delft pottery also mention round and square 'flower-pots, flower-pots in lozenge frames, round flower-pots, single marigolds' etc., which must refer to tiles of this type.

One of the most exquisite examples of this style, showing a richly-coloured bouquet in an oval medallion, is a set of four tiles surrounded by Renaissance motifs of leaves and volutes, probably dating from about 1625 or later, and deriving from the typical Antwerp style of decoration practised in the mid-sixteenth century under Cornelis Florisz (ill. 19b).

Shortly after 1600, in contrast to the flower-vases, we find a wealth of flower designs of quite a different origin. These are based on the *Flora* which began to be published at this time, with short explanations designed to encourage the study and cultivation of European and overseas plants. One of these works was the *Hortus Floridus* of Crispijn van de Passe, published at Arnhem in 1614 and, in the same year, in Utrecht in a Dutch translation entitled *Den Blomhof*. Every shade and detail is shown in its splendid hand-coloured copper engravings (ill. 31). There were also herbals, among them that of Carolus Clusius (Carel van der Sluys, 1525–1609) and 'tulip books' dating from the time of the tulip mania of 1636–7. These works contain watercolours of flowers painted from life on loose sheets of paper or copies of similar paintings. Artists such as Judith Leijster of Haarlem or Jacob Marrellus of Utrecht co-operated in their production.

Once in a way a medallion or lozenge is still used as a frame, but in general the flower naturally draws attention to itself as the dominant motif, though small blue corner-patterns maintain themselves in many variations throughout the seventeenth and eighteenth centuries.

The Dutch tulip tile is by far the most important, though various other flowers such as columbines, fritillaries, violets, poppies and the crown imperial were copied from the European *Flora*. Two types of design may be distinguished: a stylized plant with three bulbs and leaves (ill. 52), or a single flower emphasizing a particular type of bloom (ill. 20a,b). All the different flowers are shown rising from a patch of earth, later sometimes represented by an ornamental volute. The main object was to depict the flowers faithfully, and accordingly the tiles may still be regarded as poly-chrome despite the blue corners. Occasionally small flowers are shown in a square with notched corners, in which case they certainly belong to the late seventeenth century (cf. ill. 53a,b).

There is, on the other hand, a very rare design dating from early in the century in which pale pink tulips are depicted in natural size on two tiles arranged vertically. The flowers, on a stem with two shaded leaves, are painted in a lifelike style against a clear white background. These tiles, freely copied from an engraving by Crispijn van de Passe, were discovered in a cellar in Hoorn, and there is every reason to suppose that they were made there (ill. 36).

It was not only the wealth of elegant and colourful flower tiles that raised the art of Dutch tile-making to such a high level before 1650, but also the skill, ingenuity and imagination of the tile-painters and engravers. This may be seen from some of the compositions with vases of flowers, or from the single blooms—pinks, buttercups, irises and so on—combined with blue corner-patterns of oak-leaves, buds and sprays, which may be regarded as a transitional form between flowers and ornamental tiles (ill. 21a–e). One of the most remarkable designs may be of English origin; it is composed of the Tudor rose, the Scotch thistle and the Irish harp (ill. 21f).

ORNAMENTAL TILES

This is a less clearly definable group. Among traditional patterns are the chess-board motif, which already occurs in Italian majolica, and the fleur-de-lis in alternate dark blue and orange, which, as a Burgundian emblem, formed part of the ornamentation of French tiles from the thirteenth century onwards (ill. 22a,b). One finds the Hispano-Moresque style, with its Oriental pattern of intertwined and criss-crossing lines, in free adaptation and alternating with flowers (ill. 22c,d). An arrangement of rhomboids, orange and blue on a white background, with a four-petalled flower on the white surfaces, produces a perfect three-dimensional illusion (ill. 22e), and no doubt there were many other compositions of this sort. A medallion tile with traditional small white flowers in the corners bears a family coat of arms and the date 1619; this is presumed to have been made to order, but as the arms have not been identified we know nothing more of its origin (ill. 23a).

The tradition of quadrilobe and octagonal compositions was also maintained, the central rosette taking the form of a wheel with eight or sixteen spokes. The corners are sometimes painted with cognate leaf motifs; in some cases one corner is blue on reserved white, the other polychrome. All this points to a tradition persisting over a long period (ill. 23c,d).

Another abstract composition uses an octagonal yellow star on a blue ground, surrounded by four rectangles placed slantwise: these are in sgraffito technique, the pattern being produced by scratching away some of the surface layer. The same ornamentation is seen on the majolica plate made in 1623 by the Rotterdam craftsman Elias Jaspersz. and depicting a horse and rider jumping (Boymans-van Beuningen Museum). Four tiles are required to complete the pattern formed by the corner rosettes, a fact which points to a date in the second quarter of the seventeenth century (ill. 23e).

A stylized reminiscence of the marigold vases is also met with. The original corner-designs together form an eight-pointed star, reserved on a dark blue ground, which dominates the whole picture (ill. 24a); the date is about 1625. Another novel composition of this date consists of four tiles with the corner motifs forming a rosette of sixteen points in a scalloped surround. The four symmetrical bulbous plants around the rosettes are identified as artichokes (ill. 24b).

Reviewing the period of less than fifty years during which polychrome tiles were in their heyday, we should realize what an important architectural function they performed, especially at the outset, in Dutch houses, and how the introduction of blue tiles—with fleurs-de-lis and other flowers, branches of foliage and the small motifs in the corners we know as 'ox-heads' and 'spiders'—meant that this function of surface decoration was gradually lost and finally disappeared altogether. From 1650 onwards the production of blue tiles spread throughout the Netherlands as a true folk art; by the eighteenth century, the tiles were internationally renowned and became a commodity for world-wide commerce.

Notes

1 J. H. der Kinderen-Besier, *Mode-Metamorphosen. De Kleedij onzer voorouders in de zestiende eeuw* (1933), pp. 221 ff.

2 Alex Dorgelo, 'Enkele bijzondere majolica tegels met portretbusten', in *Vrienden van de Nederlandse Ceramiek*, 27 (June 1962).

   J. van Loo, 'Over een aantal kleine portret-tegels en de herkomst van de voorstellingen hierop', *id.*, 39, June 1965.

3 In agreement with the collector G. de Goederen of Woerden, who considers a Flemish origin more probable, Dorgelo's reasons for holding this view are as follows:

   The tiles show the same colours as those of Herckenrode.

   One tile of each type has the same corner-design as the middle pieces of the Herckenrode tiles, and also has a cable surround. As far as we know, neither type of corner-design occurs on any Dutch tile.

   The clay in both types is exactly like that of the circular central tiles of the inlaid floor of the Nassau castle at Breda. It cuts easily with a knife and produces the same fine-grained, light-yellow pieces. The colours, too, are the same as those of the round tiles.

   Before the English sale, three pieces were found in Holland; however, all three have a corner-design consisting of a polylobed leaf motif. The type with the Herckenrode corners was quite unknown in Holland.

   The Antwerp potters Jasper Andries and Jacob Jansen migrated to Norwich and were established in London by 1570. The tiles in question may have been made by them.

   Most of the portraits represent persons who lived in the first half of the sixteenth century. As many portrait engravings were made in the sixteenth century, these may clearly have been used for the tiles. The portrait reproductions by Chr. van Sichem are not new in the sense that a portrait of the person in question was never made before: they are copied from earlier portraits. It does not necessarily follow from the above that the tile portraits were made from Van Sichem's engravings. The conclusion is rather that they were made in the sixteenth century.

II

V   *The polychrome tile industry in Rotterdam, Haarlem,*
Delft, Gouda and Hoorn, from before 1600 to c. 1650

The North Netherlands tile industry began in Rotterdam about 1590. In that year and subsequently, inventories of bequests in the Court of Chancery there speak of *tayljoor-schilders* or painters of majolica dishes. In 1603 and 1609 we hear of tiles decorated with 'orange apples', but also of a delivery of 'two hundred plain painted tiles', as Hoynck van Papendrecht mentions in describing the development of the trade (op. cit., pp. 35 ff.). He also gives the names of several owners of potteries. Although this tells us nothing about the nature of their product, it is of historical interest to learn that Harmen Pietersz. of Haarlem, described as a *Galeyse Plateelbacker*, settled in Delft in 1602 and in 1611 is mentioned at the head of the list of members of the Guild of St. Luke. He founded a family of potters and tile-makers whom we may trace through three generations. One of his sons, Pieter Harmensz., moved to Rotterdam and established a pottery there in 1612: he adopted the surname of Valckenhoff.

One of the best-known figures in Rotterdam must have been Hendrick Gerritsz. van den Heuvel, who in 1611 became the owner of the pottery De Bergh Syon (Mount Zion) in the Hoogstraat.[1] He also went to Gouda and Harlingen to found potteries there.

Claes Jansz. Wijtmans, who is mentioned in 1614 as the owner of a pottery in Rotterdam, received permission from the Town Council of Utrecht in 1629 to exercise his profession there. Such facts as these illustrate the connections that existed between establishments in different cities.

One of the earliest works testifying to a Rotterdam origin is the important polychrome tile picture, *In Duysent Vreesen* (Amid a thousand terrors), measuring 6 tiles by 5, now in the Historical Museum there (ill. 25). It originally adorned the façade of a house on the Marktveld, later known as the Grote Markt, on the corner of the Hang Nz. The house was demolished in 1895, but a painting of 1860, also in the Museum, shows it as it originally was. A study of records has revealed that tiles were sold in the house. A separate tile bears the date 1594. The theme of the picture was regarded as historical by Hoynck van Papendrecht, but G. de Goederen is certainly right in interpreting it in the light of texts of the Old and New Testament: the Lamb, signifying Christ and the way to God, stands in front of the Burning Bush from which God spoke to Moses. In the foreground is the spring with the Water of Life, and to either side are trees with foliage and fruit. The two warriors represent the nations of the earth, and the animals signify the reign of peace promised by the Messiah.[2] In addition, the present author's studies have brought to light that the inscription *In Duysent Vreesen* has no relation to the picture and was not originally meant for it. The row of tiles bearing these words was added subsequently, and the bottom corners do not exactly match the border surrounding the picture. The tiles were painted by a Flemish potter who is said to have settled in Rotterdam at the end of the sixteenth century. A point which in my opinion still requires clarification is whether the tile dated 1594 really belongs to the house and also to the picture.

The earliest types of polychrome Dutch tiles described in Chapter IX were perhaps originally manufactured in Haarlem and Rotterdam, though the art began to spread to other cities even before 1620.

Some types, on the other hand, continued to be restricted to Rotterdam. Among these were the distinct category of polychrome tiles known as 'Turkish soldiers' or 'Saracens'. These are depicted in martial style in all kinds of battle attitudes, with sword and shield, bow and arrow, lance or cudgel, in fluttering coats with heavy sashes, with a turban or helmet as headgear (ill. 26). The style is mannerist, with impetuous lines and contours; touches of orange-brown and sometimes green fill in the space between the dark-blue lines, as in a sketch. The figures always cover the whole area of the tile, so that there is no corner decoration. Although many specimens have been discovered during excavations in Rotterdam we know nothing for certain about the provenance of these tiles, by whom they were painted or from what engravings they were made.[3]

'Kidney-tiles', an incorrect and inappropriate term, were also produced in Rotterdam. In this type of composition the reserve technique is still perceptible in the corners, and the complete pattern appears in a set of four as a rich and colourful design of geometrical or plant forms. The stylized oval leaves may be alternately green or a strong blue-green. In the spring of 1968, during the building of the Rotterdam Underground, a cellar wall of these tiles was found in the old city (ill. 27).

A third type depicts sea-monsters, nereids and tritons. These have long been regarded as peculiar to Rotterdam, a view confirmed by excavations after the Second World War. The earliest myths and legends, as well as the fine arts, feature sea-monsters, sirens and other fabulous creatures, and it is natural that in a sea port like Rotterdam this folklore should find expression in tile-painting. It occurs not only on single tiles, but in rows forming a frieze (ill. 28a). Nereids, mermen and tritons, standing on a shell or riding upon a dolphin, alternate with cupids or the goddess of Fortune, who stands on a shell drawn across the water by hippocamps, dolphins or a scorpion. Only a few tile-painters chose these subjects, which they often treated in a mannerist style. This is typified by the treatment of waves: the horizon may appear as a stiff and straight line over rippling waters, or the billows may rise up to form a triangle with the figure standing on its apex. It would seem that these imaginative marine pictures represented the most difficult challenge to the tile painters; the figures and their attributes are probably taken from Italian prints. The colours consist of light tints of sea-green and greyish-blue, yellow and orange-brown (ill. 28b–e). Apart from polychrome, sets of blue tiles in this manner are found as late as the eighteenth century.

Finally, two polychrome tile pictures belong to the Rotterdam industry, one of which bears the monogram c vi or ci v and the date 1647. These display Renaissance vases full of all kinds of flowers, and recall the paintings of the Bosschaerts, father and son, and their contemporary Roelant Saverij. The undated picture (7 × 3 tiles) was formerly in a house in the Hoogstraat in Rotterdam and is now in the Historical Museum there; the other is in the Evenepoel collection in the Musées Royaux d'Art et d'Histoire in Brussels (ill. 29a,b). The vases are not beautiful, and there is an evident relation in the choice, composition and painting of the lilies, tulips and fritillaries, though there are also differences. The Rotterdam picture was restored as early as the eighteenth century and Hoynck van Papendrecht also made some alterations to it, so that the original form has rather suffered. The Brussels specimen is ascribed by J. Helbig to the same tile-painter; the monogram is unidentified. We can thus only conclude that the pottery-painter 'c vi', who migrated from Antwerp to Rotterdam, was still active in 1647.[4]

HAARLEM

Haarlem was another city in which potters from the Southern Netherlands took refuge from an early date. They came in contact there with painters who were influenced by the Italo-Flemish mannerist style: Carel van Mander's *Schilderboeck* has proved an important source in this connection. Van Mander tells us of Cornelis Vroom, 'who took to the art of making pottery or porcelain, and being skilled in drawing he achieved wonders.' His son Hendrick (1568–1640) travelled in Spain and Italy, supporting himself by pottery-painting, and returned to Haarlem in 1596. A large number of names and facts, documenting Van Mander's account, were assembled by A. van der Willigen in 1866.[5] But the most important contribution has been made by the research and discoveries of our own time, which have brought to light specimens of pottery illustrating what was previously known only from documents.

The following data are of importance for the tile industry. In 1572 we hear of a *gheleyseplateelbacker*, a maker of glazed pottery, named Adriaen Bogaert, presumably related to Jan Bogaert who is recorded in the *Liggeren*, or Ledgers at Antwerp from 1567 to 1575. In the Musées Royaux in Brussels there is a vase by this artist, ornamented with grotesques and dated 1562, that is an acknowledged masterpiece.

In 1598 Cornelisz. Lubbersz., a *gheleyerspotbacker* at Haarlem, sold his house to Hans Barnaert Vierleger, a potter from Antwerp who is also mentioned in the *Liggeren*.

These Flemish craftsmen are mentioned here in particular because in the Huis Lambert van Meerten Museum in Delft and the Rijksmuseum in Amsterdam there are a few tile pictures bearing the monograms and dates IB 1570 and HBV 1606. The latter group are taken from engravings by the Haarlem artist Maerten van Heemskerck. The Delft pictures, which are fragmentary, represent the Prodigal Son (as does one of those in Amsterdam) and the Stoning of the Elders from the tale of Susanna. Although the original state of these rare pictures has been somewhat spoilt by restoration, they are of great importance as works of the transition between the South and North Netherlands. Eight pictures of Biblical scenes after Maerten van Heemskerck, also heavily restored, are in the Van Achterbergh collection at Amstelveen.

An especially important documented contribution to our knowledge of the Haarlem tile industry has been made by Dingeman Korf.[6] Innumerable fragments excavated in the city and its surroundings have shown that Haarlem played an important part in the growth of the Dutch tile industry from the very beginning. The relationship and co-operation with the Delft potteries should also be mentioned here in connection with the increasing production of the majolica to which Korf gives the name of 'proto-Delftware'—though in my view we should not think of this majolica as being made before the Delft type of faience, but simultaneously with it. It appears that towards 1650 the 'transitional' majolica-ware was no longer made on triangular clay wedges but in saggers. In the following decades, when Delft pottery reached its peak, the importance of Haarlem began to fade and many of its craftsmen sought their fortune anew in the Delft factories.

Apart from the best-known of the early polychrome types of tile: the chess-board motif, pomegranates, flower-vases and geometrical ornaments which, as we have seen, might be made in Rotterdam, Gouda or Haarlem, particular types may be distinguished which are peculiar to Haarlem, or at any rate are so regarded.

The recent study of the Haarlem excavations has thrown more light on the origin of two kinds of tile which show a decorative affinity with Italian ceramics, a fact not surprising in the light of what Van Mander tells us. This is the leaf motif, half blue and half white, which often occurs as a decoration of majolica plates, apothecaries' jars and tiles. Piccolpasso, in his standard work *Li tre Libri dell'Arte del Vasaio* (1545), calls it a *foglie* (leaf) design of Venetian origin. In tiles it occurs in two variations only: the leaves are wreathed about a small medallion containing the winged head of a cherub in blue and orange; in a set of four the corners form an eight-leaved rosette, also enclosed in a circle (ill. 30); in the so-called 'mirror tile', the leaves are enclosed in a wide square frame with a narrow notched outer border. These tiles are always blue.

Another Haarlem design derived from Italy consists of a medallion with delicate spiral and leaf motifs, also known as 'aigrettes', with the corner designs touching them: they are finely drawn and light blue in colour, but with notable variations in the shade and quality of the blue. In the centre there is always a very small animal figure, perhaps a hart, a dog or a hare (ill. 31a,b).

While the place of discovery is certainly some indication of the origin of these or other ornamental tiles, one should also take note of the colouring. This applies to the combination of blue with orange or brownish-yellow and also the blue tiles in these closely-related groups, for the Haarlem factories were not the only ones to decorate tiles with small animal figures of this kind; Rotterdam made these in blue, as was shown by excavations there in 1942. There is also a wreath of ears of corn which alternate with tulips to produce a new and pleasing effect. The corners are decorated with 'spiders', though there was really not enough room for these and they point to a later date (ill. 31c,d). The tradition of small animal figures persisted for a long time, as we see from the tile decoration in the cellars at Het Loo, where they still occur in about 1700 in a wide blue octagonal frame and may well be of Delft origin.

Finally, though again with caution, we may assign to Haarlem the blue composition with diagonal stylized fleurs-de-lis with sprigs pointing inward from the corners; the side of the tile shows one half of a six-petalled flower. This probably dates from the second quarter of the seventeenth century (ill. 31f).

We mentioned the relationship between Haarlem and Delft in connection with the marriage of Harmen Pietersz. of Haarlem in the latter city in 1584. In 1602 he is referred to there as a *gheleyseplateelbacker* and in 1611 he became a member of the Guild of St. Luke. It also appears from a Delft inventory that both pottery and tiles were sometimes made in a single factory. This was the case with a Frenchman named Pouwels Bourseth (d. 1620), who probably came from Rouen, as he gave the name of that city to his pottery in the Oosteinde at Delft. In those days French pottery as well as Italian was much sought by the well-to-do. Hoynck van Papendrecht found in Rotterdam inventories many 'Rouen jugs' (1603), and 'Rouen bowls, ewers, pitchers, flower-pots, dishes and platters' as late as 1647. Pouwels Bourseth, who was already recorded as a citizen of Delft in 1602, possessed, according to an inventory of 1605, 'seventy-five fine tulips, painted flower-pots, handsome dishes and small pictures', and also 'a horseman painted on earthenware and a dolphin painted likewise'. This shows how early Delftware was known, and also that tiles depicting dolphins, which have always been regarded as characteristic of Rotterdam, may also have been made at Delft.

On 5 October 1611 Michiel Nouts (d. 1615) was registered as a citizen of Delft; he is described as a 'potter and tile-painter from Antwerp'. This shows that the Twelve-Year Truce of 1609–21 encouraged the development of majolica especially in Delft, which was famous soon after 1600 for its blue imitations of Wan Li porcelain. The effect of those years was summed up by Dr. A. Pit in an article in *Oud Holland* in 1909: 'The import of Chinese porcelain was a sudden interference in the development of Dutch pottery.' It depends, of course, from what angle the history of Dutch ceramics is viewed.

However, a group of polychrome soldier tiles is also regarded as being Delft ware. They exist in two sizes: a large square of 17 cm., and the usual 13 cm. square. The composition is uniform. Under a somewhat clouded sky we see musketeers, pikemen or ordinary soldiers standing on a hilly ground and armed with halberds, swords and shields; a *vivandière* is also shown. Each scene is framed in a double circle, and the corners are decorated with white flowers. The numbers in which these tiles have been preserved suggest that they were used to cover large areas (ill. 32a). A quantity of excellent forgeries came on to the market about twenty years ago.

We do not know for what purpose the large tiles were intended. Both sizes are usually ascribed to Hendrick Goltzius or Jacob de Gheijn, although the engravings on which they were based are not known.

30

In the remaining tiles other pottery-painters may be recognized, including Adam van Breen, a painter and engraver who worked in The Hague from 1612 to 1618 and was in Amsterdam in 1629; he is later mentioned as a painter in Norway. Like Jacob de Gheijn he published in 1618 a work entitled *Nassavsche Wapenhandelinghe van Schilt, Spies, Rappier ende Targe* for which he has received a prize of 100 Dutch pounds from the States-General in the previous year. The first edition was in French: *Les évolutions militaires suivant l'idée du Prince Maurice de Nassau*, followed by German and Dutch editions. These books show only the pikemen or rank-and-file soldiers armed with a sword and shield; there are forty-eight plates with a printed commentary. The first engraving in the later edition is labelled *A. V. Breen inventor* and further the frontispiece bears the note 'printed in 1618'. The tiles with gunners therefore cannot be dated before 1618. This is confirmed by a comparison of the uniforms of about 1600 on the large tiles; the pottery-painters reproduced Adam van Breen's soldiers with less accuracy but a good deal more elegance. The origin of polychrome soldier tiles, however, is far from having been satisfactorily established (ill. 32b,c,d).[7]

Owing to the special place that Delft occupied almost from the beginning in the ceramics industry, it is natural to look to it for information about the making of tiles. As early as 1600, Pouwels Bourseth's *Rouaen* pottery was also celebrated as a tile factory; after his death in 1620 not much more is heard of it. Only in a few cases do documents show that a workshop for making lead-glaze tiles was rebuilt and equipped to make tin-glaze ones and that the craftsmen went over to the new process. However, Professor Hudig has been able to show that this was true of Aelbrecht Cornelis Keyser, who was probably born in Rotterdam. He was a *werkmeester* or foreman at Delft in the pottery De Twee Schepjes owned by Adriaen Cornelis Cater, who provided in his will that Keyser might go on living and working there for eight years; he did so from 1635 to 1642. He then bought a tile-works, and from bills that have survived we know that he still made polychrome tiles there. From 1642 he was a member of the Guild of St. Luke in Delft. By a decision of 1648 the potters and tile-makers in the Guild were eligible for the title of Dean, and he was the first to be so appointed. In December 1662 the De Paeuw pottery was sold by Dirck Hieronymus van Kessel and became the property, as to one half, of Gijsbrecht Lambertsz. Cruyck and, as to a quarter each, of Wouter van Eenhoorn and Willem Cleffius. Besides the pottery and its equipment they became the owners of 'all the made tiles and earthenware vessels, whether fired or unfired'.

These, then, are the names of some Delft potters who also took up tile-making. However, of the more than eighty tile-works that gradually spread over the whole country, only ten were established in Delft, which fact shows clearly enough that it was not the main centre of the industry. In all cases when one may speak with certainty of Delft origin, the tiles are of a higher quality, closely related to Delft decorated pottery.

GOUDA

Thanks to G. C. Helbers's research in archives[8] we now know that as early as 1596, 1598 and 1602, *geglazuurde steentgens* (glazed tiles) and 200 *glaesde Steenkens* at eleven stivers the hundred were sent by water to Gouda, almost certainly from Rotterdam; and that on 24 March 1621, Hendrick Gerritsz. van den Heuvel and his brother-in-law Willem Jansz., both of Rotterdam, were granted a sixteen-year licence to make 'glazed work *(geleyerswerck)* and all kinds of imitation porcelain' (1 May 1621 to 1 May 1637). The city withdrew this monopoly only in 1660.[9] On 18 December 1621 Willem Jansz. Oliviersz. (who had the same Christian name as his grandfather) was granted civic rights in Gouda and rented a house on the Oosthaven, which became his property in 1628. This house was called *De Swaen*; in later years he possessed three adjoining houses as a residence and tile-works. It appears from documents that he was a potter and paid tax on the tile kilns. He later used the name of Willem Jansz. Verswaen and died in 1659. The business was carried on by his descendants and those of his daughter-in-law Maria van der Saen. Helbers has done a valuable service by showing that Willem Jansz., Willem Jansz. Oliviersz. and Willem Jansz. Verswaen are all names of the same person, who with his family brought the Gouda tile industry to its fullest development. When the new Van der Want porcelain factory was being built on the Oosthaven in 1953 an unexpected accident led to the discovery of an old refuse pit belonging to the De Swaen pottery. Thanks to this it can be stated with certainty that the main output of the works belonging to Willem Jansz. Verswaen con-sisted of polychrome tiles of the highest quality.

In 1666 the municipality of Gouda issued another patent for a pottery on the Nieuwe Haven, in the hope of competing with De Swaen now that the latter's founder had died. This, however, had no lasting success, and the new factory closed down in about 1725. Gouda's importance as a centre of production gradually diminished in favour of Rotterdam, where the Aelmis family's tile-works, De Bloempot, became celebrated.

Among the Gouda tiles produced by De Swaen we may, in the light of recent discoveries, count first of all the polychrome bird and 'flower-vase' tiles. There are two types of the former, the first being a varied series showing

32

III

a single bird standing on a mound with a tuft or two of grass. The birds include cocks, chickens and ducks as well as peewits, kingfishers, tits, hoopoes and starlings (ill. 33a). The blue corner-patterns consist of fleurs-de-lis or, somewhat later, small leaves and buds. A striking example shows a bird in flight with a sprig in its beak (ill. 14a). In sets of four the corners form a fresh and decorative diagonal pattern; occasionally, within the corner-pattern, the roundel which was formerly customary is painted in with a sketchy touch.

The most famous Gouda tiles, which were also made by De Swaen, are those depicting a bird perched on a nail: the corners are undecorated, which is esthetically quite proper. A varied series of parrots, woodpeckers and parakeets with human faces are seen each perched on a long, sharp nail with a head, placed diagonally across the tile's surface and thus giving a three-dimensional look to the birds which, with their sharp and sometimes vicious expressions, seem to be eavesdropping and spying on human beings (ill. 33b, Plate III).

The colouring of both types shows the usual tints of blue, yellow and orange, green and purple, and also sometimes a bright red which, as Professor Hudig remarked in 1933, is a rarity in high-fired tiles. One of them is inscribed *Gouda* on the back, which confirms the place of origin of these splendid pieces.

It is also noteworthy that in the residence of the Verswaen family on the Oosthaven, where the last of its descendants died in 1914, huge tile-pictures were to be seen as late as the nineteenth century in the rear part of the house, where they served both as wall-decoration and to advertise the business. Two smaller pictures of 6 × 5 tiles show, in each case, a cock with bright feathers standing on a path against a white background. One of these is in the De Moriaen Museum at Gouda (see Plate 11).[10]

Also to be seen were a set of particularly striking larger-than-life scenes copied from compositions designed in 1596–8 by the Utrecht painter Joachim Wttewael (Utewael) for one of the stained-glass windows in St. John's church at Gouda. The principal one is now in the Victoria and Albert Museum in London (ill. 34: 21 × 17 tiles; dark-blue outlines, with much manganese and yellow in the shading of the drawing). The five allegorical figures represent Love, Courage, Fidelity, Concord and Stead-fastness with their attributes and emblems, drawing a triumphal chariot bearing the figure of Freedom. The whole work symbolizes The Victory of Freedom of Conscience over Tyranny. The scroll above Steadfastness bears the inscription ANNO 1640.[11]

To this group also belongs a figure of a naked boy with one foot on a globe. In the original design for the Gouda windows, now in the Nether-lands National Archives, this figure appears beside a cartouche which he is touching with his hand; the Delft picture is a mirror-image of this (ill. 35a).

In the De Moriaen Museum in Gouda, where the objects shown are taken from the family home, there are replicas of the figures of Fidelity and Concord. The figure of Hope, which is unfortunately not quite intact, is for the most part manganese in colour and is in the Boymans-van Beuningen Museum (17 × 8 tiles; ill. 35b).[12]

HOORN

As regards Hoorn and Enkhuizen, we know that Jan Lourisz. de Vogel settled in Hoorn in 1615 as a potter and that in the following year a tile-maker entered his service, by name Thomas Jansz. van Boonen of Delft, where he had been working since 1611. He did not stay long with De Vogel, for in 1617 he had his own tileworks at Enkhuizen. We know nothing further about it, but it would seem that he conducted negotiations and settled accounts through an Enkhuizen notary with Willem Verstraten's well-known tile-works in Delft.[13]

There are in Hoorn two unique products of the Dutch tile industry which were very probably made there. A niche for candles in the St. Pietershofje (built in 1617) was probably used for lighting an upper corridor at night; when the old people's home was recently rebuilt and modernized, it was removed for safety to a lower corridor. The decoration within the quatrefoil is still akin to the pomegranate motif (cf. ill. 15). The polychrome flower-vase tiles with lozenges with a toothed border are of later date and rather spoil the unity of coloration (ill. 38).

In the De Moriaen Museum in Gouda there is a similar work, painted in blue and manganese, of much later date, depicting a whaling scene: the recess is lit by a copper candle-stick with a burning candle. Around the recess are mythological scenes and Cupids in blue, carrying heavy garlands of flowers and fruit (ill. in Berendsen, *Tiles* [1967]).

The second rarity among the Hoorn tiles is the occurrence of polychrome tulips, represented vertically over two tiles (ill. 36), and copied from the *Hortus Floridus* of Crispijn van de Passe, 1614 (cf. the engraving, ill. 37). These tiles were certainly made at Hoorn. They were found in the cellar of a house at No. 57, Grote Oost, in one of the oldest parts of the town. Some of these had survived intact and are now in museums or private collections, while others had been rejected as imperfect and were used to line the walls of cellars and give them a flat surface. Fragments have even been found lining a well.

Research in archives has shown that in Amsterdam and Utrecht also, potteries were established both before and after 1600. So far it has not been possible to indicate types of polychrome tiles which have been proved by excavation to originate from these cities. In the case of some decorated blue tiles however, such origin has been established by the place of discovery or mention in old inventories. These will be discussed further below, as will the manufacture of tiles at Harlingen, which was in contact with Delft as early as 1617, and Makkum, where the tile industry was of somewhat later date.

Notes

1   The Historical Museum at Rotterdam possesses a fragment of an edging tile with SYON in dark blue Gothic letters in relief.

2   See *Vrienden van de Nederlandse Ceramiek*, 27 (June 1962). The texts are: Revelations 21 and 22; John 1 : 29; Isaiah 11 : 5–10 and 12 : 2–3; Exodus 2 : 23–5 and 3 : 1–12; Deuteronomy 4 : 24 and 24 : 22–6; and Hebrews 23 : 28–9.

3   Dr. A. Berendsen states in *Tiles* (1967), p. 126 that: 'Documentary evidence shows that these works were in existence as early as 1637' and that they 'persisted well into the eighteenth century and may have been copied from German prints.' She does not, however, give any source.

4   In 1946 Helbig went over to the view that this picture may be an early specimen of Brussels work; I do not agree, as scarcely anything is known of Brussels pottery before 1702. When the Grand'Place there was rebuilt in 1699, it appears from the sign of the Maison du Renard that this *local corporatif des Merciers* enjoyed the privilege of selling the *poteries et faïences* of the Brussels factories. See J. Helbig, *La Céramique bruxelloise du bon vieux temps* (Brussels, 1946), pp. 5–7. M. B. Keezer, in his chapter on 'Antwerp' in *Tiles* (1967), pp. 101–17, accepts this view as definitive.

5   A. v. d. Willigen, *Geschiedkundige Aanteekeningen over de Haarlemsche Schilders* (1866): appendix on Haarlem faience and pottery.

6   Dingeman Korf, 'Haarlemse Majolica en Tegels', in *Vrienden van de Nederlandse Ceramiek*, 50 (March 1968).

7   See J. G. van Gelder, 'Adam van Breen, Schilder', in *Oudheidkundig Jaarboek* (1932).

8   G. C. Helbers, 'De geschiedenis van het oude Goudse plateel', in *Vrienden van de Nederlandse Ceramiek*, 4 (1956).

9   Hendrick Willemsz. van den Heuvel, owner from 1612 of the pottery De Bergh Syon in Rotterdam, is not mentioned again at Gouda. He was more of an intermediary for the purpose of starting the tile industry, there and at Harlingen.

10 A similar picture at Rotterdam is damaged and incorrectly assembled (ill. in *Tiles* op. cit., p. 161).

11 This scene is part of the Van den Bergh Gift of 1923 to the Victoria and Albert Museum; see B. Rackham, *Catalogue of Dutch Tiles*, second printing (1931), No. 128, Pl. XIII.

12 The inventory and sale catalogue of L. A. van Straaten at Gouda, 1892, mentions '4 figures of Delft tiles (*sic*) representing Flora, Pomona, Ceres and

Diana, each of 52 pieces, and a figure of Hannibal, 39 tiles'. These probably came from De Swaen.

Finally it should be mentioned that in Gouda as in Rotterdam, tiles have been found with initials on the back, probably indicating the maker's name. The most important was probably a blue tile painted on both sides with about eight initials together with Roman and Arabic numbers: this was a kiln-record from De Swaen (Helbers, op. cit., ill. 12).

13 See *Notities Mr. A. H. H. van der Burgh*, 104, 106, 111 (Municipal Archives, Delft).

VI *Blue tiles from c. 1600 to 1700*

About ten years may have elapsed between the production of the earliest polychrome tiles and that of blue tiles in the Northern Netherlands under the influence of Chinese porcelain. There was no question of a precise imitation of the polychrome compositions with corner decoration, and thus the two types gradually developed in different ways, although the practice of placing the design in a roundel, scalloped or lozenge-shaped frame was adhered to at the outset. For many years tiles depicting human and animal figures, portraits, soldiers or flowers were produced in this style, but during the second quarter of the seventeenth century blue tiles came to be made without the traditional framing. The Biblical scenes that later became popular in the Northern provinces were at first depicted in a roundel. Similarly landscape tiles without corner-decoration are referred to in the old inventories as 'open-air work' *(open luchtjes)*.

As blue tiles developed, it is understandable that the abundant corner-decoration of earlier times was reduced to smaller isolated motifs. At the same time a vast number of new themes came to the fore, furnishing a source of inspiration for the design of blue tiles. The origin of these motifs, which gave rise in practice to almost infinite variations, may be seen from the accompanying table of corner-designs and arrangements of the main pattern.[1] If the decorations of polychrome and blue tiles are studied in their separate development, it can clearly be seen how rapidly each evolved. The group of tiles with intertwined exotic motifs is not found at all among the blue tiles: even in polychrome ones, these motifs were soon treated in the Netherlands in quite a different way.

PORTRAIT TILES

In this field there was scarcely any question of imitating polychrome tiles; portraiture in blue tiles soon rose to a much higher level, as engravings

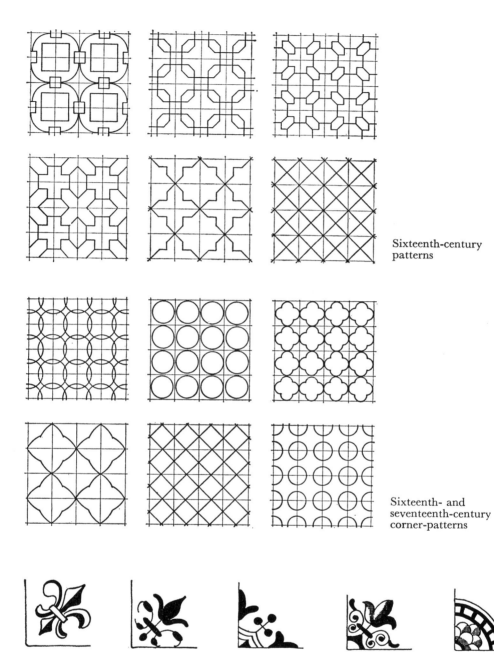

Sixteenth-century
patterns

Sixteenth- and
seventeenth-century
corner-patterns

were followed more and more exactly, a practice which stimulated the tile-painter's ability and much improved his work. Several groups of portrait tiles have been preserved from this period:

1. A series of ten historical personages may be seen in the Musées Royaux d'Art et d'Histoire in Brussels,[2] and about six belonging to this series are in the Van Gijn museum in Dordrecht. Four are reproduced here (ills. 39a–d), representing Prince William of Orange, Count Egmont, King Philip II and the Duke of Alva. The inscriptions are as follows: GVILEM D. G. PRINC. AUR. COM. NASS. & VICEC. ANTV. VES. BARO BREDÆ & GUB. HOL. SELAND; LAMORALUS COMES DE EGMOND PRINCEPS CAVERÆ PIENNÆD. &.; PHILIPPVS II. D. G. HISPANIARVM ET INDIARVM REX CATOLICVS ARCH. AVST.; FERDINANDVS A. TOLEDO DUX ALVÆ ETC. GUBERN. GENERAL BELG. A 1568.[3]

2. Portraits of the Princes of Orange must have been very popular in private homes as small tile pictures. They occur with various types of corner-design, the portraits being always taken from the same prints or paintings. Occasionally even eighteenth-century ones may be found: Professor Hudig has suggested that they may have become popular once more among Orange adherents at the time of the Patriot Party (about 1785). Some of the later ones are very poor in quality: the likenesses are bad and they are often wrongly entitled. D. F. Lunsingh Scheurleer has performed a valuable service by making an exact comparative study of these tiles representing seventeenth-century Princes of Orange and reclassifying the whole group of fifty-two portraits with the correct names of their subjects.[4] To these we may add a series of Orange portraits from the Eelco Vis collection which were sold in America in 1927 and are now in the Metropolitan Museum in New York.

First of these is a portrait of William the Silent (1533–84), in a roundel without any other decoration, after a print by Cornelis de Visscher (ill. 40a). There is a portrait in similar style (ill. 40b) of Princess Mary Stuart, the sister of Charles II (1631–60), who married Prince William II in 1641. Tile portraits of Prince Philip William (1554–1618) (ill. 40c), William III of Orange (1650–1702) (ill. 40d) and Amalia van Solms (1602–75)—at present in New York—have corner-designs of white leaves. These portraits, also from prints by C. de Visscher, derive ultimately from paintings by Gerard van Honthorst (1580–1656), who was court painter to Frederick Henry and William II. Cornelis de Visscher, who was active only for the brief span of ten years from 1652 to 1662, worked in the simple realistic style of Jacob de Gheijn, which is also typical of the court painters executing commissions for the House of Orange.

In the eighteenth century this series may be followed in a number of portraits with corner-designs of white acanthus leaves on a violet-powdered background. Their subjects include Frederick William, the Margrave of Brandenburg (1620–88), known as the Great Elector (ill. 40e); Henrietta Catharina (1637–1708), who in 1659 married Johann Georg II of Anhalt-Dessau; Philip William of Orange, and Amalia van Solms (ill. 40f). The last four, thus formed into a set despite the lack of connection between them, belong to J. G. Wurfbain's collection at De Gelderse Toren castle, Spankeren near Rheden in Gelderland (ill. 40e,f). The quality of the tile portraits was not improved by the process of imitation.

Large-scale historical compositions, more ambitious than ordinary portraits, are the full-length tile pictures of Prince Maurice and Prince Frederick Henry, represented as commanders in the war against Spain (ill. 41a,b; 13 tiles by 4). Advertisement plays a part in another princely figure (ill. 42a, 13 tiles by 5) which must be a product of the Rotterdam workshop 't Graefschap van Bueren, where Cornelis Willemsz. Sonneveldt was active from 1599 to his death in 1638. This represents a fully-armed knight, holding in his right hand a halberd and the flag of the County of Bueren, which belonged to the House of Orange through Prince William's marriage to Anna van Egmond in 1551.

3. The finest portrait tiles are those of a third group depicting famous scholars, theologians and historians who preached in the Reformed Church at Delft: see Chapter VII, below, and ills. 73a,b.

SOLDIERS

The increasingly numerous blue tiles depicting soldiers have far greater variety than the polychrome group. A new basis was afforded by the art of engraving, for which soldiers were often the subject. The tiles thus come to play a part in historical documentation, the most important series being produced in Delft.

Apart, however, from the Beauregard foot-soldiers and horsemen (ill. 43a–f), there are similar types of which no engravings are known to us. These include, for instance, musketeers framed in scalloped borders firing off their pieces (the flames are orange-red in colour: ill. 43c,d) and a series of musketeers and pikemen standing under an archway (Historical Museum, Rotterdam), with corner-designs vaguely reminiscent of the earlier reserve technique (ill. 42b,c,d). The signs point to imitation in the second quarter of the seventeenth century; this is also true of a series depicting soldiers in martial attitudes, more or less similar to the polychrome soldiers shown in action with their coat-tails blown by the wind (cf. ill. 32b,c,d). The blue tiles in question show a corner-design of fleurs-de-lis and also the so-called 'balustrade' ornamentation at the sides, so that the complete column appears when two tiles are placed together and the lilies form a star-pattern in each set of four (ill. 44a,b,c). These tiles were evidently made in the second quarter of the seventeenth century. The later the type of corner-design—ox-heads or spiders—the less skilfully the soldiers are drawn; the impression is that they are copies of copies.

HORSEMEN

The horsemen as well as the foot-soldiers can be assigned to Prince Maurice's army between the years 1607 and 1630. It is noteworthy that the Netherlands engraver's art, and in consequence the art of tile-decoration at this period, reflects a stylistic controversy. Whereas the Practice of Arms (*Wapenhande-linghe*) of Prince Maurice is depicted by Jacob de Gheijn with painstaking naturalism, in the work of Hendrik Goltzius we have a dramatic represen-tation of Roman figures, mounted and on foot.

Tiles depicting horsemen developed thereafter as a special category, and it is understandable that framing and corner-decoration gradually dis-appeared, since the rider and his mount needed plenty of space for esthetic reasons as well as in real life. Although the number of tile factories is such that the types of horsemen cannot be arranged in a single continuous development, they are each more or less recognizably of their own time, and one may also clearly distinguish the transition from Holland to Fries-land (ill. 44d,e,f; compare ills. 86a,b and 87a,b and Chapter VIII below).

Besides soldiers, attention is now also devoted to civilians and in fact all classes of society: merchant princes, craftsmen, villagers and peasants (ills. 45, 46 and 47). Some of these tiles take the form of genre pictures and may belong to moralizing literature (see ills. 66a, 67a). Tiles depicting social gatherings can also be matched with contemporary paintings and drawings by Anthony Palamedesz., Willem Buytewech, Dirck Hals, Droochsloot and others, in whose work refined fashions of dress played an important part. How closely they were copied in the blue tiles is shown by the back views of figures, some in peasant costume, which are certainly a rarity as far as tiles are concerned (ill. 46a,b). Tile painters also depicted the most diverse trades, the occupations of ordinary citizens and peasants, thus providing us with a many-sided picture of Dutch life in the seventeenth century (ills. 45, 46a–e and 47).

41

An especially typical occupation of bygone days is that of the pedlar, carrying a tray full of ribbons and thread supported by a strap slung round his neck, and offering for sale tufts of ostrich feathers to adorn warriors' helmets, as illustrated by a picture in the De Moriaen Museum at Gouda. The corner-design with the oak- or vine-leaf may point to a date around 1650. This, of course, was the period when many wares were brought to the customer's home. Equally instructive pictures show us the basket-weaver, the fishmonger with his catch balanced on his head in a basket, the thatcher, the farmer at market with a sack of potatoes and the labourer with sheaves of corn and a sickle in his hand (ills. 46e and 47a,b,c).

From the inventories of contemporary workshops we may learn not only about prices but about the vocabulary of those times; a contract of 1637, for example, speaks of *fijne schutters* (elegant marksmen) and *slechte mannekens* (plain folk), meaning evidently the common people and peasantry. A tile dated 1663 appears to confirm that this type was still much in demand.

As a minor variant in this series of human figures we may mention corner-designs of green fleurs-de-lis with a blue outline. These may be seen in the Huis Lambert van Meerten Museum at Delft, but from excavations made at Rotterdam in 1942 it seems equally probable that they may have originated there (ill. 46c,d).

ANIMALS

Polychrome and blue tiles depicting animals must have become popular about 1625. Although a variety of colours, especially with wild animals, might be expected to appeal more to the imagination, there was in fact a stronger demand for this type in blue, except for those representing birds (ills. 14c, 33a,b, Plate III). The exploration of America and other continents aroused interest in their fauna, and this was stimulated by the development of Dutch oversea connections. The foundations of exotic zoology were laid in the sixteenth- and seventeenth-century encyclopedias by the Italian Aldrovandi and the Swiss Gessner. In 1605 Plantijn of Antwerp published his *Exoticorum libri decem*. It is not surprising therefore that prints from these and similar books were imitated in tile paintings. In polychrome we find pictures of camels, lions, tigers and monkeys. Elephants must have been especially popular; they are rare in the coloured tiles with lozenge-shaped frames (ill. 13b,c) but were much sought after in blue tiles, where they appear in a variety of attitudes, sometimes tethered to a pole or with a howdah on their backs (cf. ill. 48a–d).

The variations of corner-design persist in figures of different animals, such as a dog with a collar or a stork with a fish in its beak, both with baluster decoration (ill. 48e,f).

42

The different types of corner-design make it possible to date these tiles more or less accurately until well after 1650. A general survey of the blue tiles shows striking variations in workmanship and in the quality of the models, which are generally unknown.

The animals have a sturdy, somewhat clumsy appearance; their bodies are dark blue, and in some cases the joints of the limbs are marked by shading. They are often seen running or jumping under an arch of clouds, also represented by hatching (ill. 49a–f). The tiles are thought to have been produced in Rotterdam and were evidently often imitated: in the Huis Lambert van Meerten Museum in Delft there is a large picture with compositions of this sort in a round frame with meander decoration in the corners, which clearly show the negligence of the later style.

The varying corner-designs of fleurs-de-lis, ox-heads, maze-patterns, sprigs of foliage and also the baluster pattern point to a long and varied history of imitation till late in the seventeenth century (ill. 48). With the thousands of tiles that have continued to be produced down to the present day, the essential task is to study the technique and quality and, as far as possible, to identify an earlier date and provenance.

The tile-decorators made enthusiastic use of the meander style of ornamentation, derived from Chinese Wan Li porcelain. This ascription is somewhat misleading, as the word 'meander' comes from the name of a river in Asia Minor and is used to denote a continuous band design familiar in the art of Classical Greece. However, the Greek term is also used for the more angular Chinese motif, which likewise suggests the windings of a river. Good imitations of the Chinese design can be highly elegant. Tiles dated 1630 and 1632 show us when this took place: it relates to the deep-blue porcelain of the Ming period. A set of tiles in the Gemeente Museum at The Hague gives a good idea of this, not least by its warm colouring: each tile shows a bird on a rock, wreathed round with flowers inside a scalloped frame, with a meander pattern in the corners (ill. 50). This stylistic purity was not maintained for long, as appears from a comparison of the individual tiles here.

FLOWERS

A similar unity is displayed in a composition consisting of a flowering plant in a Chinese porcelain vase, surrounded by a medallion and again with meander designs in the corners (ill. 51a).

It is understandable, however, that this new development did not last long, since the use of blue alone deprives the flowers of their natural

43

brilliance. Thus a tulip with three blooms in the same Chinese style is also a rarity: there is an example of it in the decoration of a staircase wall in a private house on the Waeze in Leeuwarden (ill. 52). These tiles may come from Rotterdam, or they may have been made at Harlingen in the eighteenth century, as they are found in the pattern-book. Often, too, in order not to lose the original colours, the flowers are rendered in subdued polychrome while the corner fleurs-de-lis, ox-heads etc. are in blue.

An attempt towards new compositions can be seen in tulips with stylized rows of leaves and a corner-design reminiscent of an earlier period (ill. 53a), and also in the more successful ovals, where blue ornamentation dominates the weaker painting of the flowers (ill. 53c). This points to a certain decline in quality and also suggests a later date in the seventeenth century.

Dingeman Korf, in his study of seventeenth- and eighteenth-century variations of the 'threefold tulip' enclosed by fleurs-de-lis and round, octagonal or lozenge-shaped frames, has identified thirteen different versions of this graceful motif.[5]

ORNAMENTAL TILES

So far as possible, blue ornamental tiles began by following the polychrome tradition, in the fleur-de-lis pattern, for example, which produces a much stronger colour effect in blue than with a single blue flower among four orange ones (cf. ill. 22b). The Venetian *foglie* motif of blue and white leaves, used to surround the Haarlem 'cherub tiles', is also particularly ornamental as it appears in the all-blue 'mirror tiles', especially when the central mirror-shape is occupied by a rosette (ill. 54a). Again, the decoration of large wall-surfaces with blue tiles was only possible with ornamental patterns of the new style, complete in one tile or spreading over four with a continuous design (ill. 54b). In any case, these blue tile designs are quite independent of the polychrome variety. It is a pity that the original decoration can seldom be found now in old Dutch houses, though large composite pictures in museums and collections give a good idea of the esthetic effect. These are all indications of how the art of making blue tiles became increasingly independent after the middle of the seventeenth century and how new possibilities arose which were to be exploited in the eighteenth (see ill. 95a,b).

Apart from these main themes there are also seventeenth-century ornamental tiles which bear witness to the painters' individual talents. Some relationship to the polychrome decoration may still be seen in tiles depicting a flower with eight or twelve leaves in an octagonal or scallop frame with a meander or flower design in the corners. The development of these and other new ideas led to harmonious blue tile compositions of high quality (ill. 55a,b,c).

There is a particularly attractive frame of a tile picture from a demolished house (No. 23 St. Laurensstraat, Rotterdam), with carefully executed Renaissance-style volutes and a handsome corner-design (ill. 56). Among the more imaginative patterns is a set of four tiles, of which unfortunately only two have been preserved (ill. 55d): branches of fruit within a lozenge-shaped frame, and above them an open umbrella and a papyrus roll, the spaces between being occupied by striped medallions. All the lines are wavy and give an impression of motion. This very original design indicates how the tilemaker's art with which the simple Dutch house was adorned made use of knowledge acquired in every domain and reflected the whole range of Dutch contacts with the outside world. Conversely, the eighteenth-century potters exported their work, which was typically Dutch in character, to practically every country in Europe and as far as Brazil.

After 1630 the tile-painter's art was enriched by entirely new subjects, such as the blue landscapes, Biblical scenes, ships, children's games and all the other themes associated with this genre, some of which imparted a completely new style of ornament to the Dutch interior. Naturally the model in such cases was almost always provided by graphic art.

LANDSCAPE TILES

A survey of the great variety of these tiles over more than three centuries illustrates the painters' endeavours to reproduce the local and rural atmos-phere of the Netherlands in their day. The design may be enclosed in the traditional roundel or medallion, the date being more or less indicated by the degree of simplicity of the corner-design. The inventories speak of landscapes in a roundel and, if there is no corner decoration, they are called *open luchtjes*. They depict an enormous variety of scenes: a peasant's cottage with its surroundings, a church among trees on a village common, windmills, a wooden bridge over a ditch, sailing-boats on a river with fishermen sitting on the tow-path, skaters, a company resting in front of an inn, or a castle with a drawbridge.

There are scenes here in plenty to give a picturesque idea of the Dutch landscape; but the development of the art was not a foregone conclusion, and its beginnings were difficult, as we may see from some rare tiles dated between 1630 and 1640. These show scalloped frame with sprigs or a meander pattern in the corners, and in the centre a castle or church standing on a small patch of ground and surrounded by a few primitive trees, with the date inscribed above or below (ill. 57a,b). A better composition and sense of space are given by placing the building between balusters, with fleurs-de-lis in the corners (ill. 57c,d,e), though even here the little farmhouse among trees and the few windmills hardly give the impression of a landscape. This comes later on, in scenes which suggest an unhindered prospect and where the signposts beside the bridge refer to the years 1674, 1677 and 1678 (ill. 58a,b,c). About forty scenes of this type exist altogether. The origin of particular tiles is hard to pin-point, since by then the industry had spread throughout the country and trade was universal. As the eighteenth century approaches we must bear in mind that some landscape themes gradually came to lose their atmosphere as a result of frequent repetition.

There is a striking difference between the rather laborious folk art of some of the landscape tiles which have been preserved and the genre of 'miniature landscapes' showing extremely fine execution; in the latter, painters like Jan van Goyen, Jacob van Mosscher, Nicolaes Berchem and Jan Martsen the Younger—to name only a few—provided in their pictures and engravings the models for scenes of dunes in the Netherlands, Italian pastoral landscapes, Biblical episodes or historic battles in open country (ill. 59a,b).[6] These attempts at lifelike portrayal also belong to the second quarter of the seventeenth century. In Van Mosscher's Dune Landscape, for instance, the tile-painter succeeded in capturing a spring atmosphere, in blue on a clear white background, which became typical of Delftware and reached its highest point in the work of Frederik van Frijtom, the most talented of the painters of landscape tiles (ill. 78a,b, Plate IV).

BIBLICAL SCENES

These are perhaps even more important than landscape as a subject of folk art in tiles. In any case they form a special group, since Biblical stories with several characters often made demands on the painters for which they were not sufficiently prepared artistically. Although they had Biblical engravings as models, they found it difficult to reproduce complete scenes with clarity. To remedy this from the technical point of view they resorted at an early stage to brownish or manganese-purple colours, which were evidently easier to draw in than cobalt blue. They also tried to solve the problem by giving a reference to the appropriate text. The Biblical tiles seldom attained a high quality, but because they involved much labour we find them more highly priced in inventories than landscapes or simpler scenes.

In the Protestant Netherlands the family Bible constituted the chief, if not the sole, reading matter, not only in the countryside but in the towns.

This is especially true of certain areas such as the Zaan district of North Holland, the County of Zutphen in Gelderland and the provinces of Overijssel and Drenthe, where, apart from the fireplace, it was common for all the walls of the single living-room, which also served as a bedroom, to be covered with tiles, including the space behind the bed. The tiles did not form a continuous Biblical story, but the Old and New Testament were clearly separated.

Besides the widespread use of Biblical tiles in Holland they began to be exported to North and West Germany and Denmark, as tiles of other kinds subsequently were.

The usual type of Biblical scene is in a circular border, the corners sometimes decorated with spiders or sprigs, pointing to a date about 1650; the common blue or manganese corner-design of carnations belongs to the eighteenth century. It is supposed that blue tiles with Biblical scenes were mostly made in Friesland and exported to the Zaan district and elswhere; but the typical Zaan *smuigers* or fireplaces of the seventeenth and eighteenth centuries in blue or manganese were probably for the most part manufactured in Amsterdam potteries (ills. 110a, 111).

As regards the subjects, these are mostly to be found in editions of the Bible and engravings from the sixteenth century onwards. Records of the delivery of tiles sometimes speak merely of 'Histories . . . with or without texts' (1664) or *beste Historien, Paerse Historijen* (1686). These items have been correctly explained by W. J. Rust as referring to an illustrated Bible published in 1659 by Nicolaes Visscher under the title *Toneel ofte Vertooch der Bijbelsche Historiën*, and an edition of 1734 entitled *Afbeeldingen van de Heilige Historiën des Ouden en des Nieuwen Testaments.*[7] The same authority has pointed out that many of these prints are based on works by the Flemish painter Maerten de Vos and the engraver Anton Wiericx, the prints having been made by Claes Jansz. and Nicolaes Visscher and reproduced in the latter's edition of Bible stories, but reduced in size and with the design reversed.

J. Pluis, in his work on Biblical tiles *Tegels met bijbelse voorstellingen*, written in 1967 for the Netherlands Bible Society, has described briefly the origin of the Biblical themes and given the names of the painters and engravers whose work can sometimes be traced in tile-decoration as late as the nineteenth century.[8] These go back to the early Renaissance period in Germany. As woodcuts and engravings by Dürer and Holbein had achieved European celebrity, copies of these works and of details recalling them began to appear in the form of tile paintings. In 1630 the Basle engraver Matthias Merian (1593–1650), who was in contact with Dutch publishers, produced his *Merian-Bibel*, etchings from which appeared in reduced size in the Dutch authorized or *Statenbijbels* of 1657 and 1741.

In Baroque art too, a connection exists between Rubens's elaborate pictures and the Dutch engraver's art. The link here was Boëtius à Bolswert of Friesland, whose engravings were reduced for the illustrated Bibles by Pieter Hendricksz. Schut (1619–1709). Schut also performed the same work for other artists and, according to J. Pluis, was responsible in this way for over sixty per cent of the Biblical stories. His manner of tile-painting was also much imitated. Later Bible illustrators who should be mentioned are Romein de Hooghe (1645–1708) and the etcher Jan Luijken (1649–1712). Pluis distinguishes four types of tile painting in the latter's work. This edition of the Bible was printed at Amsterdam in 1712; many tiles based on it have been found in dwellings in North Holland, which is a further proof of Amsterdam origin. A comparative study of the two artists would require a book to itself. Their stylistic problems may be shown by a single example. In nearly all Biblical tiles the scene is represented in a circle (ill. 60a,b,d). As opposed to the scene of Susanna and the Elders, which is deficient in perspective and has too crowded a background,[9] we have somewhat naive scenes from the Passion of Christ—the Scourging, and the Testimony of Pilate's wife to Christ's innocence—depicted in a building supported on pillars. These examples, all of mediocre quality, have leaf designs in the corners; taking into account the dates of the Bible editions, this means that the tiles belong to the last quarter of the seventeenth century or even the eighteenth.

Large tiles for window-sills and the triangular *étagère* tiles, with ornamental painted edges, frequently depict Biblical scenes, such as Tobias and the Angel or the Temptation of Christ in the Wilderness (ill. 61a,b). Biblical scenes also occurred in tile pictures even before 1700, when whole walls of tiles were becoming increasingly common. This is connected with the fact that Dutch tiles were already spreading to Spain and Portugal, where they were chiefly in demand to decorate the walls of churches and cloisters, so that more and more Biblical scenes were executed. Professor Hudig, in his *Altholländische Fliesen* (part II [1933], p. 39), refers to at least 350 Biblical scenes depicted on tiles; by 1967, further study has brought the total to over 468. A separate work on the Biblical tiles is certainly desirable, since only an outline can be given in the present study.

Apart from Biblical 'histories' there are other groups of tiles relating to the Catholic church.

In the Huis Lambert van Meerten Museum at Delft there is a set of twelve depicting the Apostles and scenes from the Life of the Virgin, among them St. Anne with the Virgin and Child and the Madonna with the Mantle which reveal the hand of a talented painter (ill. 62). The oakleaf corners point to a date in the second half of the seventeenth century. One of the figures in this series represents St. John the Evangelist. His symbol, the eagle, sits at his feet; his right hand is raised in blessing, but instead of charming a poisonous snake as in the medieval tradition, he is here seen holding a Eucharistic chalice (ill. 60f).

The prints from which these tiles are copied are not known, though they are mentioned in an inventory of 1834 from the Bloempot tile-works belonging to the Aelmis family at Rotterdam.[10]

There was also a series of manganese tiles showing the heraldic devices of the Popes. One such is in the Princessehof Museum at Leeuwarden: a deer couched in front of a row of trees, with the inscription below: MARCELLVS PAPA II. Above this device, representing the arms of the Pope's family, is a crest with the tiara and crossed keys (ill. 60e).

Tiles of this kind, related to Catholic iconography, are also found at Cadiz, furnishing further evidence of the commerce between Spain and the Netherlands.

A final example, the work no doubt of a very unskilled painter, shows a cardinal standing under an arch, holding a cross and a rosary (ill. 60c).

SHIPS

It goes without saying that ships were destined to play an important part in the decoration of blue tiles in Holland. This probably began about 1625. Professor Hudig (op. cit., p. 31) gives 1637 as the date of the oldest ship tile, but this is not a firm indication, as the design in question was repeated into the eighteenth century. In fact only the initial date of a particular type of ship tile is anything to go by. Here again, painting and engraving preceded tile painting. It is noteworthy that what inspired the artists was not a seascape with ships but above all the ship itself, the different types of construction and not least the rigging. This remained true for a long period, although there was a considerable output of tile pictures showing ships in harbour or sea-battles, witness the picture by Cornelis Boumeester in Rotterdam (ill. 72a). In the eighteenth century Harlingen and Makkum became the chief centres for producing tile pictures of ships, though here too the type of vessel remained the dominant factor until about 1730, when the shipowners of Friesland and the West Frisian Islands began to have their own ships illustrated (ill. 101b).

The pioneers of sea-painting were Reinier Nooms, known as Zeeman (d. 1668), and his contemporary Aert van Antum; their careful drawing provided what could be called an inventory of all types of ships. Willem van de Velde the Elder, nicknamed the ship-painter, worked in a similar style: like his son and namesake he illustrated the wars with England and afterwards became court painter in that country, when the glorious days of De Ruyter and Tromp were past. After their migration the Van de Veldes cease to be of importance for tile-painting.

As artists concentrated on depicting a ship's form and rigging they copied from drawings, prints and etchings. An outstanding example is a series of eight scenes showing the stages of the building and launching of a ship: this probably dates from after 1650.

The Historical Museum in Rotterdam possesses a number of tiles depicting ships with all sails spread, although they look as if they were on dry land. The ox-head corners point to a date around 1650 or later (ill. 63).

Much progress and liveliness is shown in two pictures of ships under full sail, flying the Dutch flag, framed with the baluster design and the traditional fleurs-de-lis—truly a graphic representation (ill. 64a,b). A more static approach is again seen in the pictures of warships, in which the complicated rigging seems to be the chief feature, even when three ships are engaged in battle (ill. 64d).

In the extensive view of the Battle of the Downs, commanded on the Dutch side by 'Marten Harpert Tromp in October 1638', although some ships are seen in flames the impression is more historical and topographical than realistic.[11] This work (ill. 65) is a tile picture by Abraham Verwer (1600–58) after a painting by Jacob Saverij, one of the Flemish painters who helped to modernize the art of drawing and engraving after Pieter Brueghel; Saverij was active in Amsterdam as early as 1591.

GENRE SCENES

The designers of blue tiles derived enormous advantage from the huge number of illustrated works published in the Netherlands after about 1640 and dealing with religious, educational, moral, artistic and mythological themes. It is not often possible to identify the sources of particular tile paintings, especially as the artist did not copy slavishly but tried to produce a genre picture of his own by means of small alterations. A good example is the elegant couple (ill. 67a), taken from part II *(De Misbruik der Minne)* of a work in four parts by I. H. Krul entitled *Pampiere Wereld ofte wereldsche Oeffeninge* (1681). The original engraving also shows the figure of a merchant's wife, and its spirit is expressed by the words: 'A greedy heart loves its own sorrow: people hanker after property but lose sight of love' (ill. 66a). This tile is typical of the transition to eighteenth-century style: it and the book are in the Tile Museum at Otterlo.

Genre tiles of this sort with two figures were very popular about 1700, when, like portrait tiles, they were painted with lozenge-shaped frames and used to decorate indoor walls.

A popular imaginative composition was a series depicting winged cupids floating on clouds. These three cupids are shown performing the most varied activities—making music, carrying the Cross, lugging a wine-cask or wheelbarrow or holding up the coat of arms of the Seven Provinces (Huis Lambert van Meerten Museum, Delft). The engraver of these scenes is not known; the corner-design is a spider's head (ill. 66b,c).

The extent to which tile-painting varies in quality is shown by a fragment dated 1630, representing the beginning of a text with the word *De* in ornamental script, surrounded by tendrils (ill. 67b).[12]

CHILDREN'S GAMES AND CHINESE FIGURES

The most popular type of blue tiles were those depicting children's games in simple style, with diminutive figures of one or more child playing. These continued into the nineteenth century, when the tile-painter sometimes adapted them to the fashion of his own period; some exist from about 1835. All kinds of sports and games are illustrated, including some that have long been forgotten: games with bat and ball, peg-tops and hoops, leapfrog and knucklebones, kites and windmills, or walking on stilts (ill. 68a,b).

Jacob Cats preceded his work on Marriage of 1625 with poems on children's games, which were illustrated by Adriaen van de Venne. In *De Nieuwe Zeestraet van 's-Gravenhage op Scheveningen*, Constantijn Huijgens remarks poetically that children, even 'without an Almanack', never confuse the due season for different games. This may have been another reason for the great popularity of the tiles.

To the category of figure tiles, which must have been especially popular soon after 1650, belongs a series depicting small Chinese figures in scenes typical of their life and habits (ill. 69a–f). Here we see a mandarin, a figure with a pigtail, a seated Chinese boy, an acrobat, a man examining a vase and another pigtailed figure standing in front of a small table.

Dingeman Korf, in his studies and excavations at Haarlem, has discovered fragments of majolica dishes with Chinese figures of this type.[13]

Another model may have been the series of blue tiles in the fireplace of the burgomaster's room in the Haarlem town hall, though this cannot be documented. These tiles were only placed in position after the interior of the town hall was rebuilt in 1892. They are said to have been a gift from the then registrar, M. Enschede, but no further details are ascertainable.

Tiles depicting children's games made an important contribution to the decoration of Renaissance and Baroque apartments in Holland. These developed in their own way and diverged sharply from the architectonic polychrome tiles used in decoration of kitchens, halls and cellars in the early seventeenth century.

When rooms came to be decorated with tiles in the seventeenth century, experience showed that, like stone floors, they could be kept clean with water. The Renaissance floor consisted of square slabs, green, red and grey-brown, covered with a lead glaze. In the Baroque style this was replaced by a pattern of black and white tiles of marble or Namur stone, and the walls were of white plaster. To protect the walls from damage when the floor was scrubbed, a single row of blue tiles was used as a skirting. This was the beginning; the use of tiles subsequently spread to the fireplace. After the Gothic and early Renaissance period, the hearth was modernized. On both sides of an iron fireback a tile border was laid, three or four tiles wide, and the motif of children's games was frequently chosen for this purpose. The wooden mantelshelf rested on carved limestone caryatids or marble pilasters. After 1650 these were replaced by columns of tiles, which to begin with were thirteen tiles high and one tile broad, but were soon made in a sturdier form. They are referred to in old inventories as 'hearth-pillars' *(schoorsteen-pilaertjes)*. However, when the term 'pillar tiles' *(pilaertegeltjes)* occurs, it doubtless refers to tiles having on them the baluster type of side-decoration, as Professor Hudig has pointed out. When tile 'chimney-pillars' were used, which does not occur before the Baroque period, it was necessary for the pillars in front to be made of marble so as to take the weight of the mantelshelf and fireplace.

Construction and decoration of fireplaces in the second half of the seventeenth century in the native Dutch style comes to a stop at this point, the next step being the imitation of the successive French Louis styles; tile decoration, however, persisted in the provinces and especially in the Zaan district (see ills. 110a,c, 111).

Curiously enough, late seventeenth-century dolls' houses furnish a more or less clear illustration of the transition. These are not mere toys, but elaborate pieces of craftsmanship which, when their doors are opened, give a view of the whole interior of a dwelling-house with its rooms from cellar to attic. The living-rooms and bedrooms are elaborately furnished in imitation of real life. About four of these dolls' houses have been preserved which appear to represent noblemen's houses in Amsterdam and were quite possibly made there. They usually formed part of a bride's dowry, and are a valuable illustration of Dutch culture, furniture and the general style of living before and after 1700. The most famous is that known as Peter the Great's dolls' house, which was made during the Tsar's visit to Zaandam in 1697 but which he apparently did not take back to Russia. Recent research has shown that it was made by Cornelis Beudeker (1675–1756), whose initials c.b. are in a cartouche inlaid in marquetry at the side.[14] The kitchen is decorated with gleaming white tiles, as is part of the fireplace. In the middle there is a double row of sets of four tiles with white leaves set diagonally on a purple background. These show the position of the flue; to either side are single pillar-tiles with tendrils (ill. 110b).

Notes

1 The types of pattern and a selection of corner-designs are based on the almost complete set illustrated in Dingeman Korf's *Tegels*, pp. 40-51, (third edition, Bussum, Netherlands 1964); English translation *Dutch Tiles* (London, 1963), chapter entitled 'Classification'.

2 Portraits of the following are reproduced in *Tiles*, by Anne Berendsen and others (London, 1967), p. 155: Hendrik van Brederode, King Stephen Batory of Poland, Archduke Ernest of Austria (Governor of the Southern Netherlands), Henry II of France, Francisco Valdez, the Duke of Alva, the Emperor Matthias, Emmanuel Philibert of Savoy (Governor of the Southern Netherlands), Charles IX of France and the Earl of Leicester.

3 The portraits of *Philippus Baro de Montmorency* and *Ludovicus Requesensius* are too badly damaged to be reproduced.

4 D. F. Lunsingh Scheurleer in *Antiek*, 6 (January 1969), pp. 327–36: 'Tegels met zeventiende-eeuwse Oranjevorsten'.

5 Dingeman Korf, 'De Drietulp', in *Vrienden van de Nederlandse Ceramiek*, 13 (December 1958).

6 Cf. the article by Prof. Dr. J. Q. van Regteren Altena, 'Een omlijste plaque van Delfts maaksel', in *Vrienden van de Nederlandse Ceramiek*, 37 (December 1964).

7 W. J. Rust, 'Bijbelse Tegels', in *Vrienden van de Nederlandse Ceramiek*, 40 (September 1965).

8 J. Pluis, *Tegels met bijbelse voorstellingen* (published by the Netherlands Bible Society, 1967).

9 This tile is on view at the Monnickendam Museum together with the book containing the relevant print and the legend 'Susanna is surprised by two villains and tempted to unchastity' (Daniel, 13 : 9). The signature H. Schut is on the back of the print.

10 Information kindly furnished by Prof. Dr. F. van der Meer of Nijmegen.

11 The date 1638 given on the tile should be 1639.

12 Nothing is known of the origin of this tile, which was purchased by the then director, A. Le Comte, in 1913.

13 Dingeman Korf, 'Haarlemse Majolica- en tegelbakkers', in *Vrienden van de Nederlandse Ceramiek*, 50 (March 1968), p. 16, ill. 111.

14 Th. H. Lunsingh Scheurleer, *Catalogus der meubelen in het Rijksmuseum* (1957), No. 358. Idem, 'Het Koninklijk Kabinet van Zeldzaamheden en zijn betekenis voor het Rijksmuseum', in *Oudheidkundig Jaarboek* (1945), pp. 57 ff.

The illustration in the catalogue, like that in Hudig's *Altholländische Fliesen*, ill. 49b, shows the fireplace without a fireback. See also C. W. Fock, 'Het Poppenhuis van Petronella Dubois', in *Bulletin van het Rijksmuseum*, 16, No. 3 (1968).

VII The manufacture of blue tiles in Rotterdam, Delft, Amsterdam, Utrecht, Harlingen, Bolsward and Makkum in the seventeenth century

The title of this chapter shows to what extent the tile industry came to spread throughout the Netherlands, even though the cities named above can each be proud to have taken the lead in producing a particular type named after them. It must be recognized that many kinds of tile were imitated in different workshops, especially during the eighteenth century; there was no copyright in the field of decoration. None the less, certain types of tile continued to be named after the towns where they were first produced, as will be shown.

ROTTERDAM

Here the blue tiles preserved the tradition of sea-monsters, sea-gods and goddesses, mermaids and mermen, tritons etc. The ox-head corner-designs show until long after 1650 that these were no less popular than the poly-chrome versions, though the friezes, which were also made at Hoorn, are less frequent. In the blue series, the most attractive and probably the earliest subjects are the cupids carrying torches, standing on a dolphin or on a sea-shell drawn by hippocamps (ill. 70a,b) and the tritons perched on waves that rise to form a triangle (ill. 70c). Similar figures on a dark ground representing the sea-bottom are less successful and no doubt later in date.

A series of tiles depict mythological subjects: Fortune standing on a globe and holding a spread sail, a nereid with a tulip in her hand riding a sea-monster, Icarus falling into the sea and a triton with a conch. The symmetrical, rippling waves have almost the effect of an engraving. This distinctive group is based on prints by an unknown seventeenth-century master (ill. 71a–d).

But apart from the tradition of fantastical themes there is one outstanding tile-painter who depicted both ships and the sea and, under the inspiration of Dutch painters and engravers, created impressive tile pictures of harbour scenes, sea-battles and historic events. This was Cornelis Boumeester (1652–1733), whom a chronicler of his own time calls 'an excellent painter of ships'. He worked from 1676 as chief tile-maker at the factory of Jacobus de Colonia on the Delft Canal (Delftsche Vaart), adjacent to a park of which he made a large tile painting in classical style (Rotterdam, Historical Museum; reproduced in *Tiles*, op cit. p. 171). He worked in a transitional period when, in addition to bands of continuous ornament or single tiles with landscapes, flowers, children's games etc., great interest was taken in producing larger scenes, a form which was only practicable with blue tiles. Boumeester fully appreciated the wide applications of these scenes. He was fortunate in having been able to copy all his ships from prints (some by Romein de Hooghe), though he may have used the pouncing method to represent rigging. He was thus able to some extent to disguise his lack of talent as a painter, otherwise apparent in his inability to depict rivers or the sea in a credible naturalistic style. Nearly all his works are signed, and he made his name with a number of tile pictures despite his lack of painterly qualities.

Many of his pictures show the Meuse estuary with the Rotterdam skyline in the background, for example the tile painting at Brussels, signed *C. Boumeester* (8 tiles by 12, ill. 72a). An historic scene is that of Prince William III embarking on the State yacht *Den Briel* in November 1688, bound for England where he was to be proclaimed King (ill. 72b).

As regards the history of the chief Rotterdam tile-factories, it should be noted here how they competed with one another around the turn of the century and finally merged into a single monopoly. The kiln by the Delft Canal, which originally belonged to a family named De Meijer, passed by marriage into the hands of Jacobus de Colonia, who submitted his 'masterpiece' as a tile-maker in 1662. After his death in 1700 Hendrick Schut became the owner, and when the latter died in 1709 he was succeeded by his son and namesake. The tile-works De Bloempot was flourishing at this time under Abraham Willemsz. van Lier, from whom it passed in 1697 to Pieter Jansz. Aelmis. Both owners bought up various smaller works. The Aelmis family continued to hold the monopoly of Rotterdam tile production for a century and a half, until the concern was wound up in 1853.

DELFT

Six portraits that have been preserved from a Delft pottery are justly regarded as supreme examples of the tile-maker's art on account of their porcelain-like qualities. They represent preachers in the Reformed Church at Delft, and formerly adorned the vestry there. The subjects are well documented historically: two were painted and engraved by Crispijn van den Queborn (*c.* 1604–53), while three were engraved by him from portraits painted in 1641 by Anthony Palamedesz. (1601–73) and another from a portrait of the same year by C. Dame. All were published by S. Kloeting in Delft. The two tiles now in Amsterdam are dated 1660 (ill. 73a,b).

Mevrouw J. de Loos-Haaxman has shown from archives that these portraits are the work of Isaac Junius,[1] a Delft painter of cavalry engagements (1643) and landscapes with encamped armies, who from time to time also displayed talent as a tile painter. Born in Haarlem in 1616, he came to Delft in 1625 and left in 1650, after which he seems to have been sheriff of Katwijk and Zandt. However, he maintained contact with Delft as a tile painter; it is not known for which pottery he worked, though it may have been De Dissel, the first pottery to become celebrated after 1650 for the production of 'porcelain' Delftware. The contact with Junius may have been established under the inspiration of Sinjeur Abraham de Cooge, a painter and art dealer who had a one-third interest in De Dissel from 1645 onwards and became its sole owner in 1666; he died some time after 1672.[2] No less interesting and unusual are the two tile plaques painted by Junius three years earlier and showing the front and side view of the monument of Prince William of Orange, erected in 1620 by Hendrick de Keijser. These tiles were copied from an engraving by Cornelis Danckertsz., and Mevr. de Loos-Haaxman has traced their origin also. They were offered for sale in pairs in catalogues of 1911, 1930, 1932 and 1954; all are signed and dated by Isaac Junius, with slight variations in the dating: 4 May 1657 (twice), 19 May 1657 and June 1657. These small differences suggest that Junius came specially from Katwijk to Delft to make the tiles, and then signed and dated them there (ill. 73c,d).

Another Delft pottery won international fame for its tiles depicting soldiers. Although polychrome specimens of this type are ascribed to Jacob de Gheijn, documentation is lacking. However, in the grand hall of the Château de Beauregard near Blois on the Loire there is a vast tiled floor still known as *toute une armée en marche*, representing Prince Maurice's new strategy as expounded in his *Wapenhandelinghe van Roers, Musquetten en Spiessen* (The Handling of Firelocks, Muskets and Pikes). The first edition of this work, in French, appeared at The Hague in 1608 with illustrations by Jacob de Gheijn.[3] Only ten years ago, research in the Beauregard archives showed that a consignment of over 6,000 tiles was despatched by sea from Delftshaven to Nantes and was paid for on 30 December 1627 by Paul Ardier, the owner of Beauregard. For various reasons, including the decoration of the hall with historical portraits and the death of Paul Ardier senior in 1638, the floor was not actually laid until 1646 (ill. 74).[4]

Apart from the unique historical importance of the tiles, providing as they do an idea of Prince Maurice's strategy, their composition also deserves the highest admiration. The artist has hit upon an especially happy scheme for depicting all types of cavalry and foot-soldiers in action, and has framed each in scalloped border with a bold leaf design in the corners. The musketeers, pikemen, halberdiers and ensigns, and also the cavalrymen and trumpeters, are somewhat lighter in colour than the frame, which approaches the deep blue of the Chinese Wan Li. Thanks to the *Wapenhandelinghe* and the Beauregard floor we now know that these tiles must have been made between 1607 and 1627 (ill. 75a–f).

Probably from prints by Jacob de Gheijn, but also after Goltzius, are twenty-four tile pictures of 4×3 tiles hanging in the upper gallery of the Huis Lambert van Meerten. Each depicts a soldier or horseman standing under an arch, the keystone of which is formed by a human face; the figure stands on a mound with tall plants growing on either side. Of this series, more than eighteen horsemen (as can be seen from fragments in the museum) and six pikemen or musketeers are reminiscent of De Gheijn's sober style. By contrast, Goltzius's bold planning and execution may be seen in the portrait of Manlius Torquatus, which was not engraved until 1634. The horsemen are all from designs by Goltzius (1558–1617), who originally worked at Haarlem for the engraver Dirck Volkertsz. Coornhert, and the engraver and publisher Philip Galle. He went to Italy in 1590 and as a result was strongly influenced by the Baroque style, more so than he could have been in the Netherlands. The calm pose of the Dutch soldiers should be compared with the vigorous appearance and gestures of the Roman warriors with swords and shields (ills. 76a, 77).[5]

The Goltzius engravings must have influenced Delft tile-makers considerably, since we even find them adorning the bases and capitals of the fireside pillars which gradually replaced the earlier sandstone pilasters. The main part of the column is decorated with a garland of roses (ill. 76b).

The six foot-soldiers are not identical with those to be found at Beauregard, but they were quite possibly made a few years later by Jacob de Gheijn or another tile-painter working in a similar style at Delft (ill. 77).

LANDSCAPE TILES

The Delft tile industry became especially famous for its small landscapes. An exhibition entitled 'Frederik van Frijtom and blue landscapes' was held in the Boymans-van Beuningen Museum at Rotterdam from 14 December 1968 to 3 February 1969, to mark the publication on the former date of A. Vecht's book *Frederik van Frijtom (1632–1702): Life and Work of a Delft Pottery Decorator*—an event of great importance to the study of Delft ware. Not only does Vecht's work contain data from the notarial acts of the municipality of Delft, but the greater part of Frijtom's ceramic work is for the first time brought together, catalogued and reproduced. In addition, J. Nieuwstraten has devoted a special study to his art as a painter and thus done much to enable us to appreciate this artist's many-sided work as a whole. On the basis of two or three works known to be by Frijtom, it was possible to identify seven other paintings that had been formerly ascribed to other artists. Although his output was certainly much greater, sufficient authentic works remain for us to form a clear idea. His paintings are much more individual in expression than his pottery, in which, as Nieuwstraten points out, he is essentially eclectic. Vecht's study is also valuable since it provides a conspectus of almost all Dutch seventeenth-century landscape art.

Frederik van Frijtom (b. about 1632, buried in the Nieuwe Kerk at Delft, 19 July 1702) is almost the only maker and painter of pottery who worked independently, and he has no rival in this respect. He may have been one of the 'workers-at-home' *(thuiswerkers)* such as Jeremias Godtling, who painted pottery in The Hague for Rochus Hoppesteijn, or Gijsbrecht Verhaast who worked for the Jonge Moriaenshooft, or again Pieter Vizeer, who, in the eighteenth century, painted the Orange coats of arms in his own workshop (ill. 134a,b).

To judge from the archives, Frijtom's independence and detachment may have been due to the circumstances of his life. In 1658 he was registered as a burgher of Delft 'coming from elsewhere'. Baptismal registers record the birth of eight children between 1658 and 1673 and this seems to indicate that he remained at Delft, but it is possible that those recorded after 1664 were the children of his brother Barend.

Curiously, he is not registered in the Guild of St. Luke, but in the will of his second wife, Elisabeth Verschouw, he is referred to as a 'guildsman'. In his own will, made on 14 February 1701 and amended on 3 January 1702—it was proved on 16 July of that year—he bequeathed 'to his wife Elisabeth Verschouw two small paintings fired on stone'. After her death on 9 February 1710 these are described in the inventory of her possessions as 'two earthenware paintings in wooden frames'.

In another clause he bequeaths '. . . to his brother Barent . . . small unframed paintings, being landscapes, forests . . . painted by the testator himself', which bears witness to his activity as a painter.

It has been ascertained that Frijtom was in touch with Lambert Cleffius, whose estate in 1691 included a 'porcelain landscape' by Frijtom. It is

59

also on record that Frijtom owed Cleffius 100 guilders on 25 April 1684, but this does not prove that they were in business relations or that Frijtom worked in Cleffius's pottery.

Like his contemporaries, Frijtom must have taken up tile-painting after copying pictures and engravings. In a document of 12 August 1677, where he figures as witness to a will, he is described as a 'pottery-painter'; confirmation of this is provided by a comparison between the well-known large tile picture in the Rijksmuseum and a river landscape by him (Vecht, op. cit., ills. 1 and 2), both signed in full. We do not know if Frijtom visited Italy. He did, however, paint other scenes of castles and ruins from the area round Nijmegen (Het Valkhof) and the German frontier, and among these views, one of Bentheim castle, where Vecht suggests he may have been brought up. These romantic studies no doubt belong to his early years, though a period followed in which he repeatedly produced pendants, plaques and plates, all in pairs, representing not only Dutch polder country but Italian mountain landscapes and river scenes with bridges. From his first year in Delft we have a few triangular clay wedges signed *F. Frijtom 1658*; another is signed *v. Frijtom 1684* and there are two tile pictures inscribed *F. van Frijtom 1692*, by which date he had reached the highest point of his art (Vecht, op. cit., ills. 67, 68, 93, and De Jonge, op. cit., 1947, ill. 169, and 1965, Pl. i).

By this time he had long concentrated his landscape-painting talent on the islands of South Holland, the country round Delft, Kethel, Overschee on the Vleet, Ouderkerk on the IJssel, Rijswijk and Voorschoten. In these works he developed a style of his own, distinguished as regards the drawing by hatching and a *pointilliste* use of the pen, as Nieuwstraten observes. By the gradation of blue tints he endows the painting with perspective, the clouds varying from pale blue to clear white ('double-white', as Vecht calls it) and in this way conveying the damp, rarefied atmosphere of the South Holland landscape (Plate iv).

Apart from these tile paintings with their strong esthetic sense, he painted similar scenes on round and square plaques and plates; the edges of the latter are always undecorated, and there is no blue border round the plaques. This must have been a fixed principle of Frijtom's, to avoid spoiling the transparent blue-and-white of the Dutch atmosphere. In this way his tile-painting is virtually unique. Despite the prospects afforded by Vecht's book and the exhibition, it is not yet possible to estimate the total number of authentic works by Frijtom (ill. 78a,b).[6]

Apart from one or two products of the pottery De Witte Starre which are probably imitations of Frijtom, he did not found any school and none of the Dutch pottery-painters was able to recapture the atmosphere of his landscapes. His contemporaries and successors never escaped the influence

60

of the Italian mountain landscape, which was in fact strengthened by the use of a baroque setting with flowers in relief. It is almost as though they were insensitive to Frijtom's perception of atmosphere. About the turn of the century, plaques came under the influence of the 'Louis' styles, both the blue and polychrome ones being given a more graceful form by means of a rhythmic setting. They also underwent the influence of Chinese porcelain decoration, which came to the fore especially in the Rococo period, thus bringing to an end the seventeenth-century Dutch art of landscape tile-painting.

AMSTERDAM

Amsterdam played a part in the Dutch majolica industry almost from the beginning, though it did not become so universally famous as Rotterdam and Delft until about 1700. As the city area increased, by-laws of 1597 and 1612 indicated the districts in which potters might or might not practise their craft. They were allowed, for instance, near the old convent of St. Catherine, as is shown by the early names of streets: Pottenbakkerssteegh and Geleijntgenssteegh. In 1586 Carstiaen van den Abeele (d. 1603) lived in this district: he is recorded in the marriage registry of 1584 as a potter from Antwerp, and is the first of a family which later also worked in Delft. Hudig (in *Delfter Faience* [1929]) mentions a Corstiaen van den Ambele [*sic*], also known as Christiaen, who was a master potter at De Witte Starre. A son of his (?), Cornelis Corstiaensz., who lived from 1669 to 1731, is mentioned in the Delft archives in 1704 as a potter. No works by these Delft artists are known, but the names testify to increasing activity in the various potteries.

One historic document which has been preserved is the decoration on the façade of a house in the then Carthuizerkerkhofstraat, by Haye Esdré of Oldenburg, who had a tile factory in the neighbourhood from 1623 to 1647. This is a long frieze of blue tiles, with discreet touches of green, yellow and brown, representing the Battle of the Downs after an engraving of 1643 by Claes Jansz. Visscher. A watercolour painting of the house was made in 1877, probably soon before it was pulled down, and is still extant. The frieze subsequently became the property of the Royal Antiquarian Society, and is now to be seen in the room devoted to that Society's collection in the Rijksmuseum.

In general, relatively little is known with certainty about Amsterdam tiles of the seventeenth century. However, relations existed between Rotterdam (Claes Wijtmans), Gorinchem (Jacob Claesz. Wijtmans), and the latter's brother-in-law Hendrick van Heyst or Hees, also at Gorinchem, with the result that Jacob and Hendrick became owners of a number of kilns purchased by earlier potters and known as De Oude Prins, in the Anjelierstraat in Amsterdam. In 1694 this concern, still known by the house's old name, came into the hands of the Van der Kloet family. Willem Cornelisz. van der Kloet taught the potter's craft in Rotterdam and is mentioned in the Amsterdam archives in 1670 and 1684; he died there in 1686. His sons continued the business, which became internationally known and was not wound up until 1802.[7]

The inventory of the father's property shows the variety of tiles there were and the large scale on which they were produced and purchased in Amsterdam and by other cities. From the huge stock of over a hundred thousand tiles we may mention: '. . . soldiers, horsemen, shepherds with trees, shepherds with stars (illustrating the Christmas story), cupids, children's games, white and flamed tiles, Frisian stars, Utrecht flamed tiles, imitation marble *(treckmarmer, schutmarmer)* (ill. 81a,b,c), pairs of posts (i.e. fireplace pillars: ill. 107a,b,c), roses, columbines, lilies, . . . purple tiles describing histories, Bible tales and pictures of the chase.'

UTRECHT

In our account of floor-tiles we mentioned itinerant monks who made the tiles *sur place* for the nunnery at Mariëndaal. By the beginning of the seventeenth century this industry had evidently become a concern of the City Council: on 16 December 1616 the area of the ramparts behind St. Marie was leased to Jan Gerritsz. Overmeer 'that he may erect thereon a house, treadmill and kiln wherein to bake all manner of earthenware, tiles and the like (also in the fashion of porcelain columns to stand under fireplaces and so forth)'. This pottery ceased to exist in 1664, when the rampart was razed by the city authorities.

On 7 April 1629 the City Council granted the glass-blower (and potter since 1614) Claes Jansz. Wijtmans and his son, of Rotterdam, the exclusive right for six years 'to make within this city . . . counterfeit porcelain and such-like goods', no one else being allowed either to make or to import them, the monopoly being theirs on condition that 'they shall in no wise prejudice the said Jan Gerritsz. van Overmeer or his sons'.

From 1653 the potters had their own guild, and in 1661 a corporation was formed consisting solely of pottery-painters. Both bodies are mentioned as late as 1737, 1744 and 1766. In 1752, on the guild's recommendation, François Cuvel was permitted by the City Council to found a pottery, and in 1773, as successor of the deceased Isaac van Oort, he sought a licence to make 'glazed and painted earthenware'.

Utrecht tiles were highly thought of in the seventeenth century, a fact to be explained, as in Gouda, by the establishment of a branch of Claes Jansz. Wijtmans' works. In a list of deliveries to the Amsterdam trade we read: '1664, best Utrecht shepherd tiles *(Utrechtse harders)*, round "shepherds" of Noort', these being the most expensive kind. This is significant, since in 1642 Adriaen van Oort (Noort) settled in Utrecht and secured a licence which was renewed as the years went by. The origin of these tiles is thus precisely established (ill. 80a).

The trade link with Amsterdam is not the whole story, however, as there was a Jan van Oort, possibly Adriaen's son, who worked in that city. We know from archives that he was born and married in Utrecht and moved from there to Amsterdam about 1672; he possessed his own tile-works, and died in Amsterdam in 1699. We know of two large tile pictures by him representing vases of flowers: one belonged to a fireplace in a house at Wormer (12×6 blue tiles, see Hudig, *Altholländische Fliesen*, part II [1933], ill. 32a; its present whereabouts is unknown), while the other (14×8 tiles in manganese purple) is in private ownership in Brittany, in a modern bathroom. These pictures are almost identical in design and bear the signature on white tiles at the bottom: 'JVOort—a Amste.—Anno 1697' (ill. 79).[8]

It is hard to say whether the high price of 'best' and 'round' *Utrechtse harders* was due at that time to their rarity, but I have as yet come across no seventeenth-century specimens. The Jan van Oort style may, however, be traced in the eighteenth century in shepherd tiles with a spider's-head corner-design (ill. 80a), often embellished with mythological themes such as Apollo and Daphne or Diana and Actaeon (ill. 80b).

HARLINGEN

Notarial acts of 1598, 1617 and 1621 testify to the existence of a pottery in this seaport; in 1621 it became the property of Simon Toenisz. van der Piet, or Pijpe, of Delft. His wife, Maeyke Jansdr. van de Laen, concluded an agreement in 1637 with the Delft faience-painter Cornelis van Leeuwen whereby the latter was to 'have employment both winter and summer' and receive a fixed wage for 'dishes and tiles', mention being made of 'marksmen, horsemen and ships'. In 1639 Simon and Maeyke visited Delft potteries and made arrangements for further co-operation.

Rotterdam too established a link with Harlingen. As at Gouda in 1621, Hendrick Gerritsz. van den Heuvel, the owner of the pottery De Bergh Syon, set up a tile-works at Harlingen in 1633 in association with the tile-maker Hendrick Dircksz. Coninck and a wine-merchant named Gipson, and entered into relations with Willem Jansz. Verstraten in Haarlem and Delft. Later, in 1656, Reijer and Leendert Jacobsz. Braeff of Delft settled at Harlingen and took charge of Van den Heuvel's works. The later died in 1699, after which we know nothing of the history of these potteries.

In 1681 Pytter Pyttersz. and Jan Folkertsz. Grauda are mentioned as managers of a pottery in the Raamstraat at Harlingen; by 1684 the former was sole owner. He too was no stranger to Delft, as we know from his pounced work there, some seventeenth-century examples of which are in the Huis Lambert van Meerten Museum (ill. 3a,b).

The history of the Harlingen potteries was traced by Nanne Ottema, whose conclusions were adopted by Professor Hudig. We may mention three of the chief establishments, with the names of some of their owners and the dates when they closed down:

1. In the Zoutsloot Maeyke van der Laen—Sybrand Feytema—Frans Tjallingii.
Closed in 1910 and demolished.
2. In the Raamstraat Pytter Grauda—Jan Folkertsz. Grauda (until 1684) —J. Gelinde—H. R. Binksma—taken over by Frans Tjallingii.
Closed in 1803.
3. In the Kerkpoort Theunis Claesz. Sybeda—Spannenburg—(v. d. Veen) —(v. d. Plaats)—J. van Hulst (1850), which later became 'J. van Hulst's Bouwstoffenindustrie N.V.'
Closed in 1930.

A few smaller establishments need not be enumerated.

During the last quarter of the seventeenth century the Frisian tile industry developed a character of its own, though at the same time it was much subject to Dutch influences and borrowing from other parts of the Netherlands. In 1697 it is recorded that P. Grauda's tile-works despatched to Deventer a consignment of 'landscapes with shepherds and shepherdesses, children's games and marbled tiles', almost certainly in the Utrecht style (cf. ill. 81a,b,c).

A drawer of flowers and foliage who worked in the Zoutsloot was Egbert Pietersz., whose pounces are preserved by the Frisian Society; he also drew Biblical scenes and landscapes (ill. 81d,e). Some of the pounces are marked to the effect that he re-drew them in 1730.

In 1960 a *modellen-boek* was presented to the Harlingen Museum Het Hannema-Huis; this belonged to the Van Hulst tile-works mentioned above and was a sample-book used for sales purposes. The watermark shows that

IV

it dates from the middle of the eighteenth century. The first group of specimens belongs here; the second group, in a much more academic style, were added in the nineteenth century.[9]

Of most importance, however, is the most original series planned by Sybrand Feytema of the Zoutsloot. In 1687 he received a commission from the Frisian Estates for a set of tiles illustrating the Pandects of Justinian. He attempted to execute these in the same way as the Biblical tiles that were so popular, but the result was unsuccessful. The pounces, also in the possession of the Frisian Society, show clearly how seldom they were used. Only about eight of the tiles have survived (ill. 82a–e). Seven are in the Princessehof Museum at Leeuwarden and one in the Boymans-van Beuningen Museum at Rotterdam (ill. 82a, purchased in 1947). This scene, showing the administration of justice, is rendered in sketchy fashion; the scroll underneath bears the reference to Title 4, Law 29 in the text of the Corpus Juris.[10]

BOLSWARD

We do not know when the tile factory at Bolsward was established. It may, like that at Harlingen, go back to the seventeenth century. Of unique importance is the great tile picture of 1737, showing the factory in cross-section and the entire process of manufacture (Plate i; see also the description of techniques by P. J. Tichelaar in Chapter iii above).

MAKKUM

In contrast to the Harlingen potteries of the seventeenth and eighteenth centuries, two of which remained in competition till they closed down in the twentieth, at Makkum a single concern—Tichelaar's Koninklijke Aardewerk- en Tegelfabriek N.V.—has continued active down to the present day. The records which have been preserved show that this establishment has been kept in the same family in a direct line since 1660 or even earlier, when they first became known as *Tichelaar* or tile-makers. On the occasion of their three-hundredth anniversary, the present management published a short account of the origin and fortunes of this pottery, its operations during the past three centuries and at the present day.[11]

It is not certain whether polychrome tiles were made here, but it is quite likely that the firm's products became highly popular soon after its establishment in the seventeenth century. Many bird and butterfly tiles, in the traditional round frame with the meander corner-design, which P. J. Tichelaar believes to have come from Makkum, may well have been made by his firm. One reason for dating them somewhat late is that the painter had an imperfect grasp of the meander pattern.

Makkum tiles, however, did not attain their fullest importance until the eighteenth century and after.

Notes

1 The preachers represented are:
Dionysius Spranckhuysen, preacher from 13 July 1625; d. 11 August 1650.
C. v. d. Queborn pinxit et sculp.; no date.
(Dated 1660. Amsterdam, Rijksmuseum.)
Robertus Junius, preacher from 15 January 1645 to 2 February 1653.
1645, C. v. d. Queborn effigiebat et sculp.
(Dated 1660. Amsterdam, Rijksmuseum.)
1654. Anthony Palamedesz. pinxit, C. Visscher sculp.
1644. Adriaen Souter pinxit, P. de Iode sculp.
Hermanus Tegularius, preacher from 7 December 1638, d. 17 April 1666.
1641. C. Dame pinxit, C. v. d. Quebron sculp.
A variant of this portrait, without skull-cap, by the same artist. Painted in more advanced age by Frans Hals; engraving by I. Suyderhoef. (Hamburg, Museum für Kunst und Gewerbe.)
J. G. Goethals, preacher from 22 April 1640, d. 24 December 1673.
1641. Anthony Palamedesz. pinxit, C. v. d. Queborn sculp.
The same engravings, with one or more poems, in 1645 and 1674.
Mezzotint by J. Verkolje, Limoges, Musée Adrien Dubouché, coll. Gasnault.
Leonardus Fodenius, preacher from 13 May 1632, d. 26 April 1647.
1641. Anthony Palamedesz. pinxit, C. v. d. Queborn sculp.
Limoges, Musée Adrien Dubouché, coll. Gasnault.
Volckert A. van Oosterwijk, preacher from 22 April 1640, emeritus 1 February 1672.
1641. Anthony Palamedesz. pinxit, C. v. d. Queborn sculp.
The Hague, Meermanno-Westreenianum museum.
Literature:
Mevr. J. de Loos-Haaxman, 'Isaac Junius als plateelschilder', in *Bulletin van het Rijksmuseum*, IV, 4 (1956).
H. P. Fourest, *Les Faïences de Delft* (1957).
D. F. Lunsingh Scheurleer, 'Nog een portrettegel door Isaac Junius', in *Bulletin van het Rijksmuseum*, XIV, 3 (1966).
2 Dr. H. E. van Gelder, 'Delftse Plateelbakkerij "De Dissel" (Abraham de Googe, L. Boursse, C. v. d. Kloot', in *Vrienden van de Nederlandse Ceramiek*, 17 (1959).
3 Dr. C. H. de Jonge, 'Een zeventiende eeuwse Hollandse tegelvloer in het kasteel Beauregard bij Blois', in *Vrienden van de Nederlandse Ceramiek*, 43 (1966), with Military Commentary by H. Ringoir.
For the horsemen see the present work, Chapter VI, ill. 43e,f. These figures

are presumably taken from J. J. von Wallhausen, *Kriegskunst zu Pferde* (Frankfurt am Main, 1616), part II, 'Das zweite Buch von Abrichtung und Uebung der Cavalerie'. A French translation was also published at Frankfurt: *Imprimé par Pavl Iaques aux frais de Iean Theodore de Bry L'an* MDCXVI. However, Wallhausen nowhere mentions the name of the engravers from whom he took his models.

4   However, a floor of tin-glazed Dutch tiles is impractical, as tiles of this kind are not suitable for walking on. The floor surface has deteriorated a good deal since 1646 and was much damaged during the German occupation in World War II; this was partly remedied by means of a small supply of unused tiles. The floor is now entirely covered with matting to protect it from further damage.

5   Some fragments of these Goltzius tiles are still in the bay-window of the gallery in the museum: a horseman, a pikeman and a musketeer, so that Dutch soldiers must have been included in the Goltzius series.

6   I am not, however, convinced by Vecht's conclusion that Frijtom worked for De Witte Starre before Cleffius. How can this be reconciled with the fact that he was not a member of the Guild of St. Luke? Moreover there seem to me to be stylistic objections: would Frijtom, who avoided border-decoration as a disturbing factor in his landscapes, have agreed to the pattern of birds surrounding the oval landscape medallions that bear the monogram LC (Lambert Cleffius) De Witte Starre (Vecht, op. cit., ills. 59–62)?

     Cleffius sold his share in De Witte Starre as early as 1689, while his heirs sold De Metalen Pot to Lambert van Eenhoorn in 1691. If Frijtom's landscape style was imitated at De Witte Starre this may have been due to Pieter Waelpot, though he was not engaged there as a painter till 1690.

     The set of bordered saucers for a Japanese tea service (Vecht, ills. 40–44), with the monogram MB 1684, is of course the work of another craftsman. It is not impossible that his name may some day be discovered in the Witte Starre archives, but it is unthinkable that in that case Frijtom would have gone unmentioned as a painter of small landscapes.

     Finally, the landscape framed in a baroque setting of flowers in relief (Vecht, ill. 95) can only lead the argument astray. Four specimens of this are known, based on different prints. They are certainly in the tradition of De Witte Starre, but are presumably later than 1700 and cannot belong to Frijtom's work. See De Jonge, op. cit., 1947, p. 194, ill. 167.

7   F. W. Hudig, 'Amsterdamsche Aardewerkvondsten I', in *Oud Holland*, 45 (1928), pp. 60 ff.

8   Information obtained in 1958 from the present owner in Brittany by Mej. M. A. Heukensfeldt Jansen, Research Assistant at the Rijksmuseum, Amsterdam.

9   D. F. Lunsingh Scheurleer described this book in an article in *Antiek*, 4, 5 (1968). The watermark dates it to about 1750 or 1760. The tile designs fall into two groups, the first between 1760 and 1810 and the second between about 1810 and 1890.

     The Faience- en Tegelfabriek Westraven in Utrecht also possesses two sample-books that belonged to the Tjallingii family at De Zoutsloot; these date from 1781 to 1910.

10   Nanne Ottema, 'Friesche majolica', in *De Vrije Fries* (1920); J. J. Meijer-Collins in *Tijdschrift voor Rechtsgeschiedenis*, XII (1933), ill. 4, p. 408.

11 *Vrienden van de Nederlandse Ceramiek*, 19 (June 1960): jubilee exhibition 'Wat Friese Gleijers bakten' (What Frisian potters made), celebrating the tercentenary of the Tichelaar family works at Makkum.

VIII   *Blue and manganese tiles in the eighteenth century*

While no exact date can be given, it is a curious fact that the demand for polychrome tiles began to decline before 1700, despite the high artistic level they had reached in the course of the previous century and to some extent still maintained, especially in the graceful flower patterns.

The explanation may be that by about 1650 the blue tile industry had become more and more celebrated and had developed many new decorative qualities, so that the interest in polychrome tiles fell off and they lost their predominance for some decades at least. This is one of the factors that led to a radical change in the tile industry around the middle of the seventeenth century. Another reason was the remarkable and increasing preference for tile pictures and the use of tiles to decorate walls and interiors. This led to a more monotonous type of decoration, but conversely it meant that the taste for polychrome revived at the beginning of the eighteenth century as regards flower-vases, landscapes and historical scenes.

The Delft tile industry was also influenced, as we shall see in Chapter x below, by the important effects on Delft faience of the adoption of high-fire and muffle furnace techniques from Japan.

In the eighteenth century blue tiles themselves developed a new colour-scheme by the addition of manganese, a purple or brownish-purple tint which continued to be used alone or in combination until the twentieth century.

After 1700 there is no longer any point in trying to discover the place of origin of a particular tile. By degrees each tile factory came to make whatever patterns it chose, whether they originated in Rotterdam, Amsterdam, Utrecht, Harlingen or Makkum, while Delft in this period occupied a position of its own. On the other hand, the archives of the tile-works and cities are fuller for this period, so that the documentation of products is sometimes easier. We have now only to do with universally known faience and tile-works such as those at Amsterdam (Van der Kloet), Rotterdam (Aelmis), Utrecht (Westraven), Harlingen (S. Feytema-Tjallingii, the Zoutsloot and Tjallingii-Spannenburg-Van Hulst) and Makkum (Tichelaar). The various categories each developed in its own way.

In the eighteenth century there developed a new type of portrait on 3×2 blue tiles, usually in an oval medallion or framed as a plaque. Heavy drapery hangs from above, and underneath the portrait is a cartouche giving the subject's name and sometimes his or her coat of arms, as is naturally done for members of the House of Orange. The portraits reproduced here are of WILHELM KAREL HENDRIK FRISO PRINS VAN ORANJE EN NASSAU ERFSTADHOUDER [Hereditary Stadholder] CAPITEYN GE-NERAAL EN ADMIRAAL VAN DE SEVEN PROVINCIËN DER VEREENIG-DE NEDERLANDEN & & & and Anne of Hanover (daughter of George II of England), whom he married in 1734. Her portrait shows, surmounted by a crown, the arms of Prince William IV and those of Britain and Brunswick, with the inscription: HAERE KONINKLYKE HOOGHEIT [Her Royal Highness] ANNA PRINCESSE VAN ORANJE & & &. Both portraits are from originals by Philips van Dijk of Amsterdam, who was appointed court painter in 1747; the tile portraits were made from engravings made by John Faber the Younger in 1735 (ill. 83a,b).[1]

At this period it also became customary to use tile portraits for the decoration of entire walls and rooms. Shortly before 1700 Pieter Jansz. Aelmis came into possession of the tile-works De Bloempot at Rotterdam, which had become celebrated in the previous century and which his son Jan Pietersz. did much to make known abroad. One of the most striking examples of this is the tiled drawing-room in the château at Ayeneux in the province of Liège, which according to the house-sign dates from 1743 and bears the arms of the Delcourt-Roberty family; these are repeated on the stucco ceiling of the château chapel, and also in the church at Soumagne near by, to which parish Ayeneux belonged.[2] It has not as yet been explained why the drawing-room is entirely decorated with equestrian tile portraits of the Emperor Joseph and the Empress Maria Theresa, Louis XV and Marie Leszczyńska of France and William, Duke of Cumberland (behind the fireplace). Can the person who ordered them have enjoyed some special relationship with all these crowned families? Forests, castles and riverside churches are also to be seen in the large pictures; the subjects' titles are inscribed in full on the raised foreground, and one picture bears the name of *I. Aalmis. Rotterdam* at the bottom on the left. Around these blue portraits, which measure 10 by 8 tiles, the rest of the wall is filled with sets of four tiles decorated with stylized flowers and diagonally-placed carnations in manganese tint. The portraits have a stodgy look, but are of distinct historical value (ill. 84a,b).

We should mention separately a series of portraits in blue tiles which is chiefly of importance for art history. These are the illustrations to Houbraken's *De Groote Schouburgh der Nederlandsche Kunstschilders en -schilderessen.*

Arnold Houbraken was born at Dordrecht in 1660, moved to Amsterdam in 1700 and died there in 1719. He published parts i and ii of his biographical work in 1718, while part iii appeared in 1721. A second edition dates from 1753. The historical importance of the work was justly stressed by Dr. C. Hofstede de Groot in a dissertation of 1891. A series of twelve, totalling 31 portraits, was chosen for tile-painting; three of these series have survived, and one was recently acquired by the Tile Museum at Otterlo. A second, identical series was till recently in the possession of J. G. Wurfbain at Spankeren. The third belongs to the Musée Carnavalet at Paris, whence two portraits are on loan to the Musée National de Céramique at Sèvres.

All three sets of portraits are done from the 1718–21 edition; that of 1753 is of lesser quality and not all the portraits appear in it. In the books, the names of the artists depicted are given chapter by chapter: in the tiles these are painted along the sides. The Carnavalet series is slightly larger and there are differences in the placing of the names, in which there are sometimes mistakes. The portraits of Jacobus Jordaens and Jan van Goyen, Frans van Mieris and Jan Steen are in the Tile Museum at Otterlo (ill. 85a,b); those of Jacob van der Does and Paulus Potter, and the three on a single plate representing Anna Maria van Schurmann, Rembrandt and Jacobus Bakker (ill. 85c,d), are from the Paris series, the names of Rembrandt and Bakker being transposed. It would seem that two tile-painters were at work on these series, the later one being less skilful and less conversant with the names of past and present artists; for instance, he spells Gerard de Lairesse *Gerard de Lacerd*. One of these sets of portraits, under the title 'Delft masterpieces', was exhibited for the first time in the Prinsenhof Museum at Delft, but there is no lack of proof that none of the three was made there. As Houbraken's *Groote Schouburgh* was published at Amsterdam, it is likely that the portraits were made in one of the tile-works there, in about 1720–5.[3]

HORSEMEN

The polychrome tiles depicting people and animals in a landscape in a lozenge-shaped frame, which developed in such variety in the seventeenth century, virtually ceased about 1700, as they too were supplanted by blue tiles. The illustrations to Prince Maurice's *Wapenhandelinghe* served as model for these before 1625, and there were all kinds of variations in the portrayal of infantry with pikes and muskets. Polychrome tiles showing peasants in the fields were replaced by blue tiles depicting burghers and artisans. Interest in horsemen grew, as we may see from several new compositions, and the bourgeoisie begin by degrees to appear on horseback. These tiles provide striking examples of the transition to the eighteenth century; they also began to be made in Friesland. Scarcely any prints are known, but the corner-designs, including ox-heads, point to a date after 1675, as does the style of drawing.

Special mention should be made of a number of blue and manganese tiles depicting horsemen which belong to the transition period and of which there are different examples in the two museums at Leeuwarden. The riders wear fluttering garments and are protected by shields and large hats. They are somewhat reminiscent of the Turkish or Saracen foot-soldiers (ill. 26) which may be of earlier Rotterdam origin. Both types cover the whole surface of the tile, but there are also differences. In the equestrian tiles the spider's-head motif is still used, though it is quite superfluous. The blue, green and orange colouring of the Saracen tiles does not occur with the horsemen, who are all in blue or manganese tints (ill. 86a).

Another new feature of this time is the civilian interest in riding as a pastime, giving rise to the plain blue 'riding school' tiles, each showing three horsemen riding from right to left and forming a diagonal line— trotting, galloping, mounting etc. These tiles formed the skirting-board decoration of a room in a house at Kleine Brede Plaats 8, in Harlingen, where they may have originated about 1700 (ill. 86b).

As with portraits, a way was found to combine blue and manganese in eighteenth-century equestrian tiles, although in general quality suffered. The figures were made smaller and set in a medallion in the form of an eight-lobed scallop, while the area outside this is powdered manganese. When four tiles are placed together the corners form a four-leafed clover (ill. 87a). A variant of this is seen in four tiles in the Zuider Zee Museum at Enkhuizen, where the corners join to form a rosette: this is the work of another tile-painter, after engravings of which nothing is known (ill. 87b).

BASKETS OF FRUIT AND FLOWERS

The close relationship between Friesland and the West Frisian Islands, strengthened by mutual trade, led to the appearance in both regions of a tile industry different in type and style from that found almost everywhere

else in the Netherlands. In connection with the polychrome tiles made at Hoorn we have already mentioned the relations that existed with Willem Verstraten's tile-works at Delft; but it is nevertheless clear from the interesting collection of tiles in the Zuider Zee Museum at Enkhuizen how distinctive this area was in the late seventeenth and eighteenth centuries. A brief account of this collection was given by D. F. Lunsingh Scheurleer in 1967.[4] Most kinds of the well-known polychrome tiles are represented; the later blue and manganese specimens are especially typical of the 'new style'. One has only to compare the blue baskets of fruit and flowers, in the traditional round frame with spider's-head corners, with the polychrome fruit-bowls of grapes and pomegranates, or the openwork fruit-dish set in a lozenge frame against a manganese ground and framed in a white square in reserve technique (ill. 88a,b). All these are variants that only made their appearance in the eighteenth century.

FLOWER-TILES

The wicker flower-baskets or baroque flower compositions seem to be a wholly new invention: the latter consist of bouquets resting on intertwined leaves and branches or disposed in a vase. As if this were not enough, the vase stands in a coloured rectangular earthenware dish—an original though over-elaborate device (ill. 89a).

In contrast to this excess we find an impoverishment of the stylized flower decoration of the Renaissance type. Characteristic examples are to be seen in the Enkhuizen Museum. Marigolds and a tulip are arranged in traditional fashion in vases of clumsy deformed shape, flanked by balusters and with small fleurs-de-lis in the corners (ill. 89b). Still more ungainly are the flowering plants in copper vases in a round frame, with a corner-design of stripes and blobs vaguely recalling the Chinese meander pattern (ill. 89c).

THE HET LOO PALACE

Fortunately the eighteenth century also saw new and valuable developments. One of these is seen in a cellar with cross-vaulting in the palace at Het Loo, known as the 'candied fruit' cellar: this is one of the earliest parts of the building, which was started by William III as Stadholder in 1686, the architect being Daniel Marot.[5] The tile decoration of the vaulting and dado and of the window surround is especially remarkable: it must date from shortly before 1700 to some time after that date. We find here a variety of motifs and about six principal designs in the decoration of the white dado, which shows great skill in the embellishment of surfaces (ills. 90a,b,c and 91a,b,c). Vases of flowers, landscapes and geometrical figures are varied with an elegant imitation of golden-brown marble tiles. The most striking are the blue vases in different shapes, with or without handles, containing tasteful baroque bouquets and standing against a white octagonal background; the surrounding area is of a dark manganese colour, with well-drawn small fleurs-de-lis reserved in the corners. This pattern, flanked by a border of single marble tiles, follows the ribs of the vaulting right up to the keystone, while in two corners of the cellar there is a small marble niche with decoration of the same period. The decoration of the vault springs from four blue tiles depicting tendrils and rosettes (ill. 90a,b).

The blue landscape tiles in this cellar are equally worth attention. The top row of the dado and the tiles surrounding the window are alike in composition; they are of excellent quality and may be by the same hand as the others. The scenes are full of careful detail, showing for example a jetty with two boats at their moorings and sailing craft on a river; an elegant couple with a dog walking beside a stretch of water on which ducks are swimming; two men sitting in a two-wheeled farm cart, with the waggoner leading the horse; two peasants with wide hats sitting in the shade of a tree, with cattle grazing in the foreground; skaters and a sledge on the ice, with a bridge behind and a shepherd and shepherdess sitting by the waterside, with sheep grazing on the right.

This decoration in the royal palace may make us wonder if the origin of these tiles is not to be found in Delft, more especially at the tile-works known as De Grieksche A (The Greek A), for which Marot made designs.

The cellar contains several other groups of landscape tiles, frequently showing villages by a river or churches and castles surrounded by woods (ill. 91b), small landscapes in a round with sprigs in the corners, or very small pictures of ships, villages, drawbridges and plants in a broad octagonal blue border (ill. 91c).

In the period of transition to the eighteenth century some details stand out which enable us to date the tiles if not to determine their place of origin.

CITY GATES

One such detail, in tiles depicting city gates, is an early type of carnation corner-design. These tiles with their carefully copied pictures in the traditional round frame are derived from the *Beschrijvinge der wijdt-vermaarde koopmans-stadt Amstelredam* (Description of the Renowned Merchant City of

Amsterdam), published by J. Veenhuysse in 1664. The engravings are based on paintings by Reijnier Nooms, known as De Zeeman (ill. 92a).

The new repertoire also included pictures of public squares and gardens, some from the illustrated edition of *De Zegepralende Vecht* (The Triumphant Vecht) of 1719. (See the tile picture of the residence and Zijdebalen factory of the silk manufacturer David van Mollem [1670–1746] at Utrecht, in the Central Museum there, reproduced in *Tiles*, op. cit., p. 172.) Other rural residences on the Vecht were likewise the subject of a few tile pictures of high quality.[6]

Another rare topographical scene is the view of the country house of Walenburg at Neerlangbroek near Doorn (Plate v, 17×20.5 cm.), dated 1767, copied from a print entitled *'t Huys Walesteyn bij Utrecht 1757*, after a drawing by Jan de Beijer; the etcher's name is not known.[7]

Many different themes were tried in the eighteenth century, and the new style of blue landscape also developed into an independent composition with its own character. Corner-designs and round frames disappeared, thus preparing the way for the use of the tile in landscape pictures in the same way that Cornelis Boumeester had used it for seascapes before 1700. These landscapes tended increasingly to replace paintings as a wall decoration, and in addition they were put to wider uses, first as overdoors and eventually for the adornment of chimney-pieces, whole walls, vestibules and landings. Typical examples are preserved in the Kingma house at Makkum, depicting a farmhouse and meadow with cows grazing, with a tower and windmills in the distance (4×13 tiles: ill. 92b). Another Frisian scene is the panoramic view of the canal-side village of Molkwerum, somewhat primitive in execution but clearly showing the trend towards large surface decoration (ill. 93). This led eventually to the practice of lining rooms with tiles: outstanding examples of this have been preserved, both from the northern part of the country and from Rotterdam (ills. 113, 114).

ORNAMENTAL TILES

In this field the eighteenth century brought about a total change. One may speak of a distinctive Frisian style and also a more Dutch variety influenced by the French Louis styles. The Harlingen pattern-book, already mentioned, has proved extremely valuable in this connection. In the De Moriaen Museum at Gouda and also the Zuider Zee Museum there are blue and manganese four-tile pictures painted in somewhat free imitation of a blue pattern in the book: one is called 'Alkmaar chintz' or diaper (ill. 94a).[8] The design in ill. 94b, which has no special name, is probably exclusively Frisian.

Imitations of the French styles with figures and line ornament are a great deal more delicate: they consist of traditional urns with bases, volutes, medallions and innumerable small flourishes and florets (ill. 95a). Here again both Harlingen and Rotterdam made their contribution.

At Gouda and also in the Gemeente Museum at The Hague one may see very large manganese ornamental tiles in correct Louis XIV style but suggesting the transition to French Regency and rococo by their playful little asymmetrical dancing figures with swords and flags, surmounting regular cartouches bearing the arms of cities (Utrecht, Gouda etc.), or sometimes vases of flowers, portraits and ornamental devices (ill. 95b). The patterns for these come from Rotterdam and probably from Jan Aelmis's works; they may be related to the contemporary faience of Rouen and Nevers. The small figures show the influence of Joseph Oléry's workshop at Moustiers, where from 1738 onwards all kinds of figures and grotesques were used to adorn faience in what was called the *genre Callot*.[9]

A word should be said of the development of single tiles in the transition period. These may be typically Dutch with a broad octagonal frame adorned with volutes, foliage and half-rosettes, and a delicate stripe pattern placed diagonally in the corners. Tiles of this very characteristic type often combine a scene in blue colouring with a manganese border (ill. 102f). Daniel Marot's ornamental motifs were also increasingly adapted to tiles: the classic example is a set of four in pure Louis XIV style which was made in the best-known factories (ill. 102e). The Frisian pattern-book contains a notable version in blue and white or blue and manganese.

Pounces preserved by the Frisian Society at Leeuwarden show that these ornamental tiles were also made by Egbert Pietersz. in Sybrand Feijtema's works Aan de Zoutsloot.

BIBLICAL SCENES

The clearly marked trend during these years towards decorating larger surfaces, if not whole rooms, with tiles had begun to a certain extent in the seventeenth century with the tiled fireplace, and the area thus decorated became larger and larger. This is not only true of the curved *smuigers* in the Zaan district, both blue and manganese, but was also the case in northern and eastern areas.

The general use of carnations as a corner-design is also a sign of this period, as the style of painting gradually became more open and flat (ill. 96d,e,f). For a long time Biblical scenes continued to be framed in a circle, but we also find volutes appearing on all four sides of the tile in an apparent attempt to break away from the circle motif (ill. 96a,b,c).

Old Testament scenes were probably more common at the beginning of the eighteenth century than at its end,[10] as the didactic purpose predominant in the seventeenth century was increasingly focussed on the New Testament. An example is the manganese tableau in the De Moriaen Museum at Gouda, composed of twenty-four tiles illustrating scenes from the Gospels of Matthew, Luke and John and half a dozen episodes from the Acts (ill. 97). This belongs to a later stage of development and style; the drawing is almost linear, as in the Biblical scene depicted in the fireplace of the Workum town hall which dates from 1779 (ill. 112). In this new style the tile-painter also aimed to produce a picture that could stand by itself, as may be seen from a tableau in the Frisian Museum at Leeuwarden depicting only the crucified Christ; the simplicity of this work suggests that it may well have come from this area.

SHIPS

Rotterdam tile factories, like those of Harlingen and Makkum, naturally showed a preference for tiles depicting ships. The seventeenth-century ship tiles developed with time into large pictures. The style of Cornelis Boumeester's engravings of sea-battles and harbour scenes, with choppy waves and all manner of details and accessories, is often more characteristic of Dutch design. Although Boumeester became internationally famous, he was not the only ceramic artist to specialize in this subject. His forte was seascapes, while his contemporary Jan Peeters I was much more of a river-painter. Only two tile-paintings by the latter are at present known, with views of Rotterdam[11] and Zutphen (30×50 cm, ill. 98a). Here there are a rowing-boat and another larger vessel in the left foreground, but the bridge over the Ijssel leads the eye straight to the town in the distance; clearly the artist's object was to depict the town's sky-line. The inscription on the engraving below indicates that close relations still existed between Rotterdam and Antwerp (ill. 98b). Jan Peeters I was a Dutch painter and draughtsman who supplied the engraver Casper Bouttats (1640–1695/6) of Antwerp with a collection in book form of plates representing towns involved in the Netherlands wars of the sixteenth and seventeenth centuries. The title of this work is *Thoneel der Steden ende Sterckten van 't Vereenight Nederlandt . . . verovert door Wapenen der . . . Staeten onder het gheleij van de . . . Princen van Oranien.*

The Frisian tile-makers again adopted quite a different approach, being chiefly concerned to differentiate the various types of ships, whether from copies of prints or from life.

In a nautical scene in the Dutch Tile Museum at Otterlo one may read on one of the ships the names *(Del)fland* and *Makkum*, which once again emphasizes the commercial links between Delft and Friesland.

The inn De Prins at Makkum, which dates from 1668, contains a notable display of local tile-paintings of contemporary ships, as a wall in the taproom was decorated a century later with tiles depicting twelve different types, two of which—a warship and a State yacht—are shown here (ill. 100a,b).

Towards the middle of the eighteenth century a close bond once more arose between Harlingen and Makkum, which contributed to the latter's fame and prosperity in the ensuing decades. It happened that in 1748, while Sybrand Feijtema (d. 1774) was in charge of the tile-works Aan de Zoutsloot at Harlingen, a tile picture was ordered from him by the ship-builder and shipowner Hylke Jansz. Kingma, who settled at Makkum after living for several years in Hamburg. The picture was painted by Dirck Danser, who also worked on canvas, and who mostly painted tiles with nautical scenes in addition to landscapes and 'histories'. He was probably one of the first to paint a ship tile from life and not from an engraving. The picture ordered by Kingma for his residence (now the Kingma Bank) is still to be seen there. One of the ships is inscribed *De Jonge Oranje 1748*, the year in which Prince William V was born (ill. 99a).

There was an period of rivalry at Makkum when Kingma himself started a tile-factory, which his daughter, the wife of Jan Haarsma, inherited in 1782. She and her husband died in 1811 and 1835 respectively, after which the stock was sold and the factory demolished.

One specimen from Makkum is a chimney-piece with an ornate frame of garlands. In the foreground is a two-masted sailing ship (known as a koff) with billowing sails, with a State yacht on the right and a merchant frigate to the left (ill. 99b). This work comes from the Lieuwkema-State, a building which was pulled down in 1959.

It seldom happens in the study of tiles that one is able to identify a number of signed and even dated works by a particular faience painter but not to determine their place of origin. This is the case, however, with G:D: GRAAF, whose known work includes, besides ships, a flower-piece and a salver with landscape tiles. He is mentioned by Hudig as a painter of nautical scenes and as a contemporary of Cornelis Boumeester. The latter statement is, however, not correct, as we have works of his dated 1785 and 1786: a flower-piece in a rococo frame (4×3 blue tiles, ill. 106) and a scene showing a State yacht in Zierikzee harbour.

The Rijksmuseum in Amsterdam possesses a picture by De Graaf consisting of 4 by 3 blue tiles (it may originally have been larger) and representing a Turf Ship and the Sandy Hook at Amsterdam, copied from etching No. 14 in one of Adolf van der Laan's fishery books mentioned below.

Attempts to discover De Graaf's place of residence from archives have so far been unsuccessful: no trace of him has been found in Amsterdam, Haarlem, Middelburg, Harlingen or Makkum. J. Pluis thinks he may have worked in the Zaan district. The municipal archives at Monnicken-dam mention a Gijsbert Meindertsz. de Graaf who lived at Monnickendam, married there on 14 May and died on 26 July 1815; he was buried in the church choir on 3 August. He worked for the town carpenter, but it is not known whether he also painted tiles.

Here we must mention J. Pluis's study contained in the annual reports for 1965 and 1966 of the Frisian Maritime Museum and Chamber of Antiquities at Sneek, especially the article of 1966 on the influence of A. van der Laan's etchings on the painters of ship tiles. Van der Laan lived in Amsterdam from about 1690 to 1742; his works, all based on drawings by Siewert van der Meulen, are 'Pleasures of the Sea, Land and Rivers' *(Zee, Land en Stroom Lust)*, 19 etchings; 'Deep-Sea Fishing' *(Groote Vissery)*, 17 etchings and 'Inshore Fishing' *(Kleine Vissery)*, 16 etchings.[12]

Besides Gijsbert de Graaf, subsequent faience painters also copied Van der Laan's etchings for their tile paintings. In addition it has quite recently become clear how important the tile industry of the West Frisian Islands was for the whole area along the coast to Schleswig-Holstein, Denmark and the Scandinavian peninsula. Not only is the ship itself given a name, but the owner, the skipper's name and the date are recorded in ornamental letters in a rococo cartouche like the title-page of a book (ill. 101b). To the same category belongs a three-masted galliot (6 by 4 blue tiles) surrounded by flower tiles, at present adorning the fireplace of the exhibition room in the Hannema-Huis at Harlingen (ill. 101a).

One of the most versatile faience painters in this new florescence was Pals Karsten, who presumably worked at De Grauda's in the Raamsloot works at Harlingen between 1750 and 1775, since nine of the twenty paintings known to be by him are dated there. The most elaborate specimen of his work is the fireplace that has been in the town hall at Dokkum since 1928, the superstructure and pillars being from the blue room at 't Slotsje, a miller's house on the Dokkumer Ee. In the Frisian manner, the tile decoration is almost too luxuriant. A vase of flowers, reposing on a stand and with a bird on either side, is enclosed in a fireback frame surrounded by an orchard in which fruit is being plucked. Above the frame is a picture of ships in a heavy rococo setting, after Van der Laan's etching No. 4. (See Pluis, ills. 6 and 7). Here we see 'a Netherlands warship of the second class, flying the Vice-Admiral's flag and making ready to anchor'. The work is signed *Pals Karsten 1773*. To either side of the flower picture is the usual pair of vases standing on baroque pedestals and filled with flowers. Below on the left the scenery is varied, while on the right the line of ships is partly continued (ill. 100c).

The Aelmis tile-works at Rotterdam were not slow to copy from Van der Laan's books. In a room at Altona lined with tiles in 1764 by Gijsbert van der Smissen, each of the three overdoors consists of fishing scenes. These are:

from etching No. 3 (Pluis, ills. 1 and 2):	'A Netherlands Warship of the Fifth Class, a three-masted Hooker and a Yacht';
from etching No. 19 (Pluis, ills. 17 and 18):	'A Greenland Whaler in Port at Rotterdam' (see ill. 112a below);
from etching No. 11 (Pluis, ills. 21 and 22):	'Fishing Smacks putting out to Sea'.

The first two of these are from 'Pleasures of the Sea...' and the third from 'Deep-Sea Fishing.'

Van der Laan's engravings were used as models of bygone times until the middle of the nineteenth century. In 1852 Willem Jan van Zweege, who worked for the Tichelaar factory at Makkum, produced a blue tile picture with a polychrome key-pattern border which has in the foreground a copy of *De Snelle Jager* of 1776. In the background is a paddle-steamer of 1852, the most up-to-date invention of the time but now itself a period piece (ill. 156b).

WHALING

It is perhaps also due to the influence of Van der Laan's graphic work that whaling came to occupy a place of its own in the Dutch art of painting ship tiles. Some manganese pictures that have survived make this development an object of study in its own right.

Pluis's thorough studies have shown the remarkable skill of eighteenth-century artists in the composition of large tile pictures. This is demonstrated by one of the scenes in the town hall at Wormer (Pluis, ill. 24) with men in rowing boats and whales spouting, in a composition derived from Van der Laan's etchings. These also occur in sets of four tiles in the Eelco Vis collection, since 1927 part of the Metropolitan Museum in New York. Not all ships in these scenes are taken from Van der Laan engravings; some are from other sources (ill. 110a).

We may mention finally a rare and precious tile picture belonging to the De Moriaen Museum at Gouda. This depicts a whaling scene on 6 by 8 manganese tiles (Pluis, ills. 41 and 42). It is no less valuable from the fact that this picture is copied from an etching by Adolf van der Laan. The tile-painter has achieved a fine effect by making the cloudy sky less dark (ill. 101c).

GENRE SCENES

Genre scenes in both blue and manganese developed variously in the eighteenth century as regards subject matter, though seventeenth-century fashions were sometimes preserved by way of fantasy in portraying the upper class. Pyter Grauda at Harlingen, who was in close relations with Delft, is known to have taken a special interest in these (ill. 102a).

The eighteenth century still preserved the memory of Burgundian miniatures such as those in the *Heures de Chantilly* of about 1400—a Book of Hours prefaced by a calendar of the months and seasons. Autumn was symbolized by the wine harvest, as it often is on the blue Delft plates depicting the months (ill. 102b).

More prosaic in theme, but certainly no less notable, are two scenes of about 1750 illustrating crafts: a coffin-maker's establishment and a brewery are combined in a single framed picture (ill. 103c). This presumably formed part of a larger series, but we can only guess at the other trades depicted. The engraver is still unidentified.

Folklore continued to be represented in tile design, but in a new way. The custom of the kermesse inspired series showing the acrobats, tight-rope walkers and other performers at these annual fairs. From Rotterdam come the Magito tiles, named after a family of rope-dancers who toured the country giving acrobatic performances, ballet and pantomime. The tiles are based on a series of thirty-six pictures executed for children by Tiepolo in his early years. The head of the family, Pieter Magito, is commemorated in a portrait engraving showing him towards the end of his life, in 1790, and accompanied by suitable verses; the artist is R. Jelgerhuis. Magito's feats are also celebrated in a poem of 1798 by Bilderdijk (ill. 102c).[13]

Rotterdam certainly played a new, important part in the increased use of genre tiles of this sort, but it is possible that elsewhere, for example in Utrecht, they were made for a new purpose altogether, namely as boards for parlour games. In the Central Museum in Utrecht two specimens may be seen, also based on prints for children, which originally formed part of a wall in a shop in the Predikheerenstraat. They represent the 'owl' and 'goose' games, and are entitled: HET NIEUW VERMAKELYCK UILEN-

SPEL... (ill. in *Tiles*, p. 204) and HET VER(MAKE)LIJCK GANSE SPEL: IAN. LOOT, with the inscription above *Gedrukt by Ian Loot* and the date 1710 (ill. 103d).

Examples of the Frisian style, showing the special character of the northern provinces, are the single human figures composed of 3 by 2 tiles. A rustic example shows a peasant woman with a churn and, perhaps in the kermesse context, a female dancer and a buffoon displaying the enigmatic inscription HOM HOM (ill. 103a,b).

Tiles showing municipal emblems—if these are to be classified as 'genre'—were no doubt made in Rotterdam and Amsterdam, and probably also in provincial centres; according to Tichelaar they were not made at Makkum. They are manganese in colour, artlessly drawn and came into use in the mid-eighteenth century. A canting example shows the arms of Hindelopen (*Hinloopen*, ill. 102d). This should be compared with the superior workmanship of the arms of Monnickendam in blue, executed three-quarters of a century earlier (ill. 67c).

CHILDREN'S GAMES

As a result of the radical change that took place about 1700 in the decoration of fireplaces, children's games—and also no doubt tiny landscapes and the animal figures called *springertjes*—were removed elsewhere, to halls, passages and cellars. A typical example is the well-known Johan de Witt house on the Kneuterdijk in The Hague, which was completely restored and now belongs to the Utrecht Life Assurance Company.[14] The architect C. W. Royaards states that '... the old kitchens retained their ceilings with beams and their tiled walls, ... and the lower part of the house remained essentially in seventeenth-century style to the present day.' When the house was built in 1653 the lower floor was lined with tiles depicting landscapes and children's games, and now, three centuries later, the decoration has been renovated and completed, where necessary, in the same style (ill. 104). A curious feature is the decoration of the arch with half-tiles. The reason for this probably is that in 1726 the house was extensively altered by its new owner André Girardot de Chancourt, who added rooms on the first floor and above as an enlargement of the drawing-room and dining-room, and a staircase with a carved banister leading down from the dining-room passage. To support the staircase it was necessary to build an arch underneath, just in front of the entrance to the main kitchen. When the house was restored in modern times the arch and pilasters were found to be wholly covered with tiles, and the architect rightly thought it proper to leave them. As for the tiles of the arch being sawn in two, either the new foreign owner saw no esthetic objection, or else it was thought not to matter because tiles were cheap and these, in any case, were the servants' quarters.

An exceptional specimen of genre is the oval blue plaquette showing a European lady in a rickshaw talking to a Chinese coolie. The work is edged with flowers and leaves and is rather slipshod in execution (ill. 105). It is marked with the six-pointed star of De Witte Starre and the initials JDB—most probably Justus den Bergh (van den Bergh), who bought the factory for himself and his family in 1741, though he usually signs JB or J:B:.[15] However, the tile-painter may be responsible for the difference. In any case the drawing and execution are poor. Although De Witte Starre was very popular for articles of use, especially under the management of Albertus Kiell from 1761 to 1772, a work like this shows clearly that Delft faience was in a sad state of decline.

DOORPOSTS AND HEARTH PILLARS

Shortly before and after 1700 two features of interior decoration made their appearance. The first and more formal in intention are doorposts in palaces and public buildings: on Ionic columns, sometimes topped by a royal crown, the arms of the Seven Provinces are suspended on a cord amid tendrils, while a set of four tiles display on the base some historic event or symbolize national prosperity (ill. 107a). These columns, which are very few in number, always occur in pairs; they are generally manganese or brown, and may also be decorated with small cupids. Hearth pillars developed in the same fashion with great success, originally as substitutes for the sandstone consoles supporting the mantelshelf. They continued into the eighteenth century, but it became more common to spread a more elaborate pattern over two tiles and thus increase the effect of plasticity and space. The two examples here shown come from a demolished mansion at Edam and illustrate the esthetic problems that confronted the tile-painter. Bunches of grapes, all exactly alike, hang from tall, slender stems: only the bases are different, with a peacock spreading its tail in one design while in the other it is seen walking. These pillars now adorn the kitchen in the Johan de Witt house (ill. 107b). They may be compared to the design showing a man and a woman on ladders picking grapes (specimens in the Zuider Zee Museum at Enkhuizen), with rococo ornamentation of all kinds and cupids supporting the vine at its base and tying a bow to the top (ill. 107b,c). In this case, however, the compositions are mirror images one of the other, which enhances their esthetic unity. The design for these blue pilasters can be found in the Harlingen pattern-

83

book with the title 'The Cupid and the Man on the Ladder', and can be dated about the middle of the century.

Makkum provided a rich variety of garland patterns of this sort, with flowers, fruit and cherubs or new features such as military trophies, muskets, spears or a hunting-horn and spoils of the chase (ill. 108a).

FIREPLACE DECORATION

A flower-vase tableau of 12 or 13 tiles by 8 came to replace the hearthplate (ill. 108b; see also ill. 138a). This may have its origin in the custom, seen in some paintings of interiors, of standing a vase of real flowers in the fireplace during the summer, to relieve its darkness; the chimney-piece remained the centre of the room all the year round and was probably the spot where one got most advantage from candle-light. In South Holland we are particularly well informed as regards two of these blue vase compositions, although they no longer occupy their original places. One, from the Governors' Chamber of the Sommelsdijk Orphanage, shows clearly the use of fireplace decoration at this period. A watercolour sketch made for the government by J. E. ter Grouw before the building was pulled down in 1876 shows how a Dutch provincial fireplace looked at the time, when carved pilasters were still in use and the Louis XIV style had not yet penetrated. The new fireplace may date from 1722, when the bailiff of the Sommelsdijk manor made the house into an orphanage. A flower-vase tableau is now once more on view in one of the ceramic rooms of the Rijksmuseum.

In the Cloth Hall Museum in Leiden there is a chimney-piece with carved sandstone figures on either side, and a blue vase composition in the middle; the entire work was previously in the architect's room of the house next the municipal carpenter's yard, and was transferred to the Museum in 1880 (ill. 109). Another specimen, in which the pedestal of the vase is missing, is in the Rijksmuseum reserve collection.

When the production of polychrome tiles began to develop again after 1700 it specialized first and foremost in vase compositions of this type, which were also used as panels in the walls of rooms that were entirely lined with tiles. They were mostly produced in Delft potteries, but Rotterdam may also have played a part later (ills. 135, 136 and Plate vi).

In the Zaan district (north of Amsterdam), the decoration of rooms and fireplaces developed quite differently and had a character of its own (ill. 60a,b,d). Mention should once more be made of this type, in which Biblical scenes were always the principal motif. This was still the case in the eighteenth century, which saw the development of the high chimney-piece known as a *smuiger*: this was entirely covered with tiles, as was the whole surface that curved over to meet the ceiling. One might think it impossible to follow the Biblical stories at such a height, but the tradition was maintained. The fact that these tiles came from Amsterdam probably explains the height of the *smuiger*, corresponding to the distinctive proportions of the mansions on the canals there, a result of the introduction of Louis XIV style into domestic interiors.

One of the most impressive examples of the Zaan style is the council chamber in the town hall at Wormer. The building, formerly a merchant's house, was restored in 1952–3. The *smuiger* is 3.80 metres high and is entirely decorated with Biblical scenes, each in a circle and with carnation corner-designs. The long wall to either side presents tile pictures of whaling and cattle-breeding, both highly popular themes at the time (ill. 110a). The cupids hovering above with laurel wreaths, as well as the plain tiles covering the wall and those in the fireplace itself, are new or were renovated at the time of the restoration.[16]

Another typical *smuiger*, still in its original site and decorated with manganese landscape tiles, is in a farmhouse of 1852 at Obdam north of Alkmaar. Some modernization of style is discernible here, notably in that the flower-vase tableau, which used to be a fireback, is now over the fireplace, while the cast-iron fireback typical of the seventeenth and eighteenth centuries is recalled by the carved wooden ornament, a mixture between a fireback in the hearth and a mantelpiece over it (ill. 111).[17] The last *smuiger* was made in 1863.

The different development of the construction of chimney-pieces in other areas of the Netherlands can be seen from the contrast between the one described above and that in the village of Anholt near Ruinen in the province of Drenthe, which has a nineteenth-century mantel and tiles showing the traditional Frisian star pattern (ill. 110c). In a similar way, a comparison between the tile decoration of fireplaces from all over the Netherlands would reveal their diversity.

TILED ROOMS

In many respects these rooms provide a conspectus of the variety of the products of the Dutch tile industry in the eighteenth century. Examples are not numerous, but enough have been preserved to enable us to follow the different types of blue and manganese tiles from Rotterdam or of Frisian origin; in the latter, the French ornamental style is also treated in a special way. It is equally of importance to the historian that some of these rooms are dated and that they were specially commissioned. We shall briefly describe three of these rooms below.

1. A room in a private house at Altona. The tiles were delivered to Gijsbert van der Smissen and manufactured at De Bloempot by Jan Pietersz. Aelmis, signed *Jan Aelmis à Rotterdam 1764*.[18]

The entire wall-surface of this room is in the reserve of the Hamburg Museum für Kunst und Gewerbe; it consists of four broad and two narrow panels between three double doors; the overdoor consists of 5×8 tiles in a rococo setting and the scenes above the dado measure 9×12 tiles. The overdoors are decorated with nautical scenes, including Greenland whalers with a view of the port of Rotterdam and the Ooster-Nieuwe-Hoofdpoort (ill. 112a). The large scenes are based on engravings by Jacopo Amigoni with symbolic representations of music, sculpture and astronomy. Amigoni prints, likewise published by Wagner at Venice, served as the model for Biblical scenes in the Reformed Civic Orphanage at Rotterdam. A similar tile picture representing the art of sculpture is in the Otterlo Museum (ill. 112b).

2. In 1797 the Tichelaar factory at Makkum supplied a room decoration in blue tiles, in Louis XIV style, for a house at Workum in Friesland. In a scalloped frame with rosettes in the corners, an Arcadian tile picture is suspended from a bow with garlands. Below, in the centre, is a classical vase festooned with leaves. On each wall, under the wainscot line, is another small framed tile picture. The whole nevertheless gives the impression of a white wall-surface. In contrast with this open type of decoration, the chimney-piece preserves the massive Dutch style and the fireplace combines both types of tile. Above, between the vases and garlands, is a Biblical scene (Christ and Zacchaeus, Luke 19); underneath is a koff as a framed fireback (ill. 113).

3. In the third type, the Netherlands character comes again to the fore, in a work which also marks the transition into the nineteenth century. The living quarters of the farmhouse known as the *Bouwlust*, built about 1915 in old Dutch style, have been re-erected at Bergambacht. An original 1671 fireplace was supposedly to be seen in one of the farm buildings, but on a recent visit this proved to be no longer the case. The inside of the barn was rebuilt, and behind the churn-wheel, which still exists, a living-room has been partitioned off: the whole of this is lined with manganese tile pictures or framed landscape tiles. The large scene represents a farmhouse and the surrounding area, together with livestock; in separate framed pictures round about are a horse, a cow, a dog, a cat and canaries in cages

(ill. 114).[19] These also occur frequently as fireplace decoration. In this case, there is no fireplace. The effect of this decoration, which may be quite recent, using original manganese tiles of the eighteenth and nineteenth centuries is to deprive the tiles of their true character and proportion.

In tiled rooms there is almost always a rococo tile clock; one such may be seen here standing on a console. It bears the signature *V. D. Wolk Rotterdam*. Johan van de Wolk was one of the last rivals of the Aelmis family (Laurens Verwijk) in 1791, until he too sold his factory in 1841. The tiled barn at Bergambacht is probably his work. The Central Museum in Utrecht possesses an identical clock signed: UTRECHT A: TUREL: 1775. The archives do not show whether Turel was a clockmaker or a tile-manufacturer (ill. 115c).

The origin of such tiled rooms is to be sought in Friesland, where many cellars and kitchens in well-to-do houses and public buildings are tiled in the same way. The rearing cart-horse is a typically Frisian motif (ill. 115a,b). There is no doubt, however, that the tiled room in the barn at the Bouwlust comes from Rotterdam, which supplied tile pictures and tiled rooms not only to the Krimpenerwaard, but to customers in Zealand and the country round Liège.

The tiling of kitchen fireplaces requires special mention. It is said that there is no single kitchen in Friesland that does not have a blue-tile vase of flowers set in the centre of the white wall behind the cooking-range. This may be adorned in traditional style with cherubs and volutes, as it is in the lower part of the Johan de Witt house, of West Frisian origin; but the Harlingen and Makkum faience painters also showed inventiveness in a design showing a team ploughing in front of a farmhouse in the cartouche, and with prancing horses as a link between the vase and the pattern below (ill. 116).

Finally Pieter Jansz. Aelmis of Rotterdam made a house-sign as early as 1697 for his factory De Bloempot, after a print by Carel Allard. This was a rather over-filled vase of flowers (ill. 115d) which served fifty years later as the model for the dining-room at Schloss Brühl near Bonn (ill. 122a). The original is preserved in the Historical Museum in Rotterdam.

Notes

1 Two specimens are in G. A. Bontekoe's collection at Oosterwolde. See *Vrienden van de Nederlandse Ceramiek*, 16 (1959); 'Oranje boove' exhibition, Willet Holthuysen Museum, cat. 211, 3 July—12 October 1959, Nos 66 and 67. For the polychrome coats of arms in both see Chapter x, p. 102, ill. 134a,b.

   The portrait of William IV is almost identical with the painting and also with the reproduction on a polychrome Delft teapot (unsigned, A. Vromen collection at Doetinchem) except that it does not include the right arm holding a staff; the princess's portrait, on the other hand, differs from both as regards the pose and clothing. See the present writer's 'Een particuliere verzameling Delfts aardewerk' in *Vrienden van de Nederlandse Ceramiek*, 48 (September 1967), pp. 45–6, ills. 41, 42, 43.

2 The château is now a private house (20, chaussée de la Libération). Its occupant in about 1870 was Dr. N. I. Picard, who introduced his name into the banderole of the family arms. I am indebted for this information to M. Dessert, photographer, of Angleur near Liège.

3 H. P. Fourest, *Les Faïences de Delft* (1957), p. 118, Plate xxxi, exhibition of Delft Masterpieces, Prinsenhof Museum, Delft, 2 June—15 August 1962, cat. No. 298.

   J. van Loo, 'Schilderssportretten op tegels', in *Vrienaen van de Nederlandse Ceramiek*, 45 (December 1966), pp. 16–21 with ills.

4 See *Uit het Peperhuis*, third series, 5 and 6 (September 1966): De Verzameling Tegels in het Rijksmuseum 'Het Zuiderzeemuseum' te Enkhuizen.

5 The royal domain and former castle of Het Loo were purchased by Prince William III in 1686 as a country seat with a hunting lodge. In 1694 the States of Gelderland proclaimed Het Loo to be a seigniory in the perpetual ownership of the House of Orange. The old castle, known as the Oude Loo, is mentioned in 1439 and existed in the previous century; it was rebuilt in the fifteenth and sixteenth centuries as the residence of the Bentinck family. The construction of the present-day palace was begun by William III in 1686 to plans by Daniel Marot. The flower and landscape tiles and the dado probably date back to Marot's time, though the tile work has been repaired as late as the present century.

6 R. van Luttervelt, *De Buitenplaatsen aan de Vecht* (dissertation, 1943, wartime edition); reprinted 1944 as *Schoonheid aan de Vecht*, Heemschut series, No. 40, unillustrated.

7 The print is to be found in a series made after drawings by H. Schoute, C. Pronk, J. de Beijer, A. de Haen, H. Spilman and others, etched and engraved by Rodrigues, C. Philips, H. Spilman, W. Writs and others. The collection was published at Amsterdam by P. Fouquet in about 1770; the various prints date from between 1740 and 1776. The series is rare. Information kindly supplied by Th. Laurentius, antiquarian bookseller at Voorschoten.

8 D. F. Lunsingh Scheurleer in *Antiek*, I, 4 (1966), p. 27, ills. 6d, 7c and 9: the names *servetblad* and *paneelveren* are here used erroneously. Also the same writer in *Antiek*, 5, pp. 35 ff.

9 H. C. Gallois, 'Rotterdamse Tegels', in *Mededelingenblad van den Dienst van Kunsten en Wetenschappen*, I (The Hague 1919), pp. 18-25. Other specimens

in the Huis Lambert van Meerten at Delft; ill. in Hudig, *Altholländische Fliesen*, II (1933), plate 30.

10 The scenes represented are as follows: ill. 96a, Genesis 2 : 7, the Creation and the Garden of Eden; ill. 96b, Exodus 32 : 19, Moses finding the golden calf; ill. 96c, Luke 15 : 13, the Prodigal Son's riotous living (Enkhuizen, Zuider Zee Museum); ill. 96d, Genesis 28 : 12, Jacob's Dream; ill. 96e, Job 1 : 13–19, Job receiving news of the calamities inflicted by Satan; ill. 96f, Acts 2 : 3, the Descent of the Holy Spirit (collection of Mevr. E. M. Prins-Schimmelpenninck van der Oye, Voorschoten).

11 The tile picture with a view of Rotterdam is in the possession of Messrs Nijstad at Lochum.

12 Dutch whaling and sealing in the late eighteenth century are described in a study by P. Dekker, *De laatste bloeiperiode van de Nederlandse arctische walvis- en robbevangst, 1761–1775* (1970).

13 Dr. E. Wiersum, 'De Rotterdamsche Koordansersfamilie Magito', in *Rotterdamsch Jaarboekje* (1920), pp. 104 ff., with ill. The figures seem to be copied from paintings in the Palazzo Rezzonico at Venice, reproduced in the *Guide* to the Palazzo (1930), ill. 75.

14 *Het Johan de Witt-huis*, published by N.V. Levensverzekering Maatschappij (Utrecht 1966) : 'Bouwgeschiedenis en Restauratie', pp. 45 ff.

15 M. G. van Heel collection, Twenthe Museum at Enschede, 'Oud Delfts Aardewerk', in *Vrienden van de Nederlandse Ceramiek*, 51 (May 1967).

16 The architect J. Schipper Jr. of Amsterdam adds the following information: The tiles in the fireplace itself are manganese ornamental tiles. A brass-plated fillet divides this from the piers on either side which are topped with slabs of red marble. The iron hearthplate is unfortunately concealed by the floor covering. Under the large tile pictures are long low cupboards painted in different colours. All the woodwork was repainted in its original colours at the time of the restoration.

17 H. B. J. Vlas, 'Over oude tegels', in *De Speelwagen* (1948).

18 Jan van Lier—the great-grandson of Abraham Willemsz. van Lier, owner of De Bloempot, where Pieter Jansz. Aelmis was foreman until 1691—later settled at Assen and decorated the walls of his drawing-room with tile pictures of harbours, including that of the Hoofdpoort.

Aelmis bought the tile-works at a public auction on 24 December 1691. Thereafter Abraham van Lier and his two daughters entered into partnership with Aelmis on 28 February 1692; it terminated on 7 February 1697, when Pieter Jansz. Aelmis became the owner.

19 At the Cloppenburg Museum (Lower Saxony) an exhibition was held from March to May 1970 of a collection of tiles belonging to Siegfried Stahl of Langendamm near Nienburg on the Weser: 'Alte Fliesen, volkstümlicher Wandschmuck des 18. und 19. Jahrhunderts' (with fully illustrated catalogue). The style of these tiles, both in landscape tableaux and in single tiles depicting horsemen, animals, plants and ornamental designs, often shows a strong resemblance to their Dutch models.

Blue tile pictures and tiled rooms made in Delft and Rotterdam for palaces in England, France and Germany, from c. 1690 to 1750

The great popularity of tiled rooms, which evidently began even before 1700, led to their use on a large scale and was one of the reasons why the Dutch tile industry split into two very different categories, each with its own importance as regards the export of tiles.

The potteries at Rotterdam, Amsterdam, Harlingen and Makkum turned out enormous quantities of blue tiles which found ready customers far afield in Southern and Eastern Europe, and which in their variety of design reflected the somewhat naive fantasy of folk art.

Meanwhile Delft came once more to play a major part, in association with Rotterdam. In the last quarter of the seventeenth century the Delft potteries reached their zenith as regards both blue and polychrome faience: the latter was not a little improved by the muffle furnace technique, possibly in imitation of Japanese Imari porcelain. This technique was mostly used for producing luxury objects, a category in which blue plaquettes may be included.

ENGLAND

Hampton Court (1695)
Just as it had chanced that about 1627 the illustrations to Prince Maurice's *Wapenhandelinghe* came to be reproduced in the tiled floor at Beauregard (ill. 74), so towards the end of the seventeenth century a prince of Orange once again contributed indirectly to the revival of the Delft tile industry. This time the link was between the palace at Het Loo, Hampton Court and the Delft factory known as The Greek A.

Prince William III married Mary Stuart, the daughter of James II, in 1677. They frequently resided at Het Loo before becoming King and Queen of England, and both had a strong taste for Delft faience. The collections of the British royal house still include innumerable vases adorned with their crowned arms and monograms.

90

When William and Mary visited Hampton Court as monarchs in the spring of 1689, they decided to have Henry VIII's uncomfortable palace demolished and rebuilt by Sir Christopher Wren. The Queen accordingly moved into the Water Gallery by the Thames, which architects and artists from all over the country were engaged to restore. The building accounts mention a dairy, the tiling of which was entrusted by William III to Daniel Marot. This is later spoken of as a 'dairy with all conveniences, in which Her Majesty took great delight'. It was destroyed by the King's order in 1698, after Queen Mary's death from smallpox in 1694.

In the years since 1923 over a dozen large tiles (62 cm. square) have come to light, some of which are now in the Amsterdam Rijksmuseum (ill. 117). There is also some kitchen ware, including cream-bowls, in the Victoria and Albert Museum in London. Thanks to Arthur Lane's research, the receipt for the consignment was discovered in the British Museum archives.[1] This document, of mainly historical importance, runs as follows: 'I do hereby certify that there is due unto Adrianus Koex (Kocx) of Delft for Dutch China or ware sent to her late Majesty the sum of Thirteen Hundred and Fifty Gilders 3 Styvers of English Money £122 14s. 9d' (received 30 July 1695). Presumably this amount includes both the dishes and the tiles.

The Greek A tile-works, which became celebrated under Samuel van Eenhoorn, passed on his death to his brother-in-law Adriaen Kocks, who died in 1701. The period of the latter's management marked above all the zenith of blue Delft faience, to which tiles can now be added. Arthur Lane correctly remarks that two styles of painting can be discerned in the Marot tiles, a heavier and a lighter; the scheme of the compositions is indicated by pounces. As far as our information goes today, only one faience painter, Nicolaas de Weert, is on record in 1691, but there must in fact have been several, since in those years some pottery painters were already on the staff. Further research may bring other names to light. The signature AK and the name on the receipt are confined to the owners and shareholders of the factory.

From 1701 to 1722 Adriaen Kocks's son Pieter Adriaensz. and the latter's wife Johanna van der Heul did much to confirm the leading role of this establishment in the production of polychrome Delftware (high-fire and muffle-kiln) and to increase the popularity of Dutch tiles abroad, at a time when these included both polychrome and black Delftware.

FRANCE

Beside this relationship between the Dutch-English court and Delft we may mention Delft's trade relations with Paris and some other towns with a ceramic industry, such as Rouen and Nevers, and not least the French court and the plans for Versailles.

The effect of exports of Delft faience to neighbouring countries was that potteries were established there also, in theory by way of partnership but actually as a form of Dutch competition abroad, particularly as they employed craftsmen from Delft itself. Trade relations with France were especially important in the 1660s, the key figure at this time being an agent in Paris named Claude Révérend who passed large orders to De Paauw and other tile-works and himself tried to organize the manufacture of Delftware at St. Cloud, which however ended in bankruptcy. He also made contact with Rotterdam potteries for the delivery of tiles around 1668 when Louis XIV was planning to transform Versailles into the main seat of his court. The Trianon de Porcelaine was completed in 1670; the interior and the façade were tiled, and the tympani were adorned with Delft garlands and vases. However, they turned out not to be weatherproof, so that this Trianon was pulled down in 1687. The *Comptes des Bâtiments du Roy* in the Archives Nationales in Paris show that large consignments of blue and manganese tiles were received from Rouen, Nevers and Lisieux as well as from Rotterdam, these being paid for through Claude Révérend. Robert Danis is wrong in suggesting that the tiles from the Trianon de Porcelaine were reused, over thirty years later, to decorate the summer dining-room at Rambouillet.[2]

Rambouillet (1715–30)

The Comte de Toulouse, a son of Louis XIV by Madame de Montespan, bought the château of Rambouillet in 1705. This was a medieval castle in which Francis I had lived and which had since been frequently altered, enlarged and modernized. The Comte de Toulouse, who carried out the most far-reaching alterations, was put in charge of forests and waterways by Louis XIV in 1711. After the king's death in 1715, when it became clear that he had no chance of the succession, he set about modernizing the interior of the château, where he continued to live with his wife Marie Victoire de Noailles. He had many of the rooms decorated with woodwork in French Régence style. Because of extensive rebuilding in later decades and subsequent neglect, the history of the château is in some respects difficult to follow and the use of some rooms has been incorrectly explained. This applies to the tiled room called the *salle-de-bain de Marie-Antoinette*, which can hardly be rightly named in view of the Régence ceiling with its elaborate moulded cornice and the French windows leading on to the terrace. Its use as a summer dining-room was quite in the taste of the period, as may be seen in many German castles built under the direction of the French architect François Cuvilliés. There can be no doubt that this tiled room, measuring 3.75 by 5.75 metres, is a period piece designed to meet the Comte de Toulouse's taste.

The Comte, who became Amiral de France, had a life-long fondness for everything to do with the sea and ships. Thanks to his position and circumstances he was able to achieve all he desired at Rambouillet, which became the pride of his existence.

Boumeester's work forms a bridge between the seventeenth and eighteenth centuries (ill. 72a,b). His big scenes of the port of Rotterdam are taken from the map by Jacob Quack dated 1665. He used these silhouettes frequently as the background for variously grouped warships and State yachts, surrounded by small sailing-boats and fishermen in rowing-boats casting their nets. It is thus probable that the tile pictures at Rambouillet were delivered from an existing stock (ill. 118). About six of these harbour scenes are still extant. The companion scene of the IJ river with the Amsterdam skyline and the towers of the Zuider- and Westerkerk on the horizon has more of a seaport character, with turbulent waters.

Single blue tiles are found in great variety at Rambouillet, where the object was to divide up the whole dining-room into sections. Besides the eighteenth-century landscapes without corner-designs we find hundreds of traditional themes including drawbridges, dovecotes, castles with sailing-ships in the distance, windmills, wells with windlasses, country roads and occasionally a man or woman crossing a bridge. The pounces for many of these can be found in the Rotterdam Municipal Archives.

A striking and unusual feature is the high-quality tile with a landscape in a roundel against a dark purple background with carnations in the corners, giving the desired effect of marking off a section of the wall. So far as is known, the only place where similar tiles occur in Holland is in one of the vaulted cellars at Het Loo (ills. 90a,b and 91a). At Rambouillet they occur as decoration in the dining-room round Boumeester's harbour scenes, round the four flower-vase set pieces and as a border to the dado. They are also found in Spain, where in many ways they far surpass the general standard of imported blue tiles from Amsterdam and Rotterdam. In such cases we may safely assume they were imported from Delft.

GERMANY

The Pagodenburg and Badenburg pavilions in the park at Schloss Nymphenburg near Munich (1716 and 1721)
There is no doubt that the tile decoration of rooms and halls, passages and staircases in the environs of Munich and Bonn is due to the influence of

Paris. The Versailles Trianon de Porcelaine no longer existed, but the new style of decoration at Rambouillet was to some extent imitated in Germany; the English court style of Daniel Marot was not copied in Germany.

There was, however, one important political difference between France and Germany, which led to an artistic divergence as time went on: in France there was a single royal court radiating brilliance from Versailles, while in Germany there were numerous *Residenzschlösser* both in the towns and in the country. The secular rulers and princes of the Church were responsible for the spread of a new courtly style based on their own taste and distinct from that of France. Owing partly to personal contacts and partly no doubt to chance, the stylistic result was closest in effect to Paris, and French architects and decorators were responsible for many of these castles, hunting lodges, country residences and pavilions. Tile decoration in the form of polychrome flower-vases and various composite scenes, as well as single blue and manganese tiles were supplied by Delft and Rotterdam manufacturers.

The first effects of this co-operation were seen in Bavaria. The Elector Maximilian Emanuel (d. 1726) had lived from 1691 to 1702 as Governor of the Spanish Netherlands in Brussels, where trade in Dutch tiles was naturally well known. Having allied himself with France in the War of the Spanish Succession, he was driven from Bavaria and later lived at St. Cloud. He never saw the Trianon de Porcelaine, and the works at Rambouillet were not as yet completed, but when he returned to Munich his first thought was to make Nymphenburg a princely residence comparable to Versailles.

Nymphenburg, with its stately grounds and an extensive park intersected by canals and containing the three pavilions, is thus Max Emanuel's creation. The central building had been erected in 1664 as a country house in Italian Baroque style. The reconstruction began in 1702 while the plans for extension were still being worked out. Max Emanuel largely directed their execution, but they were not completed until the reign of his son Charles Albert (d. 1745). The architect of the new palace and the Pagodenburg and Badenburg pavilions was Joseph Effner, who began his career in Paris as a student of landscape gardening; later he became a pupil of the architect Boffrand, and in 1714, returned with the Elector to Munich as court architect. In the construction of both palaces and houses he was far and away the chief exponent of the Régence style in Bavaria.

Pagodenburg (1716–19). The first of the Nymphenburg pavilions was modelled on the style of a Chinese pagoda. The original design shows that the elegantly proportioned octagonal *Salettl* was turned into the form of a cross by the addition of four rooms. The one on the south side formed an entrance; on the west, space was provided for a stairway leading to three new first-floor rooms in Chinese style; servants' quarters were on the northern side, and a tearoom was on the east. All the walls on the ground floor were tiled, as was the staircase. In the interior, the plan was to make the stucco ceiling, all the woodwork, the ceiling, the tables and chairs and the eight-branched wooden chandelier harmonize with the blue tile decoration. Altogether more than 2,000 tiles were used, among which four main groups can be distinguished (ill. 119a). Much care was taken in the selection; there are tiles with landscapes in roundels with sprig designs in the corners, in the overdoors and spandrels, while narrow panels represent outdoor life and peasants in a rural setting as well as fashionably dressed ladies and gentlemen wearing the hair-styles of about 1715.

In the staircase we find Biblical scenes, varied half-way up with two prominent tableaux (8 by 10 tiles) based on engravings which have not been identified and representing a large palace with statues on the façade and others in the park in front of it, while on the other there is a distant view of an elegant park with an avenue of trees (ill. 119b,c).

The tiles at Pagodenburg were supplied by several potters whose work is also found in other German palaces and in Spain and Portugal. Pounces preserved in the Rotterdam Municipal Archives point with certainty to De Bloempot, which at this time already belonged to Jan Pietersz. Aelmis.

Badenburg (1718–21). Work was started on this pavilion even before Pagodenburg was completed, the plans again being those of Max Emanuel and Joseph Effner. Full use was made of the waterworks which had been installed in the park. Although the façade is more or less Italian Baroque in style, various new ideas in the French Régence taste were used for the interior of the new pavilion.

Badenburg consists of a drawing-room, antechamber, gaming-room and a bedroom leading directly to the bathing pool, which is at cellar level (ill. 120). This incorporation of the pool into the main dwelling quarters is unique in the early eighteenth century. On the lower level there is also a system of pipes for heating the water, which is brought from one of the canals in the park. There are in addition a dressing-room and kitchen.

In France at this time houses were also being built with bathing pools, but those at Versailles, for instance, were only about three metres wide by one metre deep. The one at Badenburg measures 8.70 metres long, 6.10 metres wide and 1.45 metres deep. Above the water-level the walls are decorated with alternating white and blue tiles which continue up the spiral stairs that give access to the pool. The tile designs are not very varied, but repeat the well-known motifs of church-towers, windmills and little bridges over streams with sailing-ships on the horizon. There is nothing very characteristic or individual about their style, except perhaps occasionally in the rendering of clouds; they belong to the run of early eighteenth-century blue landscape tiles which were turned out by the gross all over Holland.

The decoration around the pool gives a clear idea of the Italo-French style that was coming into vogue in Bavaria. The pool is surrounded by handsome bronze open-work railings, bearing at intervals oblong shields with the Elector's monogram M.E. The gallery thus formed rests on heavy consoles, four in the corners and two in the centre, sculpted by Charles Dubut with figures in Régence style. The stucco ceiling is in the same manner. The Chinese wallpaper in the antechamber and bedroom, like that in the Pagodenburg, reflects the Elector's preference.

The Augustusburg palace at Brühl (1725–40)

A similar blending of German and French art took place in the Electorate of Cologne under Clemens August (1700–61), a son of Max Emanuel; this again was a consequence of the War of the Spanish Succession and the expulsion of the Elector of Bavaria from his dominions. The French architect François Cuvilliés (1695–1768), who had succeeded Effner as court architect at Munich, was summoned to Bonn by Clemens August in order to restore and modernize the palace at Brühl, which had been largely destroyed by an explosion in 1689, and which the Elector now hoped to turn into a centre of art and culture on the French model. The initial work of restoration was directed by Robert de Cotte with the help of a French architect and the latter's German colleagues. After 1725 the Elector himself gave direction to the work. Cuvilliés continued to supervise it until 1740, when he returned to Munich. The rebuilt palace was renamed Augustusburg after the Elector.[3]

The tiled rooms at Brühl (1740–8)

After Cuvilliés' return to Munich the rebuilding of the main edifice at Brühl continued, the tile decoration being henceforth entirely Dutch in style.

In contrast to the winter quarters on the second floor, a suite of five rooms was designed on the ground floor with a view of the park, which was modelled on that at Versailles. In 1743 the architect Balthazar Neumann received the commission for a monumental staircase which was executed in German transitional baroque-rococo style. This delayed the completion of the summer apartments. The suite of five ground-floor rooms in the south wing was planned to consist of two anterooms, the audience-chamber, a bedroom and bathroom (ills. 121, 122a,b and 123). All were completely lined with tiles of a geometrical design with tulip or carnation motifs, white on blue or the reverse. Pounces or blue watercolours of these have also been preserved. Each room has its own style of ornamentation on the basis of three different designs, and the whole is executed with judgement and good taste.

The place of the original staircase was now occupied by the summer dining-room with two service rooms, for which Neumann made an unfinished sketch. The marble fountain in the middle also belongs here (ill. 122a). Tiles left over from the tiled rooms were used for the dado. Above this, three types of tile pictures are arranged regularly along the walls: tableaux from paintings by David Teniers, a series of dancing Harlequin and Pulcinella figures from Italian drawings, and a large number of vases with tall, over-blown bouquets surrounded by birds and insects, of a type increasingly popular in Holland in the eighteenth century for corridors and kitchens. Altogether eight pictures are derived from Teniers, each composed of fifty-six tiles and depicting backgammon-players, card-players or peasants dancing in front of an inn. Two different paintings were used as models for this last scene. Pounces must have been used, as the tile pictures give a mirror-image of Teniers' work. The blue colour is vivid, but the execution is crude, showing that by the mid-century the Dutch tile industry had lost the careful quality achieved by the previous generation. This is also true of the dancing figures, which are of little artistic merit. The best are the large blue flower-vases, of which there are twenty-six, including a similar composition of twenty tiles over the entrance. Three subjects may be distinguished, each with small variations. Each tableau is of thirty-two tiles; the use of pounces is evident in the identical pose of the parrots at the base, also in the symmetry of the bouquets. The medallions on the vases are of special interest. The pounces for these have not all been preserved, while on the other hand pounces do exist for some scenes that are missing on the vases. Five scenes are still extant: they are set on a terrace bounded by a balustrade, by a fence, in front of a villa and an inn sheltered by trees; a peasant and countrywoman carry baskets, or ride past; a rustic couple dance, the woman with a harvest wreath in her hand; an elegant lady and gentleman welcome a guest and stroll in a park, followed by a servant. The most remarkable scene is of a lady and gentleman playing billiards on a terrace; unfortunately no model for this survives.

Although much has disappeared that one could wish had been preserved, the legacy of De Bloempot, which can be traced down to 1856, is especially important, since from the middle of the seventeenth century onwards it stood for the best of Rotterdam's contribution to the Dutch tile industry. Under the management of Pieter Jansz. and Jan Pietersz. Aelmis it supplied the tiles for the rooms at Brühl and the Amalienburg pavilion at Nymphenburg.

Falkenlust hunting-lodge (1729–37)

Clemens August, one of the richest and most luxury-loving princes of his day, achieved one of his dearest wishes by the construction of this lodge at the end of the park, as a scene for receptions during the hawking season. This *maison de plaisance* was Cuvilliés' masterpiece and a true reflection of his artistic ideas, which are grandiosely expressed in the decoration of the staircase. The theme of hawking for herons is most attractively treated. These scenes are varied with diagonally placed single tiles and groups of five in white and blue, representing the arms of Bavaria and also the colours of the Order of St. Hubert, founded by Clemens August himself (ill. 124). The groups, each composed of eighteen tiles, depict members of the hunt: gentlemen on horseback, ladies looking on, falconers and servants carrying hawks or herons. Other scenes show the birds, fledgling or full-grown, in flight or fighting one another. Two falcons and a heron are let loose: the falcons seize the heron and pin it to the ground while the huntsmen attach a ring to its claw in sign of victory, after which it is set free again (ill. 125a). In the main hall, too, tiles are used to form decorative panels, and as frames for portraits, and round the fireplace and dado, usually with the Bavarian arms or the symbol of St. Hubert. Set in the dado one also may find round medallions with a falcon or heron in flight or alighting on its nest (ill. 126).

These delicate Régence designs are by a French draughtsman, if not Cuvilliés himself; the compositions are executed in pastel blue tints, and match the designs in quality. Their Rotterdam origin is proved by pounces that have been preserved at the Bloempot workshop of Jan Pietersz. Aelmis (ill. 125b,c).

Notes

1   Arthur Lane, 'Delftse tegels uit Hampton Court en Daniel Marot's werk-zaamheid aldaar', in *Bulletin van het Rijksmuseum*, vii, 1 (1959), pp. 12 ff.
2   Robert Danis, *La première Maison Royale de Trianon* (1926); C. H. de Jonge, 'Hollandse tegelkamers in Duitse en Franse kastelen', *Nederlands Kunsthistorisch Jaarboek* (1959), pp. 182 ff.
3   C. H. de Jonge, 'Hollandse tegelkamers in Duitse en Franse kastelen', loc. cit., pp. 125 ff., and the literature cited there. See also, by the same author, an article: 'Aus Schloss Augustusburg zu Brühl und Falkenlust', published by W. Bader and others on the occasion of the palace being restored to use in 1961: *Kurfürst Clemens August, Landesherr und Mäzen des 18. Jahrhunderts*, Ausstellung in Schloss Augustusburg zu Brühl (Cologne, 1961).

X Tiles and tile pictures in polychrome and black Delftware, fired in high-temperature kilns or muffle-kilns, from c. 1670 to 1750

The distinctive style of polychrome tiles, dating from the very beginning of the Dutch majolica industry, was overshadowed in the second quarter of the seventeenth century by the infinite variety of subjects that came to be depicted on blue tiles. At the outset a combination of the two types was no doubt practicable, but it was restricted for the most part to the dark-blue medallion with a corner-design, as a setting for human figures or animals, in polychrome or blue. Ornamental compositions of many colours were harder to transpose into blue. Flower tiles were most adaptable to the combination of polychrome and blue, especially the group of elegant Oriental tulips, but these gradually took on the character of blue tiles with a coloured flower in the middle. Shortly after 1650 it looked as if poly-chrome tiles had had their day, but in fact things turned out differently.

We owe a debt to the Delft workshops, which concentrated on producing works of art, ornamental vases, plaquettes etc. but also made objects of household use. Some of these workshops paid special attention to technical improvements. Thus the products were often fired in round saggers or *kokers*, which helped to make them smooth. In special cases, after being painted and before the final firing they were sprinkled with the lead-glaze mixture known as *kwaart*. Red, however, was still a problem, as it fired so quickly, and attempts were also made with gold painting, the secret of which may have been discovered by free-lance workers at Jacob Wemmersz. and Rochus Hoppesteyn's factory Het Jonge Moriaenshooft (1671–92).

Shortly afterwards, however, came the importation of Japanese Imari ware, enamelled by the muffle-kiln process. Only a few Delft potteries, in particular The Greek A, were able to procure these kilns and start manufacturing the new product. The Delft Imari style with red and gold painting was a success and opened up wide prospects for the whole eight-eenth century. As regards tiles, however, this technique was rarely used.

At this time of transition, research and discovery, we should take note of Gijsbrecht Claesz. Verhaast, who in addition to carrying on his own

99

business was also, as appears from a document of 21 September 1689, employed as a faience painter, presumably at Het Jonge Moriaenshooft. We know of three small tile pictures of his, each representing a landscape or a domestic scene (ill. 127), signed in full *G. Verhaast*. The colouring is blue, purple and grey in various shades, pinkish-yellow, brown and green. The technique is skilful, but his works are only copies, the originals of which are not known.

However, the most impressive specimens of the tilemaker's art consist of five unique Delft polychrome pictures, with black for the added figures. These embody totally fresh aspects and ideas, opening up a whole new world to the beholder. All these specimens are undoubtedly based on a single composition, with variations of detail and finish. It looks also as if pounces were used, as the figures also occur in reversed image. The variations in the five pictures themselves have also made them something of a mystery.

A large picture in the Amalienburg pavilion must be the original. It is based on Chinese patterns (ills. 128, 129); Professor Hudig calls it a Dutch fantasy on a Chinese theme. The scenes are to be read in sequence like an unrolled kakemono: the Bodhisattva Kwan-Yin, seated on a lotus-flower and bathed in the rays of a golden-yellow sun, with two acolytes on her right-hand side, sprinkles the world with the dew of heavenly grace. A path then leads down among palaces and tea-pavilions, past elegant nobles and ferociously attired Chinese warriors. The two small panels represent groups of travellers among tea-pavilions.[1]

It should be said at once that the builders of the Amalienburg pavilion at Nymphenburg in 1734–9 were responsible for considerable disorder in the arrangement of the tile pictures, both in the large scene and in the accompanying panels. Thanks to the ingenuity of an official of the Museum, a photographic reconstruction of the correct arrangement has been made, although there are some gaps and also tiles whose right place cannot be found. (The reconstruction of the large picture is reproduced in ill. 129, while ills. 130–1, a and b respectively, show the present appearance of the panels and their reconstruction.)

If the Amalienburg Chinese scenes are compared with the Loudon picture in the Rijksmuseum (ill. 132) or the large fragment in the Evenepoel collection in Brussels, they will be found, in spite of close resemblances, to differ appreciably in the figures. A documented explanation of this has been provided by the studies of Dr. H. E. van Gelder and Professor J. G. van Gelder. One completely new feature is the addition of groups of Indians to the Chinese noblemen and warriors. They are Tapuya Indians, who became known in Holland through the paintings and drawings of

Albert van Eeckhout, who accompanied John Maurice of Nassau during his governorship of the Dutch colony of Brazil (1637–44).[2] After his return John Maurice created immense interest in these exotic works of art through presentations to the French, Danish and German courts. The Oranjezaal in the Huis ten Bosch in The Hague (1648–52) was decorated with representations of Indians, and in 1689–90 a set of tapestries entitled *Les Indes* was woven from Eeckhout's drawings at the Gobelins in Paris; a second series followed in 1737.

It is not surprising that the Delft craftsmen were also inspired by this exotic novelty, but they were not able to emulate it until after the successful technical experiments of Rochus Hoppesteyn and his helpers. The polychrome Delftware on a dark brown, olive or black ground, which first came into production about the same time, became known about the turn of the century, some fifty years after John Maurice's stay in Brazil; this may have been partly due to the completion of the Gobelin tapestries shortly before.

Which workshops are most likely to have produced these outstanding works of art, the supreme achievement in imitating Chinese models? Around 1700–15, three potteries may be mentioned to whom the pictures in question might conceivably be ascribed. These are De Metalen Pot under Lambert van Eenhoorn's management (1691–1721), De Dobbelde Schenckan (Louwijs Victorsz., 1688–1713) and De Grieksche A under Pieter Adriaensz. Kocks (1701–3) and his wife Johanna van der Heul (1703–22).

The painting of figures on tiles produced by De Metalen Pot is too different in style from that in the Amalienburg pictures for the attribution to be sustained. Moreover, we know one of the painters of black Delftware from this factory to have been a designer of delicate vegetation, Chinese pagodas and birds, in a style quite unlike that in the tile pictures. We shall let alone the question whether the deceptively similar monograms are those of Lambert van Eenhoorn or Louwijs Victorsz. of De Schenckan. Blue and polychrome Delftware by this skilful designer affords even less of a direct comparison with these compositions on a black ground.

We are thus left with The Greek A, and in support of it may be cited the polychrome figures of women and children and the decorative scenes of houses and hedgerows that are so common in the Imari Delftware bearing the mark PAK. After Kocks's death, Pieter van den Hurck was pre-eminent in pottery and Jan Verburgh in faience painting. Thanks to them, the style of the blue Kang Hsi décor was continued in the spirit of Pieter Adriaensz. Kocks and in a style in which one may detect an affinity with Chinese scenes on a black ground.

Finally, there is a technical link with The Greek A in that this factory produced the tiled dairy at Hampton Court in about 1690, which suggests that besides the manufacture of pottery they also had the necessary space and kilns for a tile-works on their premises.

Meanwhile, thanks to Hoppesteyn's successful refining process, Imari porcelain technique had become an integral part of the Delft faience industry. Although the results were few as regards tile production, they include a number of pictures fired in a muffle-kiln. One finds the tiles as late as the mid-eighteenth century, but after that the quality gradually falls off; the identification of subject-matter also gives rise to difficulty.

An interesting combination of green and red is shown by the polychrome muffle-kiln picture (11 by 10 tiles) of a grape-harvest in an extensive hilly landscape. Peasants are picking grapes and loading sacks in carts while in the foreground more elegant figures are seen tasting the wine (ill. 133a); the whole scene is symbolic of Autumn (cf. ill. 102b). The signature is of interest to the art historian: it reads *I: Baen: M. van Kuyk 1744*. A work by Jan Baen, representing a pot with a lid, is in the Musée National de Céramique in Sèvres; he worked at De Witte Starre and so, we may suppose, did Michiel van Kuyk, whose name appears in the Delft archives after 1700. The date 1744 supports the view that muffle-kiln tile production had passed its height by about the middle of the century.

The style and colour of *famille verte* porcelain of the Yung Chêng and Ch'ien Lung periods (1723–35 and 1736–95), which was so skilfully reproduced in Delft ornamental faience, is if anything still rarer where tiles are concerned. A coloured fragment of a 'parrot column' of only two tiles in the Bisschop collection in the Frisian Museum at Leeuwarden is an almost unique specimen of superior quality (ill. 133b). There must have been other examples of birds peeping out of hiding-places among blue-green leaves and yellow bushes, forming a colour harmony with blackish-purple, red and gold, in the style that was only possible in imitation of Chinese models in the muffle-kiln technique.

Beside the blue tile portraits of Prince William IV and his consort Anne of Hanover, from a print of 1735 (ill. 83a,b), we may set two polychrome tiles with the arms of Orange and Great Britain–Brunswick (ill. 134a,b). They were reproduced in 1909 by Havard, who gave Pieter Vizeer as the painter's name. No such person has been traced in the Delft archives, but there is a faience painter named Hendrick Visseer who made a reciprocal will with Jannetje van der Zee on 23 May 1725, and another faience painter, also Hendrick Visseer—presumably his son—who made a will with Elsje Schouten on 17 July 1779.

On both tiles the Order of the Garter encircling the arms, with the motto HONI SOYT QUI MAL Y PENSE, bears the date 1752, so that it is hard to decide between the two painters. The tiles are differently composed: ill. 134a shows the usual eighteenth-century corner motif of flowers,

102

while in ill. 134b the whole space outside the Garter is marbled with small coloured divisions, so that the general effect is obscured. There is a quarter-rosette in each corner, so that there may have been a group of four tiles. No doubt the two shown here were painted by different artists.

In general one might have expected more tiles depicting coats of arms, for it was the muffle-kiln technique that gave European popularity to escutcheons with gold ornamentation. Examples can be found of the arms of cities such as Amsterdam and Utrecht. However, the quality in these pieces is no longer remarkable (Frisian Museum, Leeuwarden).

There is a reminiscence of *famille rose*, but also of Saxon porcelain, in tiles depicting baskets of flowers, a subject which presented no problem of composition as they only display a single object (ill. 134c,d); they carry on the Chinese tradition in a refined style in contrast to the vases presented in large polychrome tableaux which introduce a new period.

At the same time a certain number of polychrome ship tiles were made; the pounces for these naturally appear to have been found chiefly in potteries in the northern part of the country, but they did not lead to a revival (ill. 134e,f).

Notes

1 See L. Hager, *Schloss, Park und Burgen* (Munich, n.d.), and C. H. de Jonge, 'Hollandse tegelkamers in Duitse en Franse kastelen', *Nederlands Kunsthistorisch Jaarboek*, 10 (1959), with literature cited there.

2 John Maurice, Count of Nassau-Siegen (1604–79), known as 'the Brazilian', was one of Prince Maurice's commanders and was governor of Dutch Brazil from 1637 to 1644. The painters Frans Post and Albert van Eeckhout accompanied him there. The Mauritshuis in The Hague, which has been a museum since 1816, was built for John Maurice in 1652 by the architect Pieter Post, after plans by Jacob van Campen.

Bibliography: Dr. H. E. van Gelder, 'Het grote tegeltableau der Collectie Loudon', in *Bulletin van het Rijksmuseum*, 4 (1956); Prof. J. G. van Gelder, 'De Oranjezaal in het Huis ten Bosch', in *Nederlands Kunsthistorisch Jaarboek*, 2 (1948–9); Th. Thomson, *Albert van Eeckhout, Ein niederländischer Maler und sein Gönner, Moritz der Brasilianer* (Copenhagen, 1938); C. H. de Jonge, 'Hollandse tegelkamers in Duitse en Franse kastelen uit de eerste helft van de achttiende eeuw', in *Nederlands Kunsthistorisch Jaarboek*, 10 (1959).

XI *Polychrome and flower-vase tableaux made in Delft and Rotterdam for French and German palaces, from c. 1700 to 1750*

The blue tile picture with the ornamental vase of flowers surrounded by birds and butterflies, which was found *in situ* in the Orphanage at Sommelsdijk, is now exhibited in the Delft rooms of the Rijksmuseum in Amsterdam (ill. 108b, 138a). It constitutes a link with a number of polychrome specimens whereof nineteen are known, in three different versions; doubtless others exist in palaces and castles in Europe. The use they were put to varied in the course of time. Originally they were set in fireplaces, but later they were used as ornamental panels on tiled walls. Undoubtedly they all come from the same workshop, for they are based on more or less the same pattern, with small variations of detail. Only a Delft pottery can have produced them.

There are fourteen of especial interest to study and compare, from the point of view both of their artistic merit and their value as historic pieces. Four of the series are at Rambouillet, three in the kitchen of the Amalienburg pavilion at Nymphenburg, three—including the blue one from Sommelsdijk—in the Rijksmuseum in Amsterdam, one in the Musée national de Céramique in Sèvres, one in the Victoria and Albert Museum in London, one in the Couven Museum at Aachen,[1] and one in the Copenhagen Museum.[2]

THE TILED ROOM AT RAMBOUILLET (1715–30)

This dining-room shows probably better than anywhere else how the flower-vase pictures were given additional importance as ornamental panels and how they contribute to the general effect. Two, measuring 14 by 8 tiles, are placed along with Boumeester's views of towns on the terrace side, and two others (13 by 6 tiles) are on either side of the chimney-piece, forming a slightly concave picture in each corner. To achieve this, some tiles had to be cut in two lengthwise: this was done in the centre of the picture, where one or two 'seams' can be seen. The frame of the picture

104

VI

was left out entirely and replaced by a narrow pattern of tendrils at the sides (ill. 135).

THE AMALIENBURG HUNTING LODGE AT NYMPHENBURG (1734–9)

An impressive result was achieved in the Amalienburg kitchen, where the breadth of the fireplace is occupied by three polychrome flower-vase pictures. After all Joseph Effner's services to Max Emanuel in the construction of Nymphenburg and the blue pavilions of Pagodenburg and Badenburg, his role under Clemens August at Bonn was taken over by Cuvilliés. The latter divided his activity in the 1730s between Bonn and Munich, where Amalienburg was built in 1734–9. The combined kitchen and dining-room is an ingenious idea of his: the hunting-party and their guests could hold picnics there, as Watteau shows huntsmen doing out-of-doors, in the forests around Paris.

From 1725 onwards Cuvilliés helped in the building of the Residenz-Schloss at Munich, and in 1728 he succeeded Effner as court architect. With the Elector's permission he also built town mansions, among them one for the Fuggers, and became highly celebrated. There is a link between the Residenz-Schloss and Amalienburg. In 1729 the *Parade-Zimmer* or Audience hall of the Residenz, then in course of construction, was destroyed by an extensive fire. The plan had been to decorate in Chinese style like Pagodenburg and Badenburg, and to line the rooms with polychrome tiles. It is almost certain that Cuvilliés used the tiles that survived the fire undamaged to decorate the kitchen at Amalienburg (ills. 128 to 131b). The same is true of the flower-vase pictures, as was confirmed during World War II. In 1944 the interior of the Residenz was completely destroyed by bombing, which brought to light fragments of the tile decoration of a ground-floor boudoir with a polychrome flower-vase picture of the same type as the three in the Amalienburg kitchen; no doubt there were similar ones in the ground-floor apartments of the palace. Clearly, then, Cuvilliés made use of the ornamental tiles intended for the Residenz in the Amalienburg kitchen ten years later.

Originally the flower-vase pictures had a setting of their own under an arch resting on columns of plant-scrolls, like the two beside the windows at Rambouillet. When they came to be used for the fireplace at Amalienburg there was no room for the entire surround (Plate VI). Only the leafy garlands enlivened with birds and cherubs were retained from the original design, though the curve of the arch over the vases is more or less in conformity with the original plan. The flower-vases themselves measure 13 by 6 tiles; the polychrome columns of tiles with cherubs amid tendrils, for which

105

there was no room in the new arrangement, were placed underneath one of the manganese flower-vases on a narrow wall, to the right as one enters the kitchen.

Superficially the effect is of an exact and harmonious composition, but as in the case of the polychrome and black Chinese scenes discussed above, irreparable mistakes were made when the tiles were fixed in their new position, as due attention was not paid to the arrangement of the flowers.

For the decoration of the remaining area in the kitchen-cum-reception room, Cuvilliés found a new solution of his own, one which was principally architectural in inspiration, created in light tones of manganese and blue. One has the impression of stepping into a spacious baroque hall with twisted Ionic columns, garlanded with flowers and resting on a discreet tiled dado. The large areas above consist alternately of blank tiles and Biblical scenes in blue. In the corners, narrow panels two tiles wide catch the eye (ill. 136, left; Plate VI). These are divided horizontally in two with a small pillar standing either above or below an urn piled high with flowers. Vertical rows of cherubs and birds amid foliage, like the polychrome border of the flower-vases, also occur, as does a simple panel with a single continuous stem. All the pillars and vases rest on pedestals depicting a Dutch landscape or a river with rowing-boats, as is customary with flower-vase tiles; one also encounters the figure of Flora bearing flowers, or a mythological or Chinese scene. These scenes are borrowed from the blue Delft of about 1700, and also occur on the square pedestals of pyramidal tulip-vases.

As in the other pavilions and at Brühl, the reception rooms of Amalienburg are of Rotterdam origin. While we lack any documentation in the form of orders, bills etc. for the construction itself, this elegant pavilion and especially its kitchen preserved the record of a particular stage in eighteenth-century interior decoration. The manganese and blue tiles also indicate that the Aelmis factory at Rotterdam entered into collaboration at this period with the Delft potteries.

FLOWER-VASE PICTURES

We shall now give a brief comparison of the flower-vase pictures themselves. Of the specimens that can be traced, eight in all went to Rambouillet, the Residenz at Munich and Amalienburg. We saw how at Rambouillet they were treated casually and mutilated for the sake of arrangement, while at Amalienburg, for a different reason, the original composition was in many ways spoilt; as has been mentioned, the specimen in the Residenz has been lost.

Eleven of the fourteen had a garlanded border, sometimes with an elaborate crown effect at the top. We see this in the Sommelsdijk specimen (ills. 108b, 137a), in a perfectly preserved polychrome picture in the Copenhagen Museum (ill. 137b) and in the specimen from the Loudon collection in the Rijksmuseum at Amsterdam; in this one the bottom row of tiles is missing and the border is also defective in places.

We may thus take the blue tile work (ill. 137a) as a starting-point for the comparison of the bouquets, which many painters are known to have worked on but which nevertheless form a single group. The urns, which stand on a marbled block of green, yellow and red, have on their sides a variety of scenes, and double, dark-blue handles. The flowers are chosen from a diversity of European and Oriental species: yellow and purple-blue tulips, daffodils, lilies, peonies, carnations, clematis and wild hyacinth, snowball-like hydrangeas and varieties of prunus. The imposing bouquets thus created recall the style of the Bosschaerts and Roelant Saverij, or at times have a more eighteenth-century look of Rachel Ruysch or Jan van Huysum. Small exotic birds flutter round them, with innumerable butterflies, dragonflies and other insects. Larger birds are perched on the branches, and half-way up on the right a peacock is on the edge of the vase.

For all his apparently casual manner the artist has clearly striven after equilibrium: witness the parrot on its perch and the cock looking backward, which fill the space to either side of the marble pedestal. In one of the pictures at Rambouillet the parrot is replaced by a heron. We have some information about these animal figures: they are taken from prints by Johan Teijler of Nijmegen (1648–1712), who specialized in the technique of coloured line engravings. He worked with Carel Allard, who designed the blue house-sign in the form of a bouquet for De Bloempot (ill. 115d).

The picture now in the National Museum at Copenhagen reached there by way of the Paris art trade. It too has undergone some changes; the top row of tiles has been restored.

To the series of these eleven pictures with borders belongs the specimen from the Isaac collection in the Rijksmuseum (ill. 138a, 5 by 13 tiles), with a half-tile edging in a well-preserved pattern of small figures among leaf-tendrils. The flower arrangement comes two tile-rows nearer the top, which does not improve the effect.

The specimen in London is in the same style, without a border of any kind (13 by 6 tiles; see catalogue, *The Van den Bergh Gift* [1923]; reproduced in *Tiles*, op. cit., p. 163); the top that replaces the arch is here better suited to the bouquet. The marble plinth is higher; the perching parrot is on the right, while the peacock spreading its tail is on the left.

Two flower-vase tableaux which differ from the type just described vary sufficiently from them to suggest the work of a different designer and painter. The bouquet is composed with new colour harmonies and the picture seems to be designed to form a special feature in a tiled room. It is certainly an improvement that the marble plinth is replaced by a carved and painted pedestal. Instead of the parrot and cock, the lower space is filled by two miniature vases of flowers, at all events in the specimen in the Sèvres Museum (ill. 138b). In the other, their place is taken by two small ornamental Delft vases with lids.

The fact that flower-vase pictures did develop in style and purpose and can be dated accordingly—there was in fact no stagnation at any time—is shown by a third group of 10 by 4 tiles, without a border, used to fill a whole pier in systematic fashion.

In four specimens, two different painters may be distinguished. In each case only part of the pedestal has been preserved; on it stands a polychrome decorated vase full of flowers, with branches sticking out to provide room for a great variety of birds. Parrots, roosters and peacocks give place to resplendent exotic birds from illustrations in books of natural history. The colour-scheme is also different, with yellow predominating over a profusion of reds, blues and greens to give the picture a different character (ill. 139a, b).

We may wonder which factory is likely to have made these pictures. In the case of the polychrome and black scenes with Chinese themes, technical arguments pointed to The Greek A. As regards the flower-vases, an investigation described in the article mentioned in Chapter x leads to the conclusion that they were very probably manufactured by De Roos.

This pottery, founded in 1662, was a flourishing concern by about 1700. Inventories exist giving an account of its stocks. In 1755 the tile-works were a separate part of the factory, as is shown by a house-sign with a red rose in flower and the inscription *De Tegelbakkerij van de Roos 1779* (Prinsenhof Museum, Delft). Research among the archives of this Delft factory may finally reveal the origin of many flower-vase pictures of the first half of the eighteenth century. Whether, in the case of the last-mentioned type (ill. 139a,b), there is any possibility of English origin, must for the present remain an open question.

Notes

1 D. F. Lunsingh Scheurleer, 'Nederlandse Tegels in het Couven-Museum te Aken', in *Antiek* (June-July 1969).
2 C. H. de Jonge, 'Hollandse Tegelkamers in Duitse en Franse kastelen uit de eerste helft van de achttiende eeuw', in *Nederlands Kunsthistorisch Jaarbo.* 10 (1959), pp. 125 ff.

The export of Dutch tiles to Southern and Eastern Europe, from c. 1665 to 1800

Portugal and Spain in the seventeenth and eighteenth centuries

Thanks in part to cultural relations with France and the Electors at Munich and Bonn, the manufacture of polychrome tiles in Delft reached an exceptionally high standard. At the same time Pieter Jansz. Aelmis's works in Rotterdam were responsible for the blue stairway at Falkenlust and the blue and manganese kitchen at Amalienburg, both by Cuvilliés. The development of the famous blue tiles and their popularity abroad did not lag behind the polychrome variety.

This trade expansion had a history of its own. It was directed in the first instance towards Southern Europe, Spain and especially Portugal, and spread further to Morocco, the Azores and the Dutch colonies of northern Brazil and Recife.

In Holland, tiles were very seldom used to decorate the outside of buildings, but in the Iberian peninsula, especially Portugal, they were, and are, used as a matter of course for both internal and external decoration in churches and cloisters, schools, factories, public buildings, palaces and houses large and small. To begin with there would be a tile picture of the patron saint over the entrance; then came the application of tiles to dadoes, staircases and corridors, to house-signs, terraces, and the walls behind fountains—in short, they were to be found everywhere. So common are they indeed in Portugal that one scarcely notices them any more: as has often been said, they seem to merge into the background.

Originally Portugal imported tiles in the fifteenth century from Spain, in particular Seville, but later they developed into a native industry. The fact that Dutch tiles nevertheless became so widespread in Portugal has an interesting history. The quality of the native product declined, probably owing to excessive demand, and when Dutch merchant ships, about 1660, brought the first consignment of tiles as a sample, they were a huge success, so much so that the native Portuguese industry was nearly extinguished. In

1687 the import of tiles was prohibited, with the result that Portuguese production survived by copying Dutch models. The ban was revoked in 1698, after which it is almost impossible to distinguish native tiles from imported ones. The earthquake of 1755 caused such devastation that it is no longer possible fully to analyze material from the Dutch-Portuguese period. From then on, imports from Holland diminished considerably.

Some interesting evidence survives of the century of contact between the two countries. Thanks to the researches of J. M. dos Santos Simões in Lisbon, the history of the Portuguese tile industry has been reconstructed with the aid of Dutch documents.[1] This study has demonstrated the scale of export production in Amsterdam, Rotterdam, Harlingen and Delft factories before and after 1700. Of the hundreds of single tiles which, for instance, formerly adorned the façade and hall of the building which became the Hôtel d'Angleterre in Lisbon, tiles which are now dispersed, there is little to be said except that they represent all types belonging to this period.

It is, however, of interest to note some large tile pictures that miraculously escaped destruction in the earthquake and whose origin has now been established.

AMSTERDAM

The tiles that were supplied in huge quantities for fireplaces and *smuigers* in the Zaan district appear to have come partly from local workshops and partly from two Amsterdam firms. The first of these was De Oude Prins in the Anjelierstraat, which retained this historic name and was bought in 1684 by the Van der Kloet family. We can now trace its activity through signatures on tile pictures in Lisbon churches and private collections, which are a source of valuable information.

The first evidence is a set of at least four scenes, now dispersed, but formerly in the palace of the Galvão Mexia family in the Rua dos Mouros, a building that ceased to exist in 1899. One of the scenes, The Dancing-lesson, is now in the Cardos collection in Lisbon (ill. 140a), and one is in the Rijksmuseum in Amsterdam: The Meal on the Terrace, dated 1707 (ill. 140b). To summarize the conclusions of Simões, it appears that all the scenes are taken from French engravings; that a third, yachting, scene existed, which according to oral tradition was signed with a Dutch name, perhaps Willem van der Kloet; and that the two pictures in the Fronteira collection represent a music party and a parlour game.[2] Simões rightly observes that the part of the house visible in The Meal on the Terrace has a decidedly Dutch look, while the clothes and especially the *fontange*

110

head-dress belong to the French fashion of about 1700–10. The Oriental servant in this scene is doubtless also a Dutch feature as Orientals were brought to Holland as a result of contacts with overseas territories. For example, there is a formal portrait of a Regent and his wife in ceremonial costume attended by a young Oriental.

In any case, works signed by Willem van der Kloet were to be found in the chapel of the Galvão Mexia palace; they are now framed separately and form part of the A. F. Coelho collection in Lisbon (ill. 141). They depict eight episodes from the life of Christ and the Blessed Virgin; the Baptism of Christ is signed below, on the left, *Willem van der Kloet fec.* (ill. 142b).

A fully documented product of this Amsterdam factory is to be seen in the church of Nossa Senhora de Nazaré, a place of pilgrimage on the high rock of the Sitio next to the fishing village of Nazaré, where all the relevant archives are also kept. Just as Claude Révérend was the agent in Paris for Rotterdam and Delft ceramics when the Trianon de Porcelaine was being designed, so in Lisbon the import of tiles from Amsterdam was arranged by one Pedro Brukhuis, Brukuis or Bruques (the correct spelling is no doubt Broekhuis) who was a shipping agent for the firm of Van der Kloet. The position and arrangement of tiles for the chapel transept was laid down precisely beforehand, and sketches of the scenes were furnished; they represent the stories of David and Joseph. Their origin is proved by the signature *W. v. d. Kloet* beneath the first scene.

Another Dutch tile-maker whose signed pictures have been preserved in Lisbon is Jan van Oort, whom we mentioned in connection with the blue and manganese flower-vase tableau of 1697 (ill. 79). He owned a factory at Amsterdam and exported very fine pictures to Lisbon. Those we are now concerned with were ordered by the church of Nossa Senhora da Conceição de Cardais, which belonged to a Carmelite nunnery. They portray the Life of St. Teresa, the foundress and patron saint of the reformed Carmelites; like those at Nazaré they were duly sketched beforehand and their dimensions indicated (ill. 142 a). The dado below is filled with putti with bunches of flowers. The documents show that the Netherlands also contributed their part to the spiritual aspect of these scenes: they are taken from a work published in Antwerp in 1613 entitled *Vita B. Virginis Teresiae a Iesu*, with engravings by Adriaen Collaert and Cornelis Galle.[3]

Although the order for the tiles dates from before 1681 they were not delivered until 1698, when the import ban was lifted. This is probably why the signature of Jan van Oort, who died at Amsterdam in 1699, is undated, though it exactly resembles that on the flower-vase pictures (ill. 142c).

A surprising form of decoration, at least to Dutch eyes, is the tiled dado found round rooms and halls in houses and palaces. It is scarcely possible even to estimate the volume of export from Amsterdam, Rotterdam and Delft, since in addition to these suppliers one must take account of the output of Utrecht, Gorinchem, Haarlem and Makkum, which were coming to the fore after 1660, and innumerable tile-works in the other provinces which joined in the export trade through middle-men. These were no doubt responsible for the large number of blue tiles with their great variety of designs. The material collected by 1959 in J. M. dos Santos Sımões' standard work seems inexhaustible. Apart from native production and Dutch imports, account must be taken of deliveries of Spanish tiles. The owners and architects of palaces and country houses were always lavish in decorating their homes and gardens. An example is the Marquês de Fronteira's palace at Benfica near Lisbon, where the grounds were laid out from about 1670 onwards with fountains backed by walls of tiles depicting horsemen. Next came the house with a chapel on the first floor and an adjoining terrace of Portuguese tiles. A wing was added shortly after 1700. The walls of the entrance hall with its imposing staircase are covered with Dutch tiles. There is a unique dining-room, with tiles instead of wood panelling, rising to a height of 1.70 metres: this is bordered by a tendril design and divided into scenes of hunting and seascapes. The landscapes recall those of Nicholaes Berchem (d. 1733), whose Italian manner frequently inspired the faience painters of small plaquettes.

The large surfaces above the panelling are entirely filled by stucco reliefs of horsemen, yellow and orange in colour, in Portugese baroque style. All this brought about a complete change in the decoration of halls and smaller apartments. Just as fresco painting had been of paramount importance to the early Italians, and Gobelin tapestries to three centuries of French kings, so now in Portugal tile decoration and grandiose stucco relief came to the fore.

In another Lisbon palace, now the Hospital de Santo António, and also in the principal museums, there are quantities of blue tiles which are said to have been part of a consignment filling several chests that was washed ashore after a shipwreck in the bay of Figueira da Foz. Many of them, with Biblical scenes, landscapes and horsemen, are in the former episcopal palace.

Despite all these discoveries, our knowledge of the trade in Dutch tiles and their use in Southern Europe and further overseas in the years 1660–1755 is still far from complete.

112

Though there is no direct evidence, it may be assumed that Rotterdam took part in export to this area, not only in respect of individual tiles whose history is not known, but also in connection with a series of views of trading cities which cannot be passed over without mentioning Cornelis Boumeester, the only faience painter to whom they can be attributed. About eight of these were found in 1944 by Simões in the *grand salon* of the Saldanha palace at Junqueira near Lisbon. João de Saldanha (1673–1723), Governor and Defender of the port of Lisbon, ordered these works, which depict the harbours or river-ports of Antwerp, Middelburg (ill. 143), Rotterdam, Hamburg, Cologne, London, Venice and Constantinople; the skylines date them between 1709 and 1723. The picture of London bears the date 1715. In that of Middelburg the dome of the Oosterkerk (1695) is visible but not the steeple, De Lange Jan, which was erected in 1713–18: the picture is probably based on a seventeenth-century print by Nicolaes de Visscher, published by J. de Roy in 1705.

The bird's-eye views or 'profiles' of all eight harbours are based on a set of original prints entitled *Grote Stadspanorama's gegraveerd in Amsterdam sedert 1609*, mostly by Nicolaes de Visscher and Hondius.[4]

As B. 't Hoff rightly points out, the foundations of Holland's Golden Age were laid during the pause in the Spanish War known as the Twelve Years' Truce (1609–21). This period saw the beginning of the construction of Amsterdam's world-famous canals and of the patrician houses in early Dutch Renaissance style, and also of work on reclaiming the marshy areas round about, the Beemster and the Purmer. The unique Dutch style of architecture spread over the whole country, as can be seen from the Chancery at Leeuwarden (1585) and the town hall at Bolsward (1616) (ill. 155a,b). At this time, too, Amsterdam became especially well known in the graphic sphere thanks to Johan Blaeu's *Steden-Atlas*, in which the townscape appears.

Although the harbour scenes in the Saldanha palace are not signed, their attribution to Cornelis Boumeester is quite justified on stylistic grounds, and it is possible that his signature below the plinth was hidden from view when the floor level was raised. If this is the case, then the agent Peter Broekhuis was very probably the intermediary for the order.

DELFT

It would take us too far afield to study in Spain—the country which, together with Italy, gave the first impulse to the Netherlands tile industry at the end of the sixteenth century—the extent to which Dutch tiles were imported via Portugal over a century later, when Holland had become the centre of the trade with Southern Europe. There is plenty of evidence of Dutch-Spanish connections, particularly as regards tiles. Seville was the main connecting link, but imports may also have taken place through Cadiz, especially for the south-western coast of Spain between Portugal and Gibraltar. The towns around Cadiz: San Fernando, Medina Sidonia and Jerez de la Frontera, can boast of tile pictures from Aelmis of Rotterdam and other series surpassing in quality anything known to exist in Portugal.

We shall, however, make an exception for one type of blue and manganese tile, the careful painting and execution of which has led Simões to suppose that it may be of Delft origin. He discovered the tiles in Commandant Lomas' house at San Fernando, a building which dates from the beginning of the eighteenth century but has lost much of its character through injudicious alteration; much of the staircase tiling has been spoilt as a result. Remnants of the blue and manganese type are found here among blue tiles. In one of the main rooms there is a red-earth floor decorated in the Andalusian manner with a pattern of stars, which in this case is filled in with Dutch tiles. Round the dado, twenty out of about sixty tiles have survived undamaged (ill. 144a,b,c): octagonal blue landscapes, flower-vases, fruit-baskets etc. are painted on a dark manganese powdered background with white fleurs-de-lis in the corners.

The various kinds of blue, manganese and polychrome Dutch tiles in this early eighteenth-century mansion would deserve a chapter to themselves, though unfortunately much of it would be conjectural. As for the blue and manganese tiles reproduced here and discovered ten years ago by Simões, chance has enabled us to say with some confidence that they were made by The Greek A at Delft, as the tiles discovered in one of the cellars at Het Loo (ill. 90a,b) appear to be of identical origin. Those at San Fernando are of especial interest, since the ones at Het Loo depict flower-vases and landscapes, whereas here there are also baskets of fruit.

Poland in the eighteenth century

P. J. Tichelaar's studies have shown on what a scale Dutch and Frisian tiles were exported to Schleswig-Holstein, Hamburg and Denmark. It is also clear that a large part of Scandinavia remains unexplored from this point of view, not to speak of England, though Lambeth Delftware has been studied in connection with Dutch potters who were active there. In his discussion of tiled rooms in Germany, Professor Hudig has indicated which

114

castles have not yet been described.[5] Eastward of Hamburg, we could cite three at Potsdam which have not yet been studied on account of the post-war situation in East Germany. Others are in the neighbourhood of Dresden, and we may presume that Danzig was a centre of the trade with Eastern Europe and that branches of Dutch tileworks may have been established there. We do not know how much of all this may have been lost in the Second World War. The whole subject of Dutch tiles in Russia also awaits study. Although Peter the Great was chiefly concerned with shipbuilding when he visited Zaandam in 1697, his journey must have stimulated trade between the two countries.

In Poland, the basis for historical research in this field was laid in 1945, when plans came to be made for post-war reconstruction. This applies especially to certain castles and palaces which reproduce the European atmosphere and style of the seventeenth and eighteenth centuries, and in which Dutch craftsmen played their part.

In the seventeenth century Tylman van Gameren of Utrecht (1631–1704), who was private architect to Prince George Sebastian Lubomirski, became famous for designing fortresses, churches and palaces in and around Warsaw. He developed his classical baroque style during long years in Italy; he then came to Poland in 1666 and continued to work there until his death.[6]

NIEBORÓW PALACE

Tylman van Gameren was the architect of this palace, the first plans for which date from 1695–7. They probably included the cupolas over the grand staircase, to which he paid special attention in all his Polish work. However, these may be repetitions or imitations, as the main work of building and furnishing was accomplished in the last forty years of the eighteenth century. From 1766 the palace was inhabited by the art patron and bibliophile Michael Kazimierz. Ogiński, and in 1774, through female members of his family and by purchase, it became the property of the Radziwills. From then on it was furnished in an international style typical of Poland, with reminiscences of Italian baroque together with French and English furniture in the salons and bedrooms. A second, less lofty storey with living accommodation was added in 1922. When the palace was restored in 1945 it was refurnished as nearly as possible in the style it had presented when lived in by the Radziwill princes after 1774. Together with the grounds, it is now State property and is under the management of the National Museum of Warsaw.

An inventory of August 1774, when the palace was purchased by Prince Michael Jerome Radziwill, states that the walls of the *escalier d'honneur* were lined with 'Dutch' tiles, as was the landing with its ceiling and also a room accessible from the staircase (ills. 145, 146). This seems to be a unique instance, as tile-decoration of this sort does not occur elsewhere in Poland. Unfortunately nothing is known of how these blue tiles, some 10,000 in number, were ordered or procured. They differ noticeably in style from the types found in Holland, though their subjects are those usually met with there from the seventeenth century onwards. We shall revert to this question after describing the tiled rooms in other Polish mansions (see ills. 149a–e and 150).

WILANÓW

Wilanów, from the Italian *Villa Nuova*, was built as a residence for King John Sobieski, and is an outstanding monument of Polish art.[7] The main edifice, with its towers, was erected to Tylman van Gameren's design in forests belonging to the king. After John's death in 1696, thirty-five years elapsed before the work of building and furnishing was completed under the Saxon monarch Augustus II. From 1733 to 1788 the palace belonged to the Czartoryski and Lubomirski families and later to their descendants by marriage. Each of the successive occupants made many changes in the structure and furnishing. The Germans damaged it severely during World War II. It was restored as far as possible in 1945 after the hostilities, and is now, like Nieborów, State property under the care and attention of the National Museum in Warsaw.

Wilanów also possesses a tiled room, but the authorities responsible for these palaces state that nothing is known of its origin, though it seems certain that the tiles were not made in Poland. The official guide to Wilanów calls this room *Cabinet des Faïences* and also *Salle de Bain de la Reine* and assigns it to the seventeenth century, when tiles were 'very fashionable'. It seems unthinkable, however, that this room with its ornamental domed ceiling, and the cornice plastered with an elaborate design of scallops and tendrils, should have been a bathroom (ill. 147a,b). A similar error occurs at Rambouillet, where the summer diningroom is described as the 'bathroom' of Marie Antoinette.

In any case this room presents problems. The tile pictures of flower-vases in oval wreaths are unique. The rows of blue tiles bordering them do not look particularly Dutch, in spite of their corner-motifs of ox-heads and sprigs. The designs are reminiscent of seventeenth-century subjects: the horsemen, the signposts dating from 1674–8 (cf. ill. 58a,b,c), the Biblical scenes, farmhouses and wells with windlasses, but yet the execution is not typically Dutch.

116

The large vases with full bouquets in an oval setting recall tile designs from pictures by the Bosschaerts and Roelant Saverij, where the bouquets are surmounted by a crown imperial, or possibly the eighteenth-century followers of Rachel Ruysch and Van Huysum, but we are left wondering where these late baroque tile pictures come from. The same may be said of the modelling and ornamentation of the vases themselves.

The combination of the highly finished baroque vases and the sketch-like tiles of the intervening rows was not considered objectionable in Poland. The mid-eighteenth century date is probably correct, this being the period when the Lubomirski family had the staircase at Nieborów lined with tiles (ill. 145).

LAZIENKI

The third palace was also partially built before 1700, under Tylman van Gameren's direction, for a member of the Lubomirski family.[8] A bathing pavilion stood on an island in the park, surrounded by marshy ground where hunting parties were held. The mention in old inventories of *faïence hollandaise* may, it is thought, refer to these pavilions.

The palace beside its artificial lake was enlarged at the end of the eighteenth century as a residence for Stanislas Augustus Poniatowski, the last king of Poland (1764–95), who bought the property from Marshal Stanislas Heraclitus Lubomirski. *Lazienki* means 'baths', but the name has remained attached to the palace itself, which is also known as the *palais sur l'eau* and was built in 1784–1795 by an Italian architect, with Saxon artists contributing to the interior. The 'Bacchus' and 'Diana' rooms were so named after their ceilings, painted with mythological scenes, which were destroyed when the Germans set fire to the palace in 1944. The Diana room was also called a *salle de bain*. The walls of these apartments were tiled in a similar fashion, the designs being chiefly landscapes (ill. 148a,b). The original tiles probably dated from somewhat later than the staircase at Nieborów, in the last quarter of the eighteenth century, but only a few dozen survived the fire; these have now been placed high up by the ceiling, some having been retouched. Both rooms have otherwise been completely re-tiled with landscapes and shepherds, windmills etc., copied from the originals and manufactured by the Husarski works at Cracow (ill. 150). Despite the variation in the trees and scenes, the general effect is monotonous.

Since 1945 the Lazienki palace has been restored as completely as possible and, like Nieborów and Wilanów, is under the administration of the National Museum.

117

We may conclude with some general remarks on the tiled rooms in Polish mansions and palaces. It may be said that thanks to the Lubomirski family, tile decoration in Poland came to be put to quite a different use than was customary in Holland. Undoubtedly the tiles of the Nieborów staircase are the finest of their kind. The late eighteenth-century style of drawing can be clearly seen in various details. We may often notice a deterioration of style and a defective understanding of the original model; however, tiles from Dutch workshops in the eighteenth and nineteenth century also show a falling-off in artistic merit.

If we compare with Nieborów the single tiles around the flower-vase tableaux at Wilanów, these appear to be of inferior quality, though the seventeenth-century models can be discerned in them. In the opinion of the Director of the National Museum in Warsaw, the tiles at Nieborów are original and date from 1774, when the palace belonged to Michael Kazimierz. Oginski. The tiled room at Wilanów is original and probably Saxon, dating from the beginning of the eighteenth century. The tile decoration in the Bacchus and Diana rooms at Lazienki dated from after 1765 and was imported from Saxony, except for the bathing pavilion on the island, which was decorated in about 1700.

As my own investigations do not extend thus far, I acknowledge with thanks the advice of the Director of the National Museum and present a full selection of illustrations from which the matter can be studied further. The present chapter may be regarded as introductory to an eventual account of Dutch tiles in Northern and Eastern Europe.

Notes

1 J. M. dos Santos Simões, *Carreaux céramiques hollandais au Portugal et en Espagne*, passim (Martinus Nijhoff, The Hague 1959), and literature cited there. A brief illustrated review of this book by J. de Kleyn is in *Vrienden van de Nederlandse Ceramiek*, 21 (January 1961).
2 J. M. dos Santos Simões, op. cit., p. 41.
3 Id., p. 51.
4 Id., p. 84. B. van 't Hoff, in *Jaarboek van het Genootschap Amstelodamum* 47, (1955), gives a full account of the seventeenth-century prints on which these city views were based, under the title 'Grote Stadspanorama's, gegraveerd in Amsterdam sedert 1609'.
5 See F. W. Hudig, *Altholländische Fliesen*, ii (1933), p. 52, n. 2.
6 J. Wegner, *Le Château de Nieborów* (1957); Dr. T. Gostwynski, 'Tylman van Gameren, Een Nederlands Bouwmeester in Polen' (translated by J. J. F. W. van Agt), in *Bulletin van de Koninklijke Nederlandsche Oudheidkundige Bond*, 13, no. 1 (1960); J. Wegner, *Nieborów*, illustrated guide published by the National Museum (Warsaw, 1964).

7 W. Fijalkowski, *Wilanów*, illustrated guide published by the National Museum (Warsaw, 1966; Polish edition with summaries in English, French, German and Russian, 1967).

8 J. Lilevko, *Le Palais de Lazienki à Varsovie* (French translation by Helena Bohosiewicz, National Museum, Warsaw, 1964).

XIII   *The Dutch tile industry in the eighteenth and nineteenth centuries and later in Rotterdam, Utrecht, Delft and Makkum*

The export market for the Dutch tile industry shrank considerably in the second half of the eighteenth century, the most obvious reason for this being the Lisbon earthquake. Exports to Germany and Poland fell off as a result of the French Revolution and Napoleon's conquest of the Netherlands. Nevertheless, this flourishing branch of applied art did not come to an abrupt end. It is remarkable how long the principal factories kept going and remained of importance, especially as regards manganese tiled interiors, the production of which expanded most after 1750, though it must be admitted that the painting became duller and of inferior quality.

To give a general idea of the next period we must return to individual cities which were formerly centres of the tile industry. It is noteworthy that Haarlem no longer plays any part and that Amsterdam more or less drops out after the period of Van der Kloet and Adriaen van Oort. The tile-works that were dispersed about the country before and after 1800 gradually went out of business or were absorbed, as at Harlingen, into related building enterprises.

The most important centres during the transition period at the turn of the century and after were Rotterdam, Utrecht, Delft and finally Makkum.

ROTTERDAM

Rotterdam had been the chief centre of the tile industry from 1600 onwards, and for two and a half centuries it maintained contact and trade relations with tile works all over the country. One of the peaks of local production had been the work of Cornelis Boumeester (1652–1733), the chief craftsman at Jacobus de Colonia's works on the Delftse Vaart. Another establishment which had become prominent in the seventeenth century under the Van Lier family became the property of Pieter Jansz. Aelmis in 1697. Later the two concerns had been merged, and absorbed existing smaller works.

120

The oldest members of the Aelmis family, Pieter Jansz. and his son Jan Pietersz., had been responsible for the tiled rooms at Nymphenburg and Brühl, at the period when co-operation with Delft was established. Including the following generation, the Aelmis family were in charge of De Bloempot for over a century.

Towards 1800, however, the tile industry declined considerably in importance, and the Aelmis concern was no exception. Jan Aelmis, the sole surviving member of the family, at the age of 73 sold the factory to Laurens Verwijk, who managed it for three years under Aelmis' supervision; however, Verwijk died in 1796. His two sons kept on the business without great success until 1843, when it was taken over by the stone-mason Willem van Traa. He managed for a time to overcome its difficulties thanks to a lively trade with some fifteen towns in Holland, about five in Belgium and also Cologne and Düsseldorf; but in 1873 he had to close down the works for lack of qualified labour.

In 1904 the Van Traa family arranged for the presentation of the entire archives of the stone-cutting and tile works to the Rotterdam city archives. The inestimable value of this gift has been shown by the research accomplished as regards Nymphenburg and Brühl. As late as the early nineteenth century consignments were apparently sent to the southern provinces of Holland which can only have come from De Bloempot.[1]

The link with Belgium had indeed existed for decades; one need only think of the portraits of princes at Ayeneux castle near Liège. Moreover there was a branch office in Brussels which took orders for Dutch tiles. Yet it is surprising to find the products of De Bloempot in small towns, villages and farms in Dutch Flanders. In a farm at Groede near IJzendijke there was a large fireplace with a chimney-piece in manganese tiles showing the embarkation of British and Russian troops for the sea-battle of 1799 off Bergen-aan-Zee (ills. 152, 153a), copied with slight alterations from the print by Dirk Langendijk; the drawing is in the Print-room of the Rijksmuseum. Through the agency of the former Mayor of IJzendijke, Jonkheer L. E. D. S. von Bönninghausen tot Jerinckhave, the picture has now found a place in the kitchen of the Willet-Holthuysen Museum in Amsterdam, where it appears as a continuous flat scene in its original blue-marbled setting (ill. 153a). To the left of the main picture is a half-length portrait of the Duke of York, to the right one of the French General Brune (these were originally the side-pieces of the fireplace); next are two military trophies, each suspended from a nail, the left-hand one marked G.R.[2] In the centre are a large scene with groups of soldiers in the foreground and a view, beyond some houses, of the sea with warships.

Other historical documents from the period of Laurens Verwijk's management of De Bloempot are two companion pictures, mentioned in the

121

archives, of the battle of Waterloo and the Anglo-Dutch bombardment of Algiers: these were probably executed soon after 1815 and 1816, as the anniversaries of these events were celebrated with enthusiasm in Rotterdam. The Battle of Waterloo, after the engraving by F. A. Langendijk (ill. 151a), is now in the Simon van Gijn Museum at Dordrecht.

The Bloempot inventory provides further historical data and information on the terminology of the tile industry: it concerns exclusively blue and manganese tiles and therefore deals with the eighteenth-century output of Rotterdam. We learn from this source that the portraits of Popes and the Virgin with Saints (ills. 60f and 62) are from a Rotterdam pottery; that 'portraits of princes and princesses on horseback' were made there in the form of tile pictures (cf. the portraits of Maria Theresa and the Emperor, Louis XV and Marie Leszczyńska supplied by Aelmis to Ayeneux in 1740: ill. 84a,b); that large whaling pictures were executed (cf. ill. 101c); and that masquerades were among the genre scenes (cf. the Magito tiles, ill. 102c).

Apart from this, the inventory gives the contemporary names for various tile designs which are now described quite differently. Not all of these can be identified, but some characteristic ones are: violet or blue landscapes 'in ornamental lace or French ribbon', or 'in a double octagon' (cf. ill. 102f), 'intertwined or Jerusalem feathers' (ill. 151b,c). Border-tiles are called *halfjes*, *slinger-halfjes* (tendrils) or *halfjes à la grecque* (a nineteenth-century term for the meander pattern, ill. 50 etc.). Twisted columns with the arms of the Seven Provinces suspended from them are called *provincie-kolommen* (ill. 107a) these are 12 by 2 tiles, in blue, brown or manganese.

The Frisian terms from the pattern book *servetstar* or *servetkant* also bear witness to these connections (ill. 94a). When manufacture had finally ceased and sales were made only from stock, customers were referred to the Tjallingii works at Harlingen. The last tiles were sold in 1873, by which time De Bloempot no longer existed.

UTRECHT

We have already spoken of the tile-works in Utrecht and the licences granted there from 1616 to the mid-eighteenth century, associated with the Overmeer and Van Oort families and that of Claes Jansz. Wijtmans. The 'Utrecht shepherd' tiles *(Utrechtse harders)* made by the Van Oorts (or Van Noort), father and son, were especially admired and are priced highest in inventories of the time. Since Jan van Oort moved to Amsterdam, it is understandable that this type of subject, together with mythological scenes such as Apollo and Daphne or Diana and Actaeon, was set in country landscapes and is frequent in North Holland (ill. 80a,b).

One of the last owners in Utrecht of an 'earthenware pottery' who is known to us by name was François Cuvel, who in 1773 sought permission from the municipal authorities concerned with the making of 'glazed and painted tiles' to take over the kilns of the late Isaac van Oort, the last member of his family, who had died in Utrecht.

Another type of tile should be mentioned, probably of Utrecht origin but clearly connected with Friesland and West Friesland. The Central Museum in Utrecht possesses a restored fragment of twelve tiles with a tendril pattern: six are yellowish-white on a purple ground, the veins of the leaves being blue; a group of four forms a complete pattern glazed with a lustre effect. The other six are similar, but are purple on a white ground (ill. 151b,c). These tiles were found in the same site on the Predik-heerenstraat as the 'goose' and 'owl' games (cf. ill. 103d).

Another twelve-tile pattern has similar white foliage on a purple ground with a small bird on one of the shoots (ill. 151 c). The composition is not made in right and left counterparts, so that in a set of four the birds in the left-hand half are upside-down. This pattern also occurs in the *Modellen-boek* in the Hannema-Huis Museum at Harlingen, where we find all the variations of design with their contemporary names. The two Utrecht specimens are designated as *Jeruzalemveeren* and *Vogelveeren*; there are also *Rooseveeren*, *Afrikaansche Veeren*, *Zonnebloemveeren* (ill. 94b) and others. Specimens of *Tulpen-Veeren* and *Anjelieren-Veeren* are in the Zuider Zee Museum, while the sets of four tiles forming rosettes are called Alkmaar chintz, or *Servetstar* (ill. 94a).

The Westraven Tegelfabriek N.V.

Out of the many Utrecht factories dating back more than three centuries only one, as in Delft, survived the French Revolution and the Napoleonic period. This was the firm of Westraven, named after part of Jutphaas which, like Hoograven, is in the immediate vicinity of Utrecht. The tile-factory here was established in 1661. On its three-hundredth anniversary the present manager published a souvenir booklet, with documentation from the archives, giving a full account of the establishment's fortunes from the beginning, under the direction of successive families.[3]

The archives of the pottery itself contain two copies of the Makkum and Harlingen pattern books, which were also used in Utrecht. They show, in nineteenth-century examples, the development of style as late as the eighties, the effect in some cases being very poor (ill. 154a).

On 1 January 1963 the works, then known as the Faience- en Tegel-fabriek Westraven, formerly Ravesteijn Brothers, became a subsidiary of

123

the Royal Delft porcelain works De Porceleyne Fles (the Porcelain Bottle) in Delft. The old Dutch craft of tile-making is carried on here without any attempt to treat the product as imitation antique. It is quite fitting that this should be so, both in order to preserve a deeply rooted tradition, and to meet the demand from tourists and others. In addition there are modern applications for tiles which did not exist in past centuries: for instance in swimming-baths, which make a more hygienic impression when tiled, and to offset the cold practicality of plastic fittings in up-to-date kitchens. Another good example of their use is the station hall in Delft. Thus, after many vicissitudes, the time has come when, without any question of imitation, we may return to the style of the best days of the Dutch tile industry.

DELFT

We may be curious as to what happened in Delft, which incorrectly came to be spoken of after 1900 as if it had been the place of origin of all Dutch tiles. Certainly it had its periods of tile production, when Delft products were distinguished from those of other centres by their high artistic quality and deep-blue colouring. They may however almost be counted on the fingers of one hand: the polychrome and blue tiles depicting soldiers and horsemen of Prince Maurice's army; Frederik van Frijtom's small land-scapes fifty years later; high-temperature and muffle-kiln polychrome tiles made by De Grieksche A at the period of Delft's chief glory before and after 1700, and finally the polychrome flower-vase decoration of tiled rooms. Each of these represents an episode of tile production linked with that of the celebrated Delft ceramics inspired by Chinese, Japanese and European porcelain.

After 1750 European production, including Wedgwood's 'hard-ware', gradually led to the decline of the Delft works: hard stoneware triumphed over brittle Delft faience. One by one, Delft firms gave up the struggle, and in these dark days scarcely any more tiles were made there. The difficulty of maintaining production became apparent soon after the time of prosperity around 1700. The Dissel factory, which was the chief source of the superior blue Delftware about 1650, was absorbed in 1701 into the glory of De Grieksche A under Adriaen Kocksz. Later, less important concerns such as De Ham, Het Hooghe Huys and China closed down in 1726, 1741 and 1743. Rouaen, known as Het Lage Huys after 1715, and famous under Paulus Bourseth for polychrome flower tiles, closed in 1742, to be followed in 1751 by the less well-known Het Gecroond Porceleijn, as well as De Metalen Pot, which had been of importance under Lambert van Eenhoorn. De Romeijn was sold to a partnership in 1767 and pulled down in 1769; De Vergulde Boot disappeared in 1770. From then on the débâcle was even more rapid, with the extinction of De Drie Porceleijnen Flesschen, De Dobbelde Schenkkan, 't Fortuyn, De Paeuw, Het Jonge Moriaens Hooft, Het Oude Moriaens Hooft, De Twee Wildemannen and De Twee Scheepjes in 1777–8 and 1792–4.

A lull seems to have set in for a few years, but the remaining factories closed down in the Napoleonic period: De Porceleijne Schotel in 1800, Hugo Brouwer's De Porceleijne Bijl in 1802, Hendrick van Hoorn's De Drie Astonnekens in 1803, De Witte Starre—so popular under Albert Kiell—in 1804, and finally in 1811 De Porceleijne Lampetkan, which had belonged to the Van der Ceel family since 1723. De Claeuw, 't Hart and De Drie Klokken struggled to continue their existence in combination until 1840; in 1841 the once famous Grieksche A closed down, as did De Roos, which had co-operated for years, through a separate tile-making department, with De Bloempot in Rotterdam. All in all, out of more than thirty factories only De Porceleijne Fles survived the general destruction.[4]

Although the nineteenth century was disastrous for the faience industry itself, this did not mean that the public lost interest in Delft work of the best period. Imposing blue and polychrome sets of three vases and two goblets, used for nearly two centuries to adorn the heavy Dutch baroque cupboards, and smaller Delft pieces competed with refined Chinese objects in glass and porcelain cabinets, while important collections of old Delft were still formed in the nineteenth century. Dutch collectors had been quick to realize the importance of Delftware. Thanks to them, the Rijksmuseum in 1916 acquired the famous Loudon bequest which has since been supplemented with many gifts, legacies and purchases. The Gemeente Museum in The Hague acquired the basis of a superior collection in 1904 through the A. H. H. van der Burgh bequest, as did the Municipal Museum in Arnhem. King William III of the Netherlands (d. 1890) presented his collection to De Porceleyne Fles Museum. Special tile collections, including the Isaac collection, were bequeathed to the Rijksmuseum in Amsterdam or bought by it. The Huis Lambert van Meerten Museum in Delft owes its name to this collector of works of art and craftsmanship, whose mansion, built in 1893, became chiefly a tile museum and was presented to the nation in 1907. The Frisian Museum, the Princessehof at Leeuwarden and the Menkema Borg near Groningen can boast outstanding tile collections, as can the museums at Hoorn, Enkhuizen and De Rijp in North Holland. Dr. Van Tijen bequeathed his collection to the museums in Alkmaar and Monnickendam.

Only a century after its decline, Delft pottery once more revived, but on quite a new technical and artistic basis. As far as tiles were concerned, the Delft industry imitated old models, though the landscapes and ships were modernized on the basis of contemporary pictures. The blue tile tradition was maintained, as the public clearly wanted it, but the attempt to revive old glories was combined with a new idea. As faience painters formerly worked from engravings or used them as inspiration for blue tiles, so the idea developed in the eighties of using a painting of an urban scene as the model for a coloured tile picture. An interesting example is Cornelis Springer's painting of the Heerengracht in winter, signed *C. Springer 1882*. The painting is in the Amsterdam city hall, while the tile picture is privately owned (ill. 154b). The houses seen at the bend in the canal are Nos. 487 to 495, the two in the foreground being the most famous of the Amsterdam patrician houses: they now belong respectively to the Dutch Life Assurance Company and the Central Sugar Company. The games on the ice, the lowering snowy sky and cosy winter atmosphere all recreate a Dutch winter's day in bygone times.

The tile picture consists of 4 by 5 large tiles, 15.5 cm. square. It is signed in the bottom right-hand corner 'H B after C. Springer', the initials being those of H. Bottelier, a faience painter at De Porceleyne Fles. The outline of a bottle, the ornamental letters J T and the name Delft form the signature patented by Joost Thooft in 1883 when the factory was turned into a limited company. The picture was probably made soon after that year. Such tile pictures of a more or less modern kind had been made possible by the revival of techniques. Landscapes, genre pieces, seascapes etc. by Anton Mauve, Jozef Israëls and Willem Roelofs also occur in the form of tile pictures.

The Royal Delft porcelain factory De Porceleyne Fles
We should not omit to mention here the name of Auguste Le Comte (d. 1921), who from 1877 was Professor of Decorative Art at what was then the Delft Polytechnic College. He was the most important designer of revived Delft ceramics for De Porceleyne Fles, then owned by Joost Thooft and Labouchere, the work being carried out in Delft under the direction of Leon Senf. We owe to Le Comte the tile decoration of the palace of the Grand Duke of Saxe-Weimar, the entrance-hall of the Ministry of Justice in The Hague and the wall-decorations of the Lucas Bols premises in Paris and Berlin. Special mention should be made of the frieze of blue tiles in the bodega of the Poort van Cleve restaurant in Amsterdam: this shows a joyful procession of putti and children celebrating the wine harvest, some dancing and others riding in ornamental cars (ill. 153b).[5]

At the same time it became clear that no new development or future was in store for the time-honoured art of decorating interiors by means of

126

tiles. It therefore seems a practical decision to have transferred the manufacture of traditional tiles to the Westraven concern in Utrecht, thus giving De Porceleyne Fles room to develop the modern industry of building, decorating and crafts as is its present policy.

The signs of a new future along these lines were in fact already visible about 1900. In the same way as at Makkum, there was a search for technical change, while the sense of an imminent esthetic and artistic revolution could no longer be ignored. A wave of new ideas, as yet indefinite, spread over Western Europe: they are associated with William Morris (1834–96), the founder of the British Arts and Crafts movement and an enthusiast for the revival of applied art. The new style was known in Germany as *Jugendstil* and in France as *Art nouveau*. Soon after the turn of the century, the inspiration of the Bauhaus became of great importance for De Porceleyne Fles among others. The modern art of decorating house façades developed in the Delft workshop and was taken up by it on a large scale. Since 1955 artists and architects have been able to execute their designs, or have them executed, in the studio of the architectural section of the works themselves, whether on the basis of a colourful tile composition or a figurative representation. Many works by younger artists are exhibited in the museum attached to De Porceleyne Fles.

MAKKUM

In Friesland the fortunes of the tile-works can be clearly followed around the end of the eighteenth century. The Bolsward factory, which appears such a flourishing concern in the well-known picture of 1737 (Plate I), was sold to an Amsterdam owner in 1790, after which little more is heard of it.

The history of the Harlingen factories after 1800 has been described along with the development of the art of tile-making. As long as contact with Rotterdam was preserved, they were able to keep one another in being. One establishment lasted until 1930 in combination with a building works.

In contrast to these changing fortunes the Tichelaar family concern rests on a firm basis and long tradition, though at the end of the eighteenth century it had briefly to meet competition from a tile-works belonging to the shipowner Kingma; this went out of business around 1830, apparently because the market was too small. Since then the Tichelaar factory, which for over three centuries has been producing majolica, pottery and tiles, has been supreme not only in Northern Holland but in North Germany and Scandinavia, while it also figured prominently in the export trade to

Spain and Portugal. It had its setbacks, as, for instance, in 1824 when the whole factory was destoyed by fire, but it was quickly rebuilt.

It is an important fact about this firm that it has always moved with the times and has succeeded thereby in maintaining a character of its own. In the eighteenth and nineteenth centuries it used the Frisian style that was widely known from the pattern-books preserved in its archives, but also followed the general line of development of the Dutch tile industry. Makkum, however, at no time adopted the Chinese style of decoration introduced by Delft and taken up by other centres.

Eighteenth-century Makkum pottery is usually distinguished by a bright, mid-blue colour, which was superseded about 1840 by a harder blue and a purple-brown shade of manganese.

In the introduction to the catalogue of the exhibition marking the factory's three-hundredth anniversary, attention is drawn to the deliberate modification of the product, which is also the case with tiles.[6] It states that from about 1880 there was a period of search for new possibilities, which did not bear fruit until the twentieth century.[7]

Tichelaar's Royal Makkum Pottery and Tile-Works
It is worth while tracing the independent development of the works in the nineteenth and twentieth centuries. We have already mentioned a panoramic tableau (9 by 6 tiles), made at Makkum, of the village of Molkwerum (ill. 93). This idea was used in other ways. For instance, in the family's private possession there is a tile picture of a pastoral landscape in summer with a treeless carriageway in the middle; Makkum village is seen on the horizon with its church-towers and windmills, and on the left are ships at sea. It is typical of nineteenth century style that the whole picture is a *trompe-l'oeil*, with its dark frame hanging by a cord from a rosette-headed nail against a wall of white tiles (ill. 156a). The Fitzwilliam Museum in Cambridge possesses a similar picture on a single large tile. Both must have been made between 1843 and 1851.

A tile picture in dark blue, manganese and yellow, signed wJTZ in yellow and dated 1855, is noteworthy for the up-to-date addition of a paddle-steamer in the background (ill. 156b). Willem Jacobus ten Zweege was chief faience painter at Tichelaar's from 1849 to 1896. In the foreground, as a contrast, is the sailing-vessel *De Snelle Jager*, from an engraving by Adolf van der Laan; the pounce for this had already been used at Makkum in 1776 for a tile picture by Gerke Gerbrants.[8] The Greek key patterned border is also from the factory's pattern-book.

It was fortunate that new technical and artistic methods were consciously sought in the eighties, and the good effect of this is also to be seen in Frisian

128

tiles. As examples we may mention two small pictures (23.5 × 20 cm.) representing the Chancery at Leeuwarden (a former law-court) and Bolsward town hall (ill. 155a,b). The Renaissance-style Chancery (1585) stood by the Turfmarkt, which had not yet been filled in. This picture in modern style was offered as a gift on the occasion of a prize-distribution in 1890. In such works the execution has reached a high level, and evidently new life has been infused into the tile industry.

At the beginning of the twentieth century the Makkum works, through a combination of circumstances, took part in the general development of Dutch style. The painter Christoffel Bisschop (b. at Leeuwarden 1828, d. at Scheveningen 1904), who specialized in Hindelopen interiors, bequeathed his studio to the Frisian Museum. It was transferred in two stages, the second in 1914, on which occasion a wall painting of a peacock on a flowering branch, which for technical reasons could not be moved from his home at Scheveningen, was copied in Indian ink: the drawing is signed *Jan R. Steensma 20/5 1914* (ill. 157a). From it was made the tile picture that now catches the eye as one enters the Bisschop room at Makkum (ill. 157b). Steensma was engaged as a painter at the Makkum factory in 1917 and died in 1967. The tile picture is signed with two capital T's, crossing diagonally. The wall painting, presumably by Bisschop himself, is typical of the decorative art of about 1900 and is reminiscent of the Jugendstil.

Flower trophies and trophies of the chase were also affected by technical innovation. As regards composition they retain their original appearance though slightly modernized, but they are promoted to the rank of tile pictures (ill. 158a,b).

In our own day Makkum has actually produced work in the Chinese style, though this has no connection with Delft pottery, which was modelled on Wan Li porcelain of the seventeenth century and Ch'ing porcelain to the end of the eighteenth. The modern polychrome tiles produced at Makkum and representing Chinese figures, with carefully copied ideograms, are commissioned copies of actual Chinese tiles (ill. 158c).

Among the recent designs of 1969 is the tile with the manganese seahorse (ill. 158d) commissioned by the Kingma Bank at Makkum on its centenary and presented to customers as a souvenir. With inventions such as these, Tichelaar's Royal Makkum Pottery and Tile-Works remains an up-to-date, progressive and active concern.

Notes

1 A. Hoynck van Papendrecht, op. cit. (1918), pp. 189 ff.
   Dr. E. Wiersum, 'De laatste Rotterdamsche Tegelbakkerij', in *Rotterdamsch Jaarboekje* (1921), pp. 102 ff.
2 Presumably the monogram of the faience painter G.R., whose name has not come to light in the Rotterdam municipal archives.
3 C. de Jonge, *Westraven 1661–1961. Van Pannen en estriken tot tegels en plastieken* (1961).
4 H. W. Mauser, 'De Porceleyne Fles', in *Vrienden van de Nederlandse Ceramiek*, 5 (August 1956), on the occasion of the firm's tercentenary.
   Th. H. Lunsingh Scheurleer, 'De collectie John F. Loudon veertig jaar in het Rijksmuseum', in *Bulletin van het Rijksmuseum* (1956).
   O. A. van der Want, 'Kanttekeningen bij een catalogusinleiding', in *Vrienden van de Nederlandse Ceramiek*, 30 (March 1963).
5 *Faïencerie d'Art de Delft de Joost Thooft & Labouchere*, 'De Porceleyne Fles' Anno *1672* (n.d.).
6 Catalogue of the exhibition for the tercentenary of Tichelaar's Royal Makkum Pottery and Tile-Works, with introduction by P. J. Tichelaar, in *Vrienden van de Nederlandse Ceramiek*, 19 (June 1960).
7 See introduction to catalogue of the exhibition of Frisian pottery in the Pothuis at Makkum (De Waag Museum), 1 June—15 September 1963.
8 J. Pluis, 'De invloed van de etsen van A. van der Laan op de tegelschilders van schepentableaux', in *Jaarboek 1966 van Fries Scheepvaartmuseum en Oudheidkamer*, Sneek, Frisia.

XIV *Literature and collections*

Four centuries of the Dutch tile industry, reflected in the literature and collections of the past fifty years

We have attempted in the foregoing pages to trace the rise and development of the Dutch tile industry in all its variety.[1] In so doing, we have often had occasion to point out its close connection with historical and cultural events in the Netherlands. It is certainly an encouraging fact that when the interest in collecting Delftware revived about 1900 it extended in full measure to the collection of tiles. The development and significance of this characteristically Dutch art can now be studied in the principal Netherlands museums. The great diversity of decorative schemes clearly emerges from the present account; the importance of the place accorded to the tile in art can be judged from the wealth of literature on the subject. Recent research has provided much new material and raised new problems to be solved. It is now time, fifty years after the first major studies, to draw up a bibliography.

Professor F. W. Hudig, in his first book *Delfter Fayence* (1929: chapter 1, pp. 12–24), gave an illuminating summary of the Dutch and international literature and glossaries, and also the catalogued collections up to and including the works of Henry Havard. Reference may well be made to Hudig's work at the present day even though it is partly out of date.

The works published between 1866 and about 1900 were subjected to justified criticism, until A. H. H. van der Burgh of Delft laid the basis, which still remains valid, for the archival study of Delft pottery.

The general literature covering old Dutch majolica, tiles and Delft pottery includes the following works:

Dr. Elisabeth Neurdenburg and B. Rackham, *Old Dutch Pottery and Tiles* (1923).

Eelco Vis and C. de Geus, *Altholländische Fliesen*, I (1926).

Prof. Dr. F. W. Hudig, *Delfter Fayence* (1929).

C. de Geus, Member of the Association of Netherlands Architects (BNA), *Oud-Nederlandsche Tegels. Bijdrage tot de kennis van de Nederlandsche Ceramiek. De collectie Isaac in het Rijksmuseum te Amsterdam* (1931, second edition 1939).

Prof. Dr. F. W. Hudig, *Altholländische Fliesen*, II (1933).

Dr. Elisabeth Neurdenburg, *Oude Nederlandsche Majolica en Tegels, Delftsch Aardewerk*, Heemschut series, 35 (1943).

Dr. C. H. de Jonge, *Oud-Nederlandsche Majolica en Delftsch Aardewerk* (1947).

IJsbrand Kok, Member of the BNA, *De Hollandse Tegel*, Heemschut series, 67 (1949).

Dingeman Korf, *Dutch Tiles* (London, 1963; third Dutch edition, 1964).

Arthur Lane, *A Guide to the Collection of Tiles* (London, Victoria and Albert Museum, 1939, second edition 1960).

Dr. Anne Berendsen, Marcel B. Keezer, Dr. Sigurd Schoubye, Dr. J. M. dos Santos Simões, P. J. Tichelaar, *Fliesen* (1963); English edition, *Tiles* (London, 1967).

Dr. C. H. de Jonge, *Delfts Aardewerk*, part 5 of the Oud-Delft series (1965).

Also various articles in *Oude Kunst*, 1916–20, and the bulletin *Vrienden van de Nederlandse Ceramiek* since its foundation in 1953.[2]

The principal collections of tiles are in the museums listed alphabetically below with information concerning exhibitions of new acquisitions, donations, excavations etc. Many provincial museums in Holland have collections of tiles produced locally; for these the official guide should be consulted (*De Nederlandse Musea*, 1967).

Alkmaar	*De Nieuwe Doelen Museum*
	Part of Dr. van Tijen's collection was presented to the museum in 1968.
Amsterdam	*Stedelijk Museum*
	Exhibition of Dutch decorative wall-tiles of the 16th and 17th centuries, Eelco Vis collection, 29 March—10 April 1919. See catalogue with notes by C. de Geus. The collection was sold to America in 1927.
	Rijksmuseum
	The Arthur Isaac tile collection was acquired partly by purchase in 1944, the remainder from his heirs in 1955.

See C. de Geus, *Oud-Nederlandsche Tegels* (1939);
Dr. Elisabeth Neurdenburg, *Oud-Aardewerk* (1917, second edition 1920);
Marie-Anne Heukensfeldt Jansen, *Delfts Aardewerk* (1955), and *Majolica* (1961).

Arnhem	*Rijksmuseum voor Volkskunde* This museum has a large collection of Dutch tiles.
Delft	*Huis Lambert van Meerten Museum* See Guide by Ida C. E. Peelen (Delft, 1922).
Enkhuizen	*Zuider Zee Museum* See Catalogue of tile exhibition, by D. F. Lunsingh Scheurleer (1967).
Enschede	*Twenthe Museum* In 1966 the museum acquired on long loan from the Chamber of Antiquities at Rijssen an important collection of Delft pottery including some tile pictures, property of the late Mevr. G. J. M. van Heel-Willems.
Franeker	*Dr. Coopmanshuis Museum* Collection of pottery manufactured in Makkum, Harlingen and Delft.
Gouda	*Catharijne-Gasthuis Museum* and *De Moriaen Museum of pipes and earthenware* See Guide to both museums by Dr. J. Schouten, 1955, 1966; G. C. Helbers, 'De geschiedenis van het oude Goudse plateel', in *Vrienden van de Nederlandse Ceramiek*, 4 (1956).
The Hague	*Gemeente Museum* See A. J. Servaas van Rooyen, Catalogue of the Van der Burgh bequest (Delft pottery collection) (1905); Ida C. E. Peelen, Catalogue of Dutch pottery collection (1917). A small part of the loan collection of J. W. N. van Achterbergh (1935) was purchased in 1941. See Dr. Beatrice M. L. J. M. Jansen, Catalogue of Dutch pottery 1500–1800 (1949), and Guide to the department of old crafts (1950).
Harlingen	*Hannema-Huis Museum* Small collection of Frisian tiles; a Harlingen fireplace is on exhibition.

133

Tile pattern-book from the Van Hulst family of potters, 18th-19th centuries, see D. F. Lunsingh Scheurleer, 'Een modellenboek voor tegels', in *Antiek*, 4 and 5 (1968).

Hoorn　　　*West Frisian Museum*
Collection of old Dutch majolica and tiles, many of Frisian and West Frisian origin.
In the St. Pietershofje at Hoorn is an original polychrome tiled niche for a candlestick (*post* 1617).

Leeuwarden　　*Frisian Museum*
Small but important collection of northern Dutch tiles.
Princessehof Museum
Large collection of tiles and Delft pottery, assembled by Nanne Ottema. After the present expansion this collection will be exhibited together with the Van Achterbergh collection at Amstelveen (Amsterdam).

Leiden　　　*De Lakenhal Museum*
See exhibition catalogue, *Tegelschouw*, Dec. 1970—Jan. 1971;
Dingeman Kat, *Majolicavondsten in en om Leiden* (1970).

London　　　*Victoria and Albert Museum*
Rich collection of tiles and Dutch pottery.
See B. Rackham, *Catalogue of the Van den Bergh gift* (1923; second edition 1931).

Makkum　　　*De Waag Museum*
Frisian earthenware.
Het Pothuis
Permanent exhibition of Makkum pottery.
See Tichelaar's Royal Makkum Earthenware and Tile Factory, 1660–1960:
300 jaar Makkumer aardewerk (1960).
'Wat Friese gleiers bakten' (1960), reprinted in *Vrienden van de Nederlandse Ceramiek*, 19 (June 1970).

Monnickendam　*De Waag Museum*
See Dr. J. B. Knipping, 'Ikonografie van de tegels der verzameling Van Tijen', in *Vrienden van de Nederlandse Ceramiek*, 26 (1962);
Guide to exhibition of old Dutch tiles and majolica in the Van Tijen collection (1963).

134

Otterlo	*Tegelmuseum It noflik Ste* (Tile Museum). See O. Feenstra, 'Een klein tegelmuseum te Otterlo', in *Bouw* (1962).
Rotterdam	*Historical Museum* Important collection of tiles and excavated objects; catalogue in preparation. See H. C. Gallois, 'Over Rotterdamsche Tegels', in *Mededeelingen van den Dienst van Kunsten en Wetenschappen* (1919); A. Hoynck van Papendrecht, *De Rotterdamsche Plateel- en Tegelbakkers en hun product, 1590–1850* (1920); Dr. E. Wiersum, 'De Rotterdamsche Koorddansersfamilie Magito', in *Rotterdamsch Jaarboekje* (1920) and 'De laatste Rotterdamsche Tegelbakkerij', ibid., (1921), pp. 102 ff. *Boymans-van Beuningen Museum* See Catalogue: exhibition of old pottery from the Bastert-van Schaardenburg collection, under the auspices of the Boymans Museum Foundation, 1940, purchased 1942; Catalogue of exhibition *Uit de bodem van Rotterdam* (From the soil of Rotterdam), 1942. Museum exhibits show an extensive survey of the Dutch tile industry. J. W. N. van Achterbergh collection at Amstelveen, purchased 1943, partly on loan.
De Rijp	*Rijper Museum In 't Houten Huis* See Dr. J. B. Knipping, 'Ikonografie van de wandtegels in het museum "in 't Houten Huis", De Rijp, N.H.', in *Vrienden van de Nederlandse Ceramiek*, 24 (October 1961).
Utrecht	*Centraal Museum* Catalogue of the municipal Historical Museum (1928), pp. 92 ff.

EXPLANATORY NOTES

The pioneering work, especially as regards Rotterdam, is A. Hoynck van Papendrecht's important and well-documented *De Rotterdamsche Plateel- en Tegelbakkers en hun product* (1920). A spur was given to this work in 1914, when excavations for the building of a new town hall on the Coolsingel led to the discovery of thousands of potsherds and fragments, richly varied in decoration, which showed with certainty that a pottery had existed.

After the bombardment in May 1940 former tile-works came to light in many parts of the devastated old city of Rotterdam, as well as tiled walls in passages and cellars. An account of these is given in the catalogue of the exhibition *Uit de bodem van Rotterdam* (1942).

The Delft municipal archives contain valuable documentation concerning the earthenware industry in the form of notarial acts referring to the potteries and their owners, the artists, the products themselves and their fortunes at home and abroad.[3]

By the purchase of the J. I. Schouten collection in 1920, the Huis Lambert van Meerten became the Dutch tile museum *par excellence*, and efforts are still devoted to enlarging it.

Research on the subject of Delftware is still based on the method laid down in Professor Hudig's thorough study *Delfter Fayence* (1929). Part I of the standard work on Dutch tiles—*Altholländische Fliesen*, by Eelco Vis and C. de Geus— appeared in 1926, and in 1933 Professor Hudig published the second part, in which he paid particular attention to the archives of Dutch tile-works. He collected historical and economic data concerning over eighty factories, whose owners he traced in archives and notarial acts. Old inventories listed thousands of tiles with their subjects and prices. It repeatedly came to light how soon the different factories were in contact with one another and how close their relations were. Craftsmen would often move to another town to try their luck by starting a factory there. Between 1609 and 1629 at least twenty-five new concerns were founded, including, Hudig tells us, six in Rotterdam, five in Delft and Utrecht and others in Amsterdam, Gorinchem, Gouda, Enkhuizen and Hoorn.

The establishment of tile-works in Friesland shows how quickly contact was made between the provinces of North and South Holland and the rest of the country. Thanks to the interest of the lawyer Nanne Ottema at Leeuwarden, attention was directed towards Dutch majolica in Friesland in the years after the First World War.

At Leeuwarden, alongside the existing fine collections of Oriental porcelain and Delftware, the present direction of the Princessehof Museum is endeavouring, in connection with the current rebuilding, extension and re-organization, to provide a general view of the Dutch tile industry.

The history of the Bolsward factory speaks for itself thanks to the unique tile picture, a modern copy of which is in the Pothuis Museum in Makkum.

The early seventeenth-century contacts between Harlingen and Delft have been fully described in the relevant chapters. Makkum also deserves close attention, since its earthenware and tile factory is the only establishment in the country which carries on the original spirit and tradition of Dutch tile-making, adapted to modern times. In addition Westraven in Utrecht, an offshoot of De Porceleijne Fles, maintains the tradition of blue tiles.

136

Since the Second World War there has been an especially lively interest in the study of Dutch majolica, Delft faience and tiles. As a result of successful research in Delft notarial acts, Dr. H. E. van Gelder published articles on early Delft craftsmen and the factory De Dissel in *Vrienden van de Nederlandse Ceramiek*, 12 and 17 (1958 and 1959).[4] The same years marked the publication of works on the trade with Portugal and Spain by the outstanding expert J. M. dos Santos Simões, whose excellent knowledge of Dutch has enabled him to study the archives thoroughly. His masterpiece *Carreaux hollandais au Portugal et en Espagne* was published by the Calouste Gulbenkian Foundation in Lisbon.

P. J. Tichelaar has given impetus to the study of tile exports to North Germany, the Schleswig-Holstein and Danish coast and Scandinavia. Dr. Sigurd Schoubye, in *Hollandske Vægfliser* (1963), has begun the study of Dutch tiles in Denmark, where innumerable specimens are to be found, including those in the Museum at Tønder.

Contact with Poland was presumably established through Danzig, Finland and St. Petersburg, where many Dutch architects were active in the eighteenth century. In Chapter XII above, a first attempt, largely of an illustrative character, has been made with regard to the thousands of Dutch tiles in castles and palaces in and near Warsaw, which are a subject of active research under the direction of the Polish National Museum. In the days of the last King of Poland, Stanislas Augustus Poniatowski, who bought the Lazienki palace, tile decoration was carried out by artists from Saxony, but today Poland has tile factories of her own.

Notes

1 For books and articles on detailed subjects, see notes to Chapters II to XIII.
2 The quarterly journal *Vrienden van de Nederlandse Ceramiek* focusses attention on the whole range of Dutch ceramics, both antique and modern. On the tenth anniversary of this Association, Professor H. L. C. Jaffé contributed an article to the journal (28, 1962) entitled 'From Havard to the present day', in which he reviewed the literature on Dutch ceramics and illustrated its importance at all periods.
3 The documents, which also record marks and signatures, have been copied (1,654 pages) by A. H. H. van der Burgh and are preserved in the municipal archives. With the help of the municipal authorities they are being organized into a card-index system so that they can be consulted with ease.
4 This shows clearly what useful data the Van der Burgh notes provide for the knowledge and understanding of the Delft industry.

Illustrations

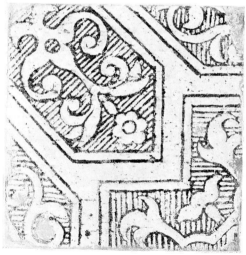

2 a
b c

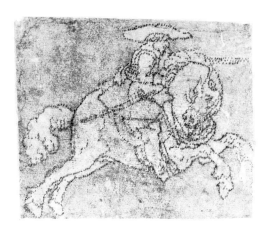 

4

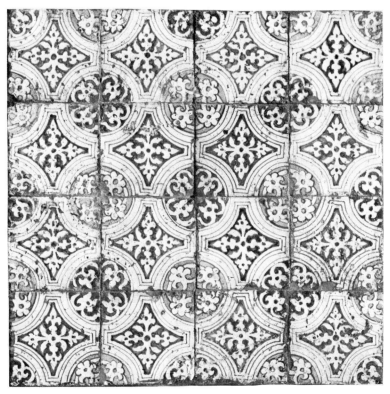

a   5
b

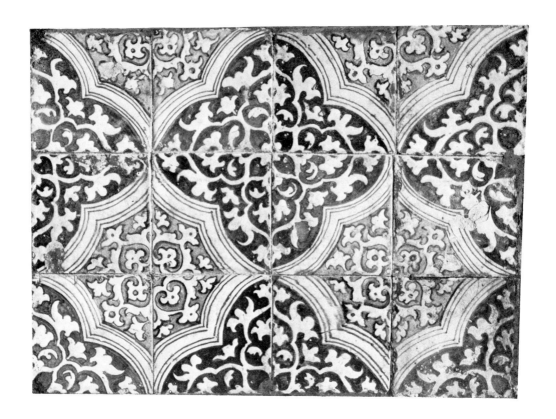

6 a
b

a
b
c

7

8 a   b
    c   d
    e   f

a
b
c

9

10   a
     b   c

11

12   a   b
      c   d
      e   f

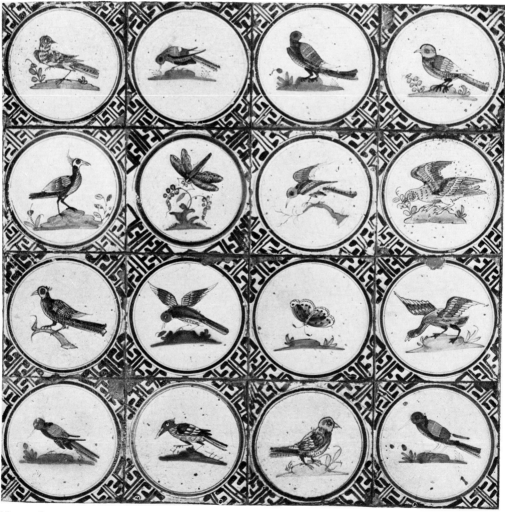

14   a   b

c

16   a   b
     c   d
     e   f

a   17
b

18 a
b

a 19
b

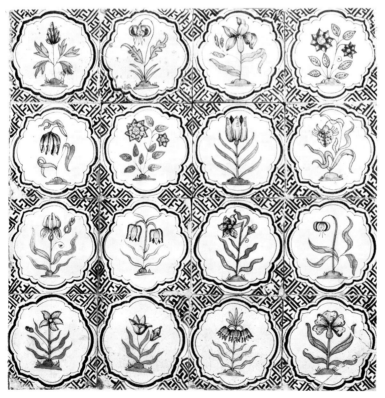

20   a

b

a   b 21
c   d
e   f

22   a   b
      c   d
      e

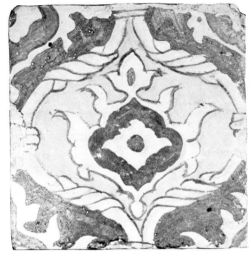

a b 23
c d
e

24   a
      b

28   a
      b   c
      d   e

a b 31
c d
e f

32 a b
    c d

a 33
b

34

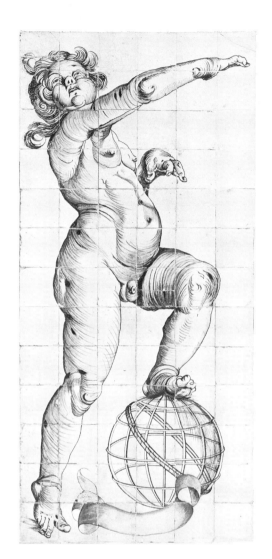 

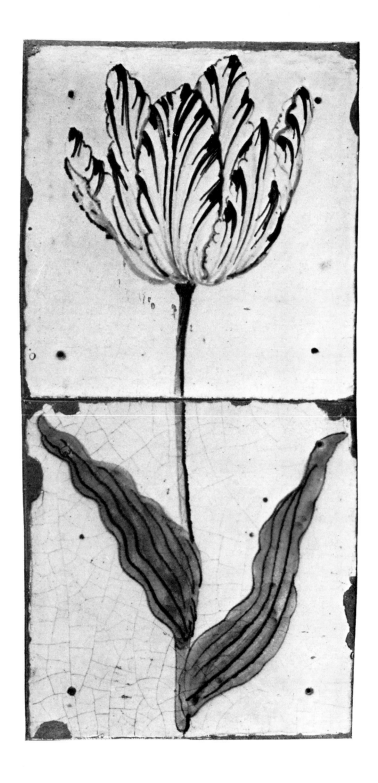

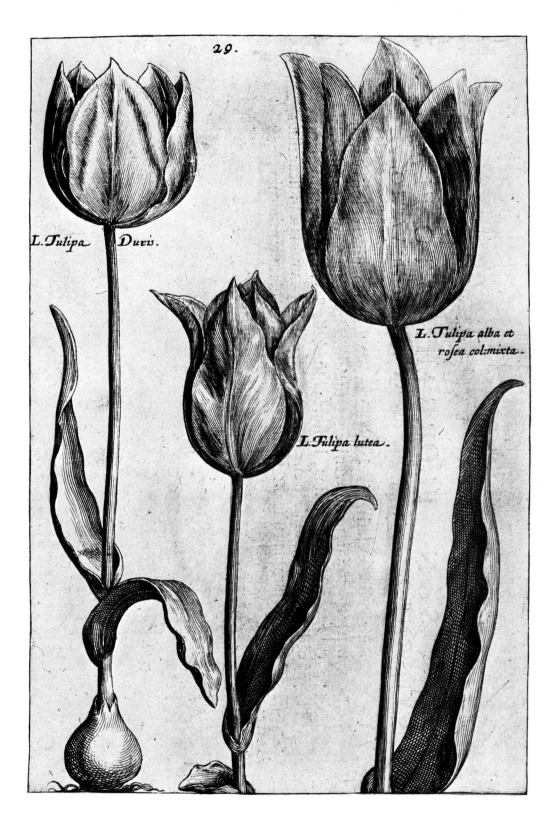

L. Tulipa Duris.

L. Tulipa alba et
rosea col:mixta.

L. Tulipa lutea.

a b 39
c d

40   a   b
     c   d
     e   f

MAVRIT^S PRINS VAN ORAENGEN
1615

PRINS HENDRICK VAN NASSAV
1619

42   a   b
        c
        d

a   b 43
c   d
e   f

44 a b
    c d
    e f

46 a b
      c d
      e

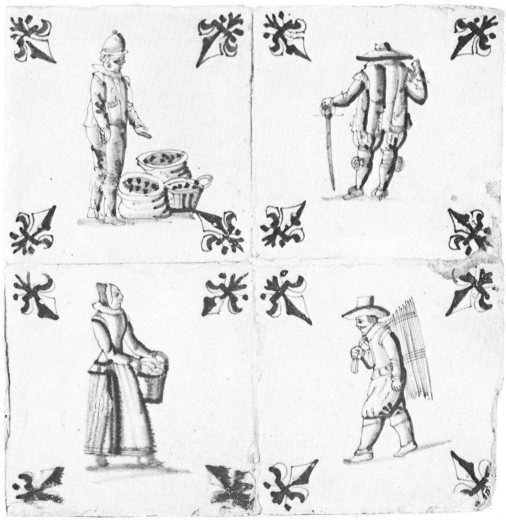

a b 47
c

48   a   b
       c   d
       e   f

a b 49
c d
e f

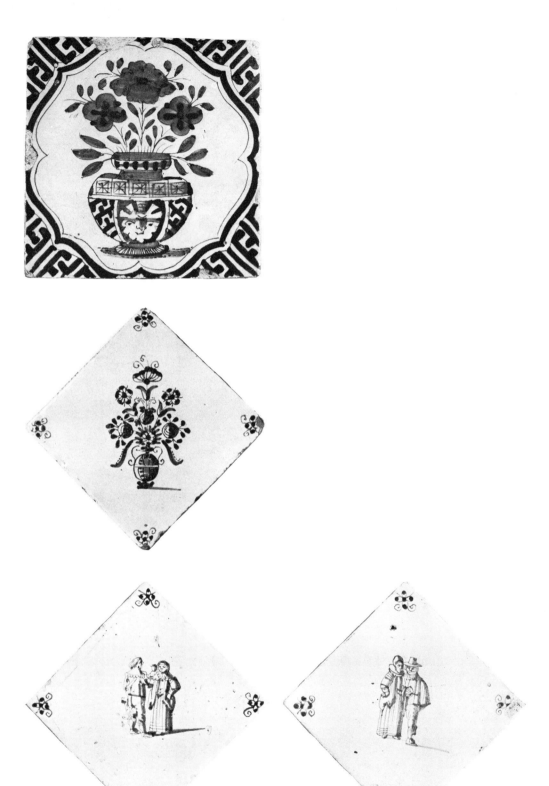

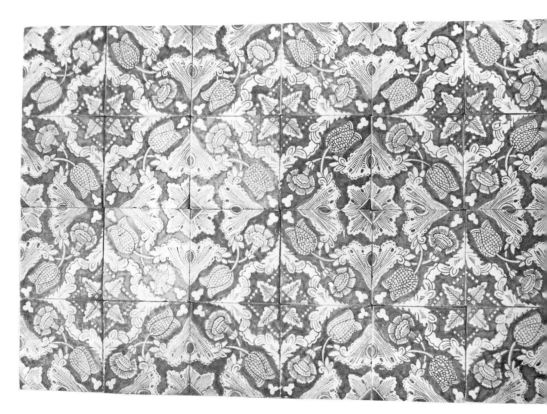

54 a
b

a b 55
c
d

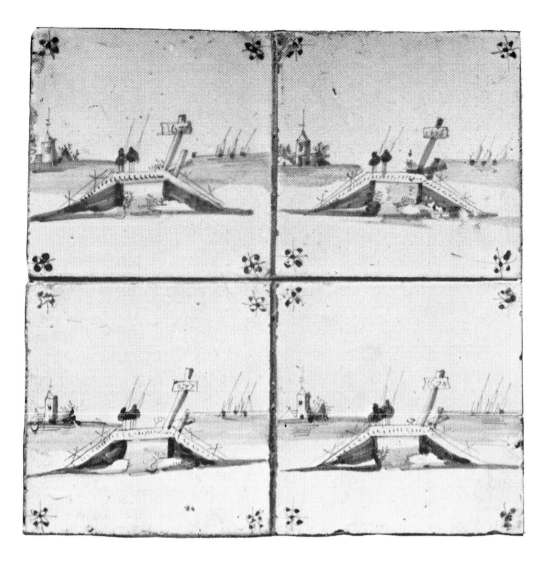

58   a
      b   c

60   a   b
        c   d
        e   f

64 a b
      c d

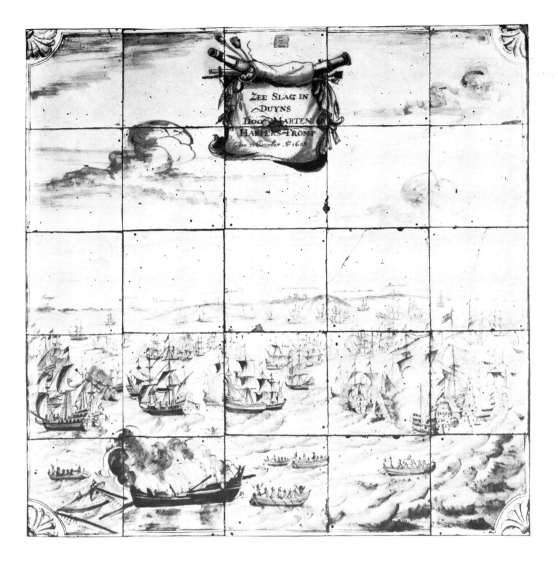

ZEE SLAG IN
DUYNS
DOOR MARTEN
HARPERS TROMP
den 21 October A° 1639

66   a

    b c

a 67
b
c

68 a b

70 a b
c

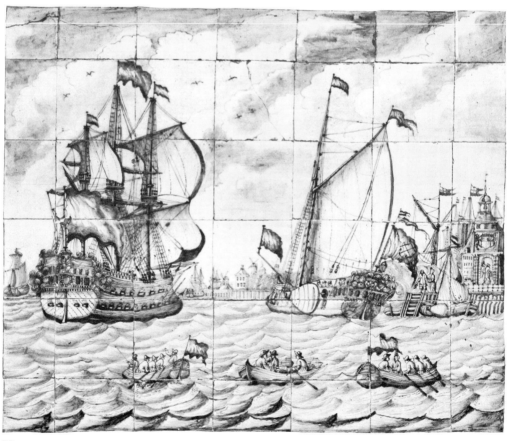

72　a
　　b

a b 73
c d

a b 75
c d
e f

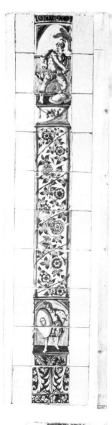

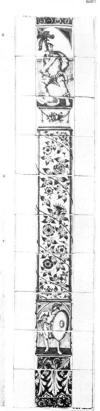

76 a b

78 a
    b

80　a
　　b

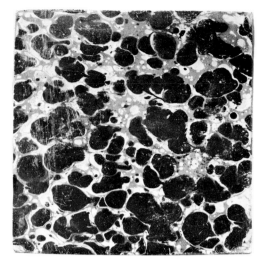

a b 81
c
d e

.T.4.L.29.

T.J.L.j6.

T.4.L.19.

T.6.L.28.

.T.6.L.29.

82   a   b
      c   d
      e

84 a
     b

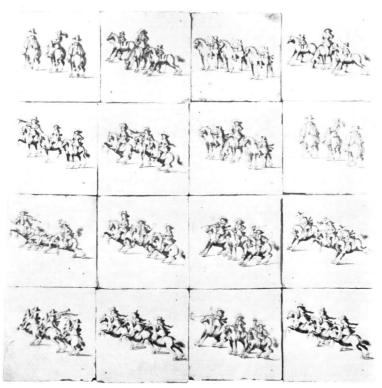

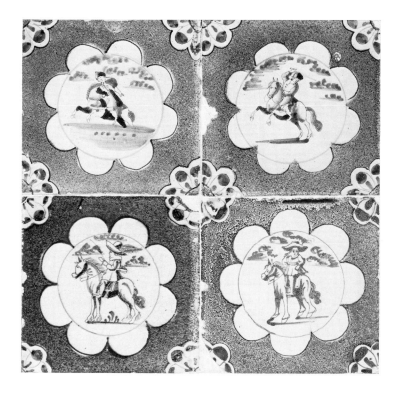

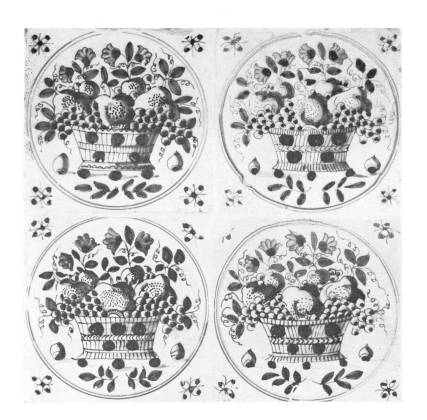

88 a
     b

a 89
b
c

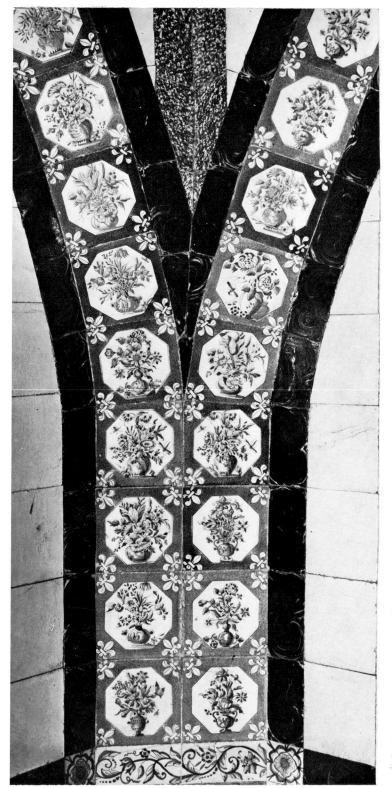

90 a b
         c

a
b   91
c

92   a
     b
     c

94   a
      b

96 a d
      b e
      c f

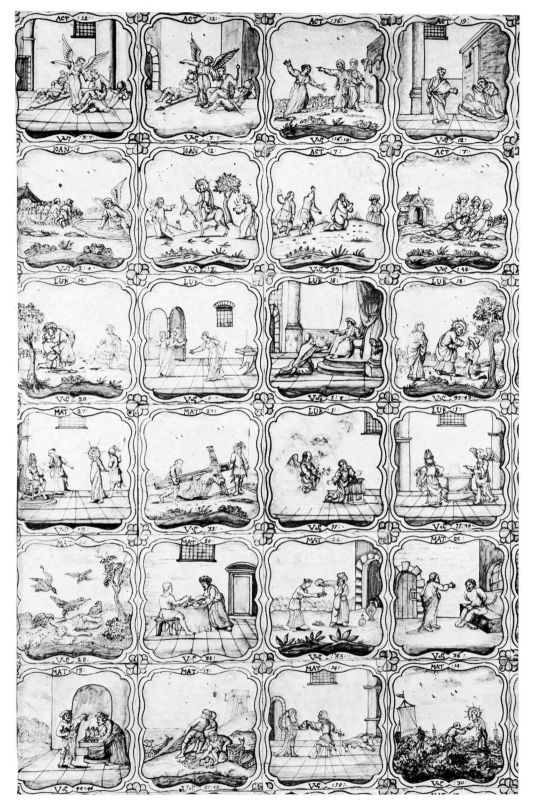

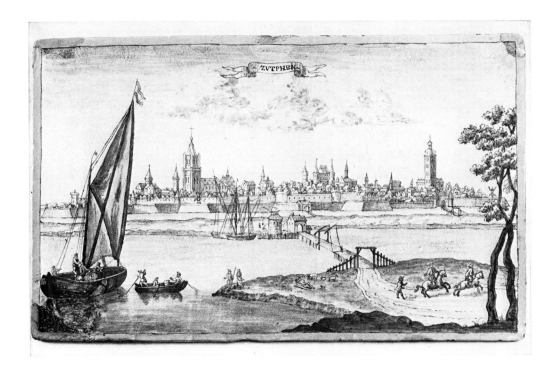

Ioannes Peeters delin: Casper Bouttats fecit aqua forti et excudit Antverpia Cum privilegio

ZVTPHEN in Ghelderlandt leyt op de rechte zyde des Waeter-vloets Yfel, een ander half myl van Doesborgh, vier van Aernhem ende fes van Nijmmegen, een goede ende wel betimmerde Stadt, wel verfien van huyfen, Kercken ende Cloofters. In 't Iaer 1583, den 23. September heeft den overften Taxis van weghen den Prince van Parma de Stadt met liftigheyt inghenomen, ende ten deele gheplundert. Anno 1584. beftont den Grave van Hohenle, ende 1585. den Grave van Leycefter de Stadt wederom te belege-ren, maer wierden beyde opghellaeghen door den Prince van Parma. In 't Iaer 1591, op 25. Mey wiert Zut-phen aengheraft van Prins Maurits, die (naer dat fy twee daeghen dapper befchoten was) haer, heeft over-gegeven; nu ghedwongken door Bernard' van Galen Bifschop van Munfter Anno 1672.

ZVTPHEN Pays de Gelare, eft fitué fur le cofté droit du Rivage de l'Yffel lieu & demy de Doesborgh, auatre d'Arnhem, & fix de Nimmegen : Ville affez bonne & bien bâty, embelly, & ornée de beaux Edifices, Eglifes, & Monafteres : L'An 1583. le 23. Septembre, le General Taxis l'a furpris par fubtilité de la parte du Prince de Parme & en partie pillée, l'Année 1584. le Comte de Hohenla & l'Année 1585. le Comte de Leycefter ont penfé la r'affieger, mais furent tout deux lattus & repouffz, du Prince de Parme. L'An 1591. le 25. Mey elle fut attaquée du Prince Mauris, & apres deux jours de fiege s'eft rendue, & en l'Année 1672. pris par Bernard van Galen Evefque de Munfter.

98 a
b

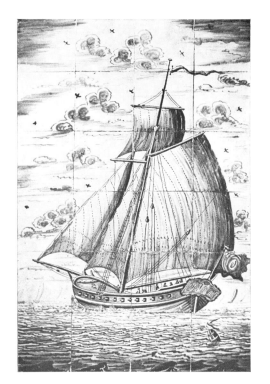

100 a b
      c

a b 101
c

102   a   b
       c   d
       e   f

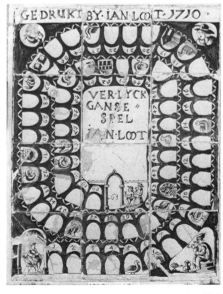

a b 103
c d

a b c 107

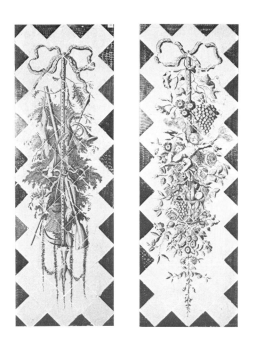

108   a
        b

110 a
      b c

112 a
b

113

a b 115
c d

117

122 a
b

124

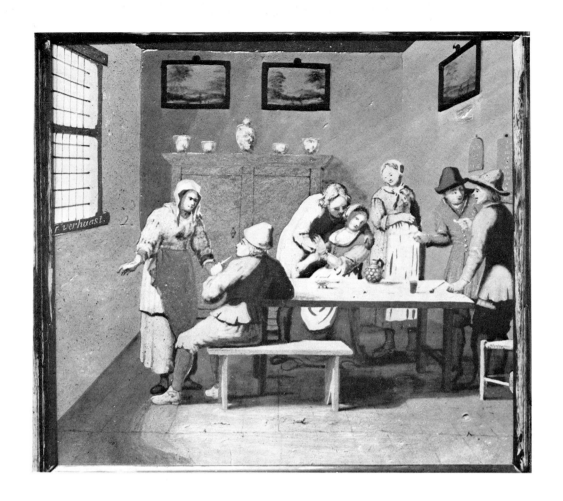

127

130   a   b

132

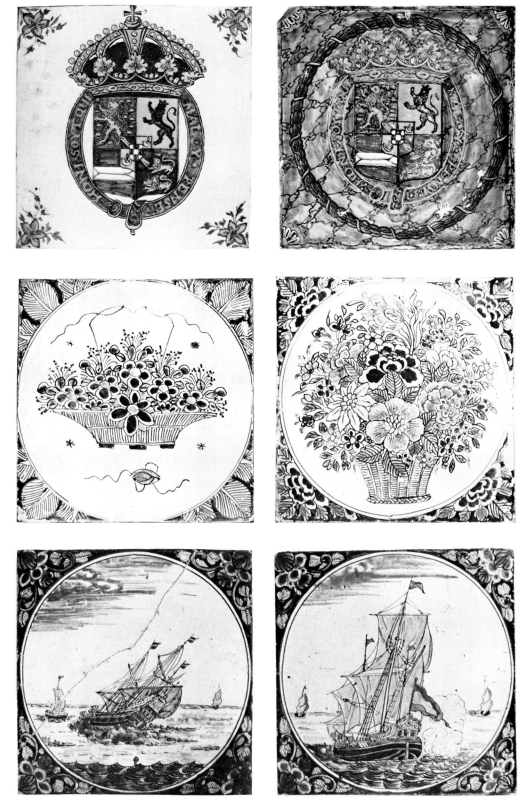

134   a   b
       c   d
       e   f

138   a   b

140　a
　　b

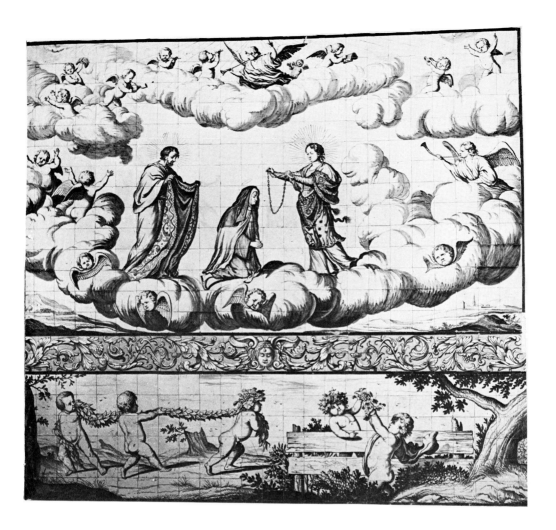

143

145

147 a
b

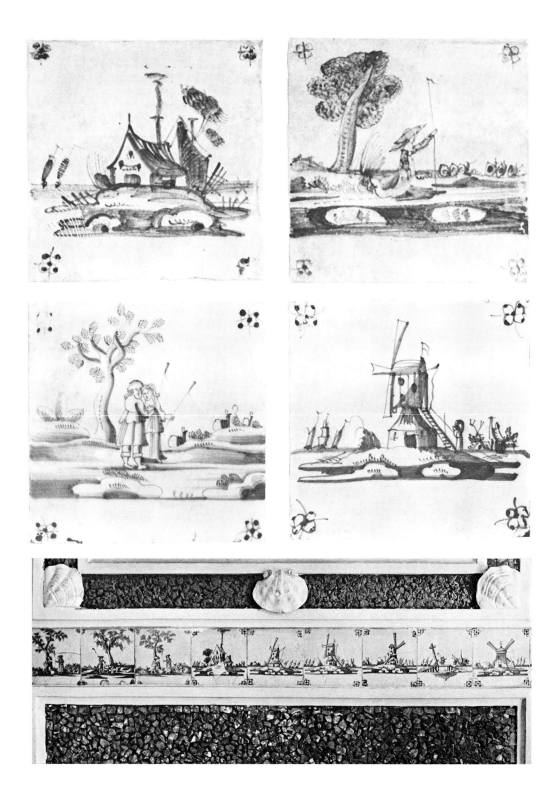

151   a
      b c

154   a
      b

a 155
b

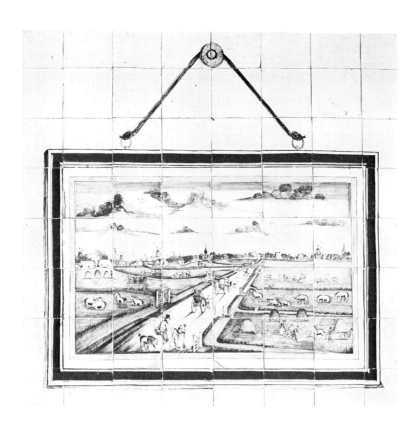

156   a
       b

a b 157

158 a b
    c d

List of illustrations

Plate I

Picture composed of 9 by 11 blue tiles showing a cross-section of the interior of the Bolsward tile factory: ground floor and two storeys. Above it, a picture (5 by 11 tiles) with flower-garlands to either side and the arms of the founders of the firm suspended from ribands. The names are IOH. TICHELAAR – IAN. STEENSMA – HEROD. IAGER – WYBE STEENSMA. A cartouche at the top is inscribed:

De Stichters van dit Werk
Zijn deese met haar Vieren
Wiens Waapens met haar naam
Doen deese muier versieren
Anno 1737

(The founders of this factory are these four, whose arms and names adorn this wall.)

Amsterdam, Rijksmuseum. A copy, made in 1967, is in the De Waag Museum at Makkum.

Plate II

Polychrome tile picture of a cock. *De Moriaen Museum, Gouda*

Plate III

Polychrome bird perched on a nail (detail of ill. 33b). *De Moriaen Museum, Gouda*

Plate IV

Blue tile painting (31.6 × 42.2 cm.). View of the village of Ouderkerk on the IJssel. The village is seen on the right in the bend of the river, to the left are farms; tall trees on either side. Signed on the back: F. van Frijtom, 1692. *Vught, collection of the heirs of Dr. F. H. Fentener van Vlissingen*

Plate V

Blue tile plaque in a dark manganese setting from Walenburg castle (1767), after a drawing by Jan de Beyer, 1757

Plate VI

Amalienburg: interior of the kitchen as seen from the reception-room. Between manganese columns are three flower-vase pieces under a trellis of vines peopled with small figures. Each bouquet in its ornamental vase stands on a marble block with birds and butterflies round about, a peacock on the right-hand edge of the vase; below, a parrot is on a perch to the left and a cock to the right. The arched frame is uncut only in the centre panel. Composition by François Cuvilliés. *Amalienburg pavilion in the grounds of Nymphenburg palace near Munich*

1a	Fragment of tiled floor from Utrecht Cathedral, *c.* 1350. *Utrecht, Centraal Museum*
1b	Floor-tile from the refectory of St. Paul's abbey, Utrecht: portrait of a woman, *c.* 1350. Cat. Hist. Museum (1928), No. 1555. *Utrecht, Centraal Museum*
1c	Floor-tile from Mariëndaal monastery, Utrecht. Portrait of the founder Theodoricus, known as Kovelwaet (1245?). First half of the sixteenth century. *Utrecht, Centraal Museum*
2a	Fragment of a tile floor: set of four, with inscription in Gothic script in a diagonal setting. Fourteenth–fifteenth century. *Rotterdam, Boymans-van Beuningen Museum*
2b	Tile with diagonal setting, dated 1556. *Delft, Huis Lambert van Meerten Museum*
2c	Tile from a set of four: hatched pattern of Greek and saltire crosses with foliage motifs, alternating with an octagon: *c.* 1550. *Gouda, Catharijne-Gasthuis Museum*
3a,b	Two pounces for tiles depicting horsemen: *c.* 1700, possibly from Harlingen. *Delft, Huis Lambert van Meerten Museum*
3c,d	Pounce and tile showing an officer with his squire. The pounce is marked PG for Pieter Grauda of the Raamstraat tile-works at Harlingen, 1681–4. *Leeuwarden, Frisian Museum*
4	Picture (3 × 3 tiles) with Hispano-Moresque motifs, in reserve technique. *London, Victoria and Albert Museum*
5a	Set of 16 blue tiles with Hispano-Moresque motifs, in reserve technique. *Delft, Huis Lambert van Meerten Museum*
5b	Set of 16 polychrome tiles with Hispano-Moresque motifs, in reserve technique. *Amsterdam, Rijksmuseum*
6a	Set of 12 polychrome tiles with Hispano-Moresque motifs, in reserve technique. *Amsterdam, Rijksmuseum*
6b	Set of four tiles with leaf motifs inside an outlined square and a similar circle. *Rotterdam, Boymans-van Beuningen Museum*
7a	Polychrome tile, divided diagonally into quarters, with stylized floral motif in reserve technique. *Rotterdam, Boymans-van Beuningen Museum*
7b	Tile with diagonal leaf and tendril design, white on dark blue. *Epse (Gelderland), J. van Loo collection*
7c	Tile of identical design, dark blue on white. *Rotterdam, Boymans-van Beuningen Museum*
8a	Polychrome tile with bust of a man, facing right, with large hat and flat collar, in ornamental medallion; corner-design of white buds. *Delft, Huis Lambert van Meerten Museum*

8b	Polychrome tile with bust of a man, facing left, with doublet and ruff, in ornamental medallion; corner-design of white buds. *Delft, Huis Lambert van Meerten Museum*
8c	Polychrome tile with bust of a man, facing right; large hat and 'millstone' ruff; polychrome diagonal lozenge frame, corners in reserve technique. *Rotterdam, Historical Museum*
8d	Polychrome tile with bust of a man, facing left; narrow-brimmed hat and doublet, millstone ruff; corners in reserve technique. *Woerden, G. de Goederen collection*
8e,f	Two polychrome tiles: busts of a woman and a man facing each other. The woman wears a heart-shaped cap, the man a broad-brimmed hat; both wear large ruffs; polychrome lozenge frames, corners in reserve technique. *Amstelveen, J. W. N. van Achterbergh collection*
9a	Polychrome tile, bust of a woman facing left; heart-shaped cap, millstone ruff and pearl necklace; polychrome medallion, white buds in corners. *Rotterdam, Historical Museum*
9b	Polychrome tile with similar portrait of a woman, in left profile; dark green diadem cap and ruff; polychrome medallion, white buds in corners. *Rotterdam, Boymans-van Beuningen Museum: gift of Mevr. E. M. de Kock-Pijpers, Rotterdam*
9c	Polychrome tile, head and shoulders of a woman in semi-profile; white cap with pleated border, ruff tilted upwards at the back; polychrome medaillion, white buds in corners. *Rotterdam, Boymans-van Beuningen museum, on loan from J. W. N. van Achterberg*
10a	Six polychrome tiles in scalloped frames; busts facing right or left, two in white wigs; drapery around the shoulders. In the same series, two cherubs heads with wings. *Otterlo, Tegelmuseum*
10b,c	Two polychrome tiles, portraits of the Anabaptists Johan Mathys van Haerlem and Jan Beuckelsz. van Leyden; in a lined circle; corners. reserved. *Amstelveen, J. W. N. van Achterbergh collection*
11	Tableau of 25 polychrome tiles showing men and animals in a landscape, in lozenge frames; corners reserved, with leaf design. *The Hague, Van Stolk family*
12a	Polychrome tile: a galloping horseman with a sword raised in his right hand, in lozenge frame; corners reserved. *Epse, J. van Loo collection*
12b	Polychrome tile: a pikeman standing, with his pike in his left hand, in a lozenge frame; corners reserved. *Oudewater, Mevr. F. van der Lee-de Blécourt collection*
12c	Polychrome tile: an eagle perched on a sprig; decorated medallion, white buds in corners. *Rotterdam, Historical Museum*
12d	Polychrome tile: a monkey sitting in a field; polychrome circular frame, white buds in corners. *Rotterdam, Historical Museum*
12e	Polychrome tile: a sea-monster breaking the surface; decorated medallion, white buds in corners. *Delft, Huis Lambert van Meerten Museum*
12f	Polychrome tile: a swan swimming among water-plants; quadrilobe frame, corners reserved. *Woerden, G. de Goederen collection*
13a	Polychrome tile: a peacock on a wooden stile, spreading its tail; diagonal frame, corners reserved. *Haarlem, Frans Hals Museum*
13b,c	Two polychrome tiles, each with an elephant facing left; diagonal frame, corners reserved. *Amsterdam, J. W. N. van Achterbergh collection*

13d	Polychrome tile: a crouching rabbit nibbling plants; medallion framed with dots and a zigzag pattern, corner-design of blue sprigs on white ground. *Amstelveen, J. W. N. van Achterbergh collection*
14a	Polychrome tile: a bird in flight with a sprig in its beak; corner-design of foliage. *Epse, J. van Loo collection*
14b	Polychrome tile: a goose looking for food in the water; ox-head motifs in corners. *Rotterdam, Historical Museum*
14c	Tableau of 16 polychrome tiles with a variety of birds and butterflies in circular setting; meander pattern in corners. *Amsterdam, Rijksmuseum*
15	Large tableau of 48 polychrome tiles. Each group of four has an eight-pointed star in the centre, surrounded by four pomegranates and diagonally placed tulips and bunches of grapes. *Amsterdam, Rijksmuseum*
16a	Polychrome tile with an eight-leaved rosette in the centre; in the corners, placed diagonally, are two burst pomegranates and two bunches of grapes. *Woerden, G. de Goederen collection*
16b	Polychrome tile with eight-pointed star in the centre; around it are four pomegranates and in the corners, placed diagonally, are tulips and bunches of grapes. *Woerden, G. de Goederen collection*
16c	Set of four polychrome tiles: flowering pomegranates in a quadrilobe; corners reserved. *Delft, Huis Lambert van Meerten Museum*
16d	Polychrome set of four tiles: diagonal composition of pomegranates and grapes, the design between forming an eight-petalled flower. *Amstelveen, J. W. N. van Achterbergh collection*
16e	Polychrome tile: a burst pomegranate; ornamental medallion; corners reserved. *Delft, Huis Lambert van Meerten Museum*
16f	Polychrome tile: burst pomegranate surrounded by leaves and buds in an ornamental medallion; corners reserved. *Delft, Huis Lambert van Meerten Museum*
17a	Two tiles from a set of four with burst pomegranates in a many-sided frame, alternating with reserved corner-design. *Woerden, G. de Goederen collection*
17b	Polychrome tableau of four tiles, each showing three burst pomegranates on a stem within a quatrefoil; corner-design of inverted sprigs. *Amstelveen, J. W. N. van Achterbergh collection*
18a	Set of four polychrome tiles with round fruit-bowls on short stems, containing pomegranates and bunches of grapes; corner-design of inverted sprigs. *Rotterdam, Historical Museum*
18b	Polychrome set of four tiles with ornamental fruit-bowls on tall stems, containing pomegranates and bunches of grapes; ox-head corner-design. *Rotterdam, Historical Museum*
19a	Set of four polychrome tiles, each showing a Renaissance vase with high handles, filled with marigolds and foliage, the design alternating with eight-petalled rosettes in medallions. *Gouda, De Moriaen Museum*
19b	Two polychrome tiles, part of a group, each showing a Renaissance vase with high handles filled with various flowers, in an oval frame; to either side, Renaissance-style leaves and volutes in reserve. *The Hague, Gemeente Museum*
20a	Set of four polychrome tiles, each showing a flower from one of the *Flora*. The bulb is seen in a dark patch of earth, and sketchy clouds are indicated. *Amsterdam, Rijksmuseum*

20b Set of 16 polychrome tiles depicting different flowers from the *Flora* in scalloped frame, with meander pattern in the corners. *Rotterdam, Historical Museum*

21a Polychrome tile: a plant from the *Flora*, with the bulb visible in dark earth, in a polychrome circle; corner-design reserved. *Epse, J. van Loo collection*

21b Polychrome tile: a tulip planted in the ground, in a polychrome lozenge frame; corner-design reserved. *Amstelveen, J. W. N. van Achterbergh collection*

21c Polychrome tile: a carnation in bloom with stylized leaves in polychrome lozenge frame; corner-design reserved. *Hoorn, West Frisian Museum*

21d Polychrome tile with two carnations and two lilies arranged in a cross; inverted corner-design of leaves. *Delft, Huis Lambert van Meerten Museum*

21e Diamond-shaped polychrome tile with stylized buttercup, showing stamens. *Rotterdam, Historical Museum*

21f Polychrome tile showing the emblems of Great Britain: in the centre a Tudor rose in bloom and, hanging to right and left of the stem, a Scotch thistle and an Irish harp; at the foot of the stem is a knot with three loops; inverted corner-design of leaves (English?). *Woerden, G. de Goederen collection*

22a Polychrome tile with chess-board motif in a lozenge frame; reserved corner-design. *Woerden, G. de Goederen collection*

22b Four polychrome tiles with overall pattern of fleurs-de-lis in round and octagonal frames, alternately dark blue and orange. *Delft, Huis Lambert van Meerten Museum*

22c Polychrome tile with Hispano-Moresque plaited design, placed diagonally between inverted plants in flower. *Woerden, G. de Goederen collection*

22d Polychrome tile with Hispano-Moresque motifs of interlocking circles, the centre of each filled with a many-petalled floret. *Amstelveen, J. W. N. van Achterberg collection*

22e Polychrome tile with pattern of lozenge-shaped blocks piled on one another, with a coloured four-petalled flower on each white surface. *Delft, Huis Lambert van Meerten Museum*

23a Polychrome tile with coat of arms in round frame of different colours; corner design of white buds. The shield hangs from a branch, with two snakes coiled on either side and the date 1619. The device on the shield is a three-branched tree with three pewter cans and a fish horizontally across the trunk. *Leeuwarden, Frisian Museum*

23b Polychrome tile with a stylized burst pomegranate; reserved corner design of leaves(?). *Woerden, G. de Goederen collection*

23c Polychrome tile with striped sixteen-sided frame in different colours. In the centre is a wheel with eight spokes, and around it four inverted flowers; Renaissance corner-design in reserve technique. *Woerden, G. de Goederen collection*

23d Polychrome tile with square-on-circle design; in the centre is a wheel with sixteen spokes in a circle, and around it a fourfold leaf-design with fruit(?); Renaissance corner-design in reserve technique. *Rotterdam, Historical Museum*

23e Polychrome tile: in the centre an eight-pointed star on a dark ground in a roundel, with a fourfold design of leaves and fruit around it; outside these, four rectangles with sgraffito decoration. Variations of the centre motif are repeated in the corners, and to either side is the outline of a flower(?). *Rotterdam, Historical Museum*

24a   Set of four polychrome tiles with white stars on a dark ground in an octagon, alternating with marigolds and tendrils in a pomegranate-shaped vase(?) on a white ground. *Delft, Huis Lambert van Meerten Museum*

24b   Set of four polychrome tiles, the corners forming a sixteen-leafed rosette enclosed in a scalloped frame. A stylized artichoke leaf is placed diagonally on each tile, and in two corners, a bearded head in profile: the heads in the centre of each group of four are enclosed in an oval setting. *Delft, Huis Lambert van Meerten Museum*

25   House-sign. Polychrome tableau of 30 tiles with ornamental border. Symbols of the Old and New Testament: the warriors represent the peoples of the earth and, with the animals, prefigure the future reign of peace. *Rotterdam, Historical Museum*

26   Set of six polychrome tiles showing Turkish soldiers or Saracens in action. *Delft, Huis Lambert van Meerten Museum*

27   Six polychrome 'kidney' tiles, fragment of a common wall-decoration composed of sets of four tiles with oval medallions facing one another and a pattern of foliage; corners in reserve technique. *Rotterdam, Historical Museum*

28a   Polychrome two-tile picture of a triton with a twisting tail, against a calm sea. *Amstelveen, J. W. N. van Achterbergh collection*

28b   Polychrome tile showing a cupid sitting on a dolphin in the sea and holding a staff with a snake twined round it. *Amstelveen, J. W. N. van Achterbergh collection*

28c   Polychrome tile showing a cupid sitting on a dolphin in the sea and holding a purse. *Amstelveen, J. W. N. van Achterbergh collection*

28d   Polychrome tile showing a nereid and merman standing in the water, the former holding an ear of corn(?) and the other blowing a conch. *Otterlo, Tegelmuseum*

28e   Polychrome tile showing a triton blowing into a serpent. *Epse, J. van Loo collection*

29a   Polychrome tableau (21 tiles) of an ornamental vase of flowers. The vase stands on a table and the tall bouquet is surmounted by a double scroll; to either side, on the table, is a bird with a pomegranate and a bunch of grapes. *Rotterdam, Historical Museum*

29b   A similar tableau (65 tiles), with the table-top chequered in white and coloured squares; small birds perch around the vase and bouquet. At the top are the date 1647 and a monogram CIV or CVI. *Brussels, Musées Royaux d'Art et d'Histoire*

30   Fragment of a polychrome and blue tile picture with winged heads of cherubs alternating with eight-leaved rosettes in a round medallion; the space between is filled with *foglie* decoration, half blue and half white. *Delft, Huis Lambert van Meerten Museum*

31a,b   Two blue tiles with small animal figures: a leaping hart and a water-fowl with a worm in its beak, each enclosed in a circle with aigrette decoration. Corner-design of inverted sprigs. *Otterlo, Tegelmuseum.*

31c,d   Similar blue tiles showing a running hare and a seated dog respectively, enclosed in a wreath of tulips and ears of corn. Spider motif in corners. *Rotterdam, Boymans-van Beuningen Museum*

306

31e   Blue tile with polychrome bird on a branch, in a circle with aigrette decoration; corner-design of inverted sprigs. *Delft, Huis Lambert van Meerten Museum*

31f   Blue tile with diagonal composition of a stylized fleur-de-lis extending to touch the inverted corner-design of leaves. Half a six-petalled flower is seen in the centre of each side. *Woerden, G. de Goederen collection*

32a   Polychrome tile showing three musketeers in a double circle of different colours; reserved corner-design of white buds. *Delft, Huis Lambert van Meerten Museum*

32b,c, Three polychrome tiles, each depicting a soldier in a warlike stance, armed
   d   with sword, shield and spear and loading a musket, within a lined circle; reserved corner-design of white buds. *Amstelveen, J. W. N. van Achterbergh collection*

33a   Set of nine polychrome tiles, depicting birds and flowers alternately; corner-design of fleurs-de-lis pointing inwards. *Oudewater, Mevr. van der Lee-de Blécourt collection*

33b   Set of nine polychrome tiles, each showing a bird perched on a slanting nail. *Gouda, De Moriaen Museum*

34   Tableau of 357 polychrome tiles representing a group of five allegorical figures after a design by Joachim Wttewael (Utewael) for one of the windows of St. John's church in Gouda. *London, Victoria and Albert Museum*

35a   Tableau of 78 polychrome tiles representing a naked youth with his left foot on a terrestrial globe, a figure intended for the window of St. John's church in Gouda. *Delft, Huis Lambert van Meerten Museum*

35b   Polychrome tableau of 136 tiles with a female figure representing Hope; she wears a draped garment and is standing in front of an anchor, with a hooded hawk perched on her right hand (damaged). *Rotterdam, Boymans-van Beuningen Museum*

36   Polychrome picture, on two tiles placed vertically, of a pink-striped tulip with two leaves. A specimen of this rare series has been lent to each of the chief Netherlands museums. *Rotterdam, Boymans-van Beuningen Museum*

37   Engraving of three stylized tulips from the *Hortus Floridus* of Crispijn van de Passe, which served as the model for the above tile. *The Hague, Royal Library*

38   Niche composed of large polychrome tiles with a quadrilobe design enclosing stylized flowers and pomegranates round a central eight-leaved rosette. The corner-designs combine to form an octagonal leaf pattern in reserve technique. The niche, rectangular in shape with an arched top, is set into a wall of tiles depicting stylized tulips in lozenge frames, the corner-design consisting of inverted fleurs-de-lis. *Hoorn, St. Pietershof*

39a–d   Four blue tiles from a set of six portraits: Count Egmond, Prince William I, the Duke of Alva and Philip II of Spain, the name of each being inscribed in an oval medallion. *Dordrecht, Simon van Gijn Museum*

40a   Blue tile portrait of William I the Silent, Prince of Orange (1533–84): bust, almost full-face, in a circle of three lines. *Delft, Huis Lambert van Meerten Museum*

40b   Blue tile portrait of Princess Mary Stuart (1631–60), who married Prince William II in 1641. Bust, facing slightly left, in a three-lined circle. *Spankeren, De Gelderse Toren castle, J. G. Wurfbain collection*

40c   Blue tile portrait of Prince Philip William of Orange (1554–1618): bust facing right, almost full-face, in a three-lined circle; corner-design of white buds in reserve technique. *New York, Metropolitan Museum of Art*

40d Blue tile portrait of William III, Prince of Orange and later King of England (1650–1702). Bust facing right, almost full-face, in a three-lined circle; corner-design of white buds in reserve technique. *New York, Metropolitan Museum of Art*

40e Blue tile portrait of Frederick William, Margrave of Brandenburg, the 'Great Elector' (1620–88). Bust facing right, almost full-face, in a three-lined circle; corner-design of spread leaves in reserve technique on a manganese ground; eighteenth century. *Spankeren, De Gelderse Toren castle, J. G. Wurfbain collection*

40f Blue tile portrait of Amalia van Solms (1602–75). Bust facing left, almost full-face, in a three-lined circle; corner-design of spread leaves in reserve technique on a manganese ground; eighteenth century. *Spankeren, De Gelderse Toren castle, J. G. Wurfbain collection*

41a,b Two portraits, each composed of 13 by 4 blue tiles, of Prince Maurice and Prince Frederick Henry attired in armour as military commanders, standing under a curtain beside a chest covered in Gobelin tapestry, on which their plumed helmets are lying. *Amsterdam, Rijksmuseum*

42a Portrait (13 by 5 blue tiles) of Count van Buren as a knight in armour, standing on a grassy plot on which plants are growing. In his raised right hand he holds a spontoon with the flag of his county attached. A cartouche below is inscribed HET GRAEFSCHAP VAN BVEREN. *Amsterdam, Rijksmuseum*

42b–d Three blue tiles from a series of six showing musketeers and pikemen, each standing under an arch on a hillock with plants growing from it; reserved corner-designs in spandrels. *Rotterdam, Historical Museum*

43a,b, Four blue tiles depicting two musketeers and two cavalrymen, each in an
e,f, accolade medallion with corner-designs of foliage. Specimens from the tiled floor at *Beauregard castle near Blois*

43c,d Two blue tiles, each with a musketeer firing his piece to right and left respectively, in a scalloped frame; corner-designs of foliage. *Monnickendam, De Waag Museum, Dr. Van Tijen collection*

44a–c Three blue tiles showing an ensign-bearer, a musketeer and a pikeman in action; corner-design of inverted fleurs-de-lis; baluster pattern on either side. *Dordrecht, Simon van Gijn Museum*

44d–f Three blue tiles showing riders on rearing horses, armed respectively with a gun, a spear and a sword; corner-design of ox-heads. *Monnickendam, De Waag Museum, Dr. Van Tijen collection*

45 Set of six blue tiles, showing figures in action: an officer drawing his sword, an elegant couple dancing, a drummer, a soldier saluting, another carrying a spear, and a peasant walking along with a heavy basket attached to a stick over his shoulder. Each figure is in a scalloped medallion, with meander pattern in the corners. *The Hague, Gemeente Museum*

46a Blue tile with a female figure (a dancer?) seen from behind: her left arm is extended and in her right she holds a fan. The fashion is that of about 1630; ox-heads in corners. *Alkmaar, H. B. J. Vlas collection*

46b Blue tile with rear view of a woman in peasant dress carrying a bucket over her right arm. The frame is a three-lined scalloped medallion; corner-design of fleurs-de-lis. *London, Victoria and Albert Museum*

46c Blue tile showing a man with a spade over his shoulder, walking towards the right; corner-design of inverted green fleurs-de-lis. *Rotterdam, Historical Museum*

46d Blue tile showing a woman, dressed in the fashion of about 1630, walking towards the left; corner-design of inverted green fleurs-de-lis. *Rotterdam, Historical Museum*

46e Eight blue tiles from a group of 20 showing various figures from behind and in profile, among them an officer with hat in hand, a fishmonger with a basket on his head, a pedlar; corner-design of inverted sprigs. *Monnickendam, De Waag Museum, Dr. Van Tijen collection*

47a–c Six blue tiles from a large tableau with full-length pictures of men and women, in profile and from behind, representing various trades: a basket-weaver, a peasant with a sheaf of corn over his shoulder and a sickle in his hand, a potato-seller, a nobleman with a sword, a woman with a basketful of loaves and a thatcher; corner-design of inverted fleurs-de-lis. *Gouda, De Moriaen Museum*

48a–d Four blue tiles representing elephants. The corner-designs, all pointing inwards, consist respectively of fleurs-de-lis, ox-heads, sprigs and fleurs-de-lis with a baluster at either side. *Nijmegen, H. L. Houtzager collection*

48e,f Two blue tiles: a dog with a collar, facing right, and a stork with a fish in its beak, facing left, standing on a patch of sand(?) with plants on either side; corner-designs of inverted fleurs-de-lis, with a baluster at either side. *Leeuwarden, Princessehof Museum*

49a,b Two blue tiles: a lion and a bird on a patch of grass in a meadow, under a streaky sky. *Otterlo, Tegelmuseum*

49c Blue tile showing a wild boar leaping over a patch of sand and grass, with growing plants, under a streaky sky. *Apeldoorn, D. J. A. A. van Lawick van Pabst collection*

49d–f Three blue tiles: a barking dog, a running fox and a leopard, on a dark and stippled patch of ground under streaky clouds. *London, Victoria and Albert Museum*

50 Tableau of six blue tiles. Four show a bird in a roundel amongst flowers, and two, flowers only; the roundel is framed in a scalloped border; corners in meander pattern. *The Hague, Gemeente Museum*

51a Flowering plant in an ornamental Chinese vase, in a scalloped frame; corners in meander pattern. *Rotterdam, Boymans-van Beuningen Museum*

51b Blue lozenge-shaped tile depicting a vase of flowers; spider motif in corners. *De Bilt, Mejuffrouw M. A. H. van Es collection*

51c,d Two lozenge-shaped tiles, each showing a man and woman walking together; spider motif in corners. *Monnickendam, De Waag Museum, Dr. Van Tijen collection*

52 Staircase wall decorated with blue tiles showing a tulip plant with the blooms in a scalloped medallion; meander pattern in corners. *Leeuwarden, Het Waeze No. 25.*

53a,b Two blue tiles: a stylized tulip and sunflower with symmetrical foliage, in an octagonal setting; corners reminiscent of reserve technique. *Epse, J. van Loo collection*

53c Tableau of four blue tiles with tulip and other plants in oval medallions, surrounded by small leaves and S-shaped volutes; corner-design of inverted fleurs-de-lis. *Monnickendam, De Waag Museum, Dr. Van Tijen collection*

54a Six blue 'mirror tiles' from a panel of twelve, each with a border of *foglie* ornamentation in a frame with a toothed edge; an eight-petalled flower in the centre. Each group of four tiles is linked by diagonal lines. *Oudewater, Mevr. F. van der Lee-de Blécourt collection*

54b Twenty-four blue tiles from a tableau of 32 with a continuous pattern of lozenge shapes enclosing an eight-pointed star. The lozenges are formed of tulips and carnations on a dark ground. *Otterlo, Tegelmuseum*

55a Blue tile with eight-petalled flower on a rosette of twelve leaves within a scalloped frame; meander pattern in corners. *Woerden, G. de Goederen collection*

55b Blue tile with eight-petalled flower on a rosette in an octagonal medallion; corner-design of rosettes and leaves, forming a further pattern in each set of four. *Epse, J. van Loo collection*

55c Blue tile with a small snail in the centre, surrounded by flowers and leaves placed diagonally; symmetrical flower decoration at the sides. *Monnickendam, De Waag Museum, Dr. Van Tijen collection*

55d Two blue tiles forming half a pattern of four. The main design consists of ornamental plants placed diagonally in a volute-type setting bordered by three lines; the plants alternate with four lozenge motifs and open umbrellas. The corners combine to form a similar pattern in the same setting, but with a papyrus roll taking the place of the umbrella. *Woerden, G. de Goederen collection*

56 Fragment of a blue tile border: design of symmetrical volutes and stylized foliage. *Epse, J. van Loo collection*

57a Blue tile showing a farm, with a haystack and trees, in a scalloped medallion; above, the date 1633; meander design in corners. *Rotterdam, Boymans-van Beuningen Museum*

57b Blue tile showing town-gate with trees in a scalloped medallion; below, the date 1640; corner-design of sprigs. *Rotterdam, Boymans-van Beuningen Museum*

57c,d Two blue tiles, each depicting a church. The first also shows a town-gate and some vegetation, with the date 1630 underneath; the second has a smoking chimney, trees on the left and a fence on the right, with the date 1638; corner-design of inverted fleurs-de-lis, baluster ornament at the sides. *Rotterdam, Boymans-van Beuningen Museum*

57e Blue tile showing a farmhouse among trees; two windmills in the distance on the left, a man fishing on the right; corners-design of fleurs-de-lis and baluster ornament at the sides. *Rotterdam, Boymans-van Beuningen Museum*

58a Set of four blue tiles showing landscapes with a wooden bridge over a river. To the right of each bridge is a signpost bearing one of the dates 1674, 1677 and 1678; spider motif in corners. *Amstelveen, J. W. N. van Achterbergh collection*

58b,c Two blue landscape tiles: one shows a farmhouse among trees, the other a farmhouse with barn and haystack. An expanse of foreground is vaguely suggested; sailing-ships on a river in the distance. *Rotterdam, Boymans-van Beuningen Museum*

59a Blue tile picture of a battle at the foot of a hill; a fortress is being besieged in the background. Ascribed to an engraving by Jan Martsen the Younger (1609–47). *Enschede, Twenthe Museum, M. G. van Heel collection*

59b Blue tile picture showing the prophet Elijah being fed by ravens in the wilderness: after the engraving by Nicolaes Berchem (1620–83). *Amsterdam, Rijksmuseum*

60a   Blue tile showing Susanna and the Elders, in a double roundel; sprig design in corners. *Monnickendam, De Waag Museum, Dr. Van Tijen collection*

60b   Blue tile showing the Scourging of Christ, bound to a stone column; framed in a double roundel, with sprig design in corners. *Otterlo, Tegelmuseum*

60c   Blue tile with the figure of a cardinal holding a cross in his right hand and a rosary in his left, standing under an arch; meander design in the corners. *Monnickendam, De Waag Museum, Dr. Van Tijen collection*

60d   Blue tile showing Pilate's wife trying to convince him of Christ's innocence; behind her is Christ with a guard; double roundel, with sprig design in corners. *Otterlo, Tegelmuseum*

60e   Blue tile with the arms of Pope Marcellus II (*reg.* 1555): the ornamental shield is surmounted by a crest with the tiara and crossed keys. Inscription below: MARCELLUS PAPA II; spider motif in corners. *Leeuwarden, Princessehof Museum*

60f   Blue tile showing St. John the Evangelist standing on a grassy patch with the eagle at his feet. He raises his right hand in blessing and holds a Eucharistic chalice in his left; corner-design of inverted oak-leaves pointing inwards. *Leeuwarden, Princessehof Museum*

61a   Large blue tile depicting the meeting of Tobias with the Angel on the bank of a river; double roundel with sprig design in corners; zigzag and flower decoration on the front edge. *Gouda, De Moriaen Museum*

61b   Blue triangular tile from a window-sill, showing a scene from the Temptation of Christ in the wilderness; volute decoration on the curved edge. *Gouda, De Moriaen Museum*

62   Tableau of twelve blue tiles showing the Apostles and scenes from the Life of the Virgin, including St. Anne with the Virgin and Child and the Madonna of the Mantle; corner-design of inverted oakleaves. *Delft, Huis Lambert van Meerten Museum*

63   Tableau of eight blue tiles showing moored ships of different types; ox-head motif in corners. *Rotterdam, Historical Museum*

64a,b   Two blue tiles showing sailing-ships with their crews in the open sea; corner-design of inverted fleurs-de-lis; baluster ornament on either side. *Rotterdam, Boymans-van Beuningen Museum*

64c   Blue tile showing a merchant vessel in the open sea, in a three-line roundel with toothed border; corner-design of inverted sprigs. *Leeuwarden, Princessehof Museum*

64d   Blue tile showing three warships in combat; corner-design of inverted oak-leaves. *Leeuwarden, Princessehof Museum*

65   Picture consisting of 25 blue tiles, representing the Battle of the Downs. Above, a cartouche with martial trophies is inscribed: ZEE SLAG IN DUYNS DOOR MARTEN HARPERS. TROMP den 21 October A° 1638. *Rotterdam, Historical Museum*

66a   Engraving from *Pampiere Wereld ofte wereldsche Oeffeninghe*, by I. H. Krul, 1681. *Otterlo, Tegelmuseum*

66b   Blue tile showing three angels floating in clouds and carrying the Cross; spider motif in corners. *Woerden, G. de Goederen collection*

66c   Blue tile showing three amorini with a wine-cask: one of them is sitting

311

on it like Bacchus with a beaker in his left hand and a bunch of grapes in his right; spider motif in corners. *Amsterdam, De Wildeman, wine and spirit merchants, formerly Levert & Co*

67a   Blue tile with detail of the engraving from *Pampiere Wereld* (ill. 66a). *Otterlo, Tegelmuseum*

67b   Blue tile: detail from a group with the ornamental initial D, dated 1630, under a decoration of foliage. *Delft, Huis Lambert van Meerten Museum*

67c   Blue tile with the arms of Monnickendam: a monk walking along while two winged griffins hold a laurel wreath over his head; ox-head motif in corners; about 1675. *Monnickendam, De Waag Museum, Dr. Van Tijen collection*

68a,b   Two sets of three blue tiles, from a large number showing children playing various games singly or in pairs, which form the decoration of fireplaces in the Renaissance and Baroque rooms of the Museum; spider motif in corners. *Utrecht, Central Museum*

69a–f   Six blue tiles with small Chinese figures representing different classes and occupations. *Amsterdam, Rijksmuseum*

70a,b   Two blue tiles with cupids carrying torches: one is riding a dolphin, the other, a scallop drawn by two hippocamps; ox-head motif in corners. *Amstelveen, J. W. N. van Achterbergh collection*

70c   Four blue tiles showing a sea with waves rising in a triangular shape in the foreground, and a mermaid or triton riding on them; ox-head motif in corners. *Rotterdam, Historical Museum*

71a–d   Four blue tiles from a set of six: Fortune standing with one foot on a globe holding a billowing sail; a nereid on a sea-monster, with a tulip in her right hand; Icarus falling into the sea, and a triton with a conch. *Rotterdam, Boymans-van Beuningen Museum*

72a   Cornelis Boumeester: estuary of the Meuse with the skyline of Rotterdam behind. *Brussels, Musées Royaux d'Art et d'Histoire*

72b   Cornelis Boumeester: embarkation of Prince William III for England on the State yacht *Den Briel* at Rotterdam, 1688. *Rotterdam, Historical Museum*

73a,b   Two blue tiles with portraits of preachers at the Reformed Church in Delft.
a. Hermannus Tegularius: half-length, almost full-face, in a gown with ruff and skull-cap. In the upper part of the tile is a hole for hanging. *Hamburg, Museum für Kunst und Gewerbe*
b. Dionysius Spranckhuysen: half-length, almost full-face, in a gown with ruff and skull-cap. The back of the tile is dated 1660. *Amsterdam, Rijksmuseum*

73c,d   Two blue plaques with a front and side view of the monument of William the Silent in the Nieuwe Kerk at Delft, erected by Hendrick de Keijser (1620). The tiles were made by Isaac Junius in 1657 after an engraving by Cornelis Dankertsz. *Delft, Prinsenhof Museum, and Amsterdam, Rijksmuseum*

74   The great hall of the Château de Beauregard with its floor of blue tiles illustrating the military dispositions of Prince Maurice, ordered by Paul Ardier, the owner of the castle, in 1627 and laid in 1646. *Château de Beauregard, Cellettes, near Blois, Loir-et-Cher, France*

75a–f   Six blue tiles from the great hall at Beauregard (which contains about 6,000 in all), showing a pikeman, two infantry officers, two musketeers, a halberdier and a standard-bearer, after engravings by Jacob de Gheyn. Each is framed in a three-line scalloped medallion, with leaf designs in the corners. *Beauregard castle, near Blois*

76a   Tableau of 4 by 3 blue tiles representing Titus Manlius Torquatus after an engraving by Hendrick Goltzius, *Anno 1634*. The hero is standing on a mound under an Ionic arch, with an imposing plant on either side. A mask forms the keystone of the arch; the spandrels are decorated with foliage. *Amsterdam, Rijksmuseum*

76b   Two chimney pilasters, each ten blue tiles high, with floral garlands. At the foot of each is a soldier with a shield; the capitals depict warriors after prints by Goltzius, the bases bear stylized acanthus leaves. *Delft, Huis Lambert van Meerten Museum*

77   Tableau of 4 by 3 blue tiles representing a soldier standing under an arch in a hilly landscape with a staff in his left hand; tall flowering plants on either side. The spandrels are decorated and a mask forms the keystone. From a design in the style of Jacob de Gheijn. Damaged. *Delft, Huis Lambert van Meerten Museum*

78a   Circular blue tile picture of a rocky Italian landscape with a river and bridge; tall trees on the right. To the left, further off, are the ruins of a castle and a town. Diameter 37 cm. In the upper part is a hole for hanging. *London, Victoria and Albert Museum*

78b   Tile painting, 34.5 cm square, of the village of Overschie. To the left, figures are seen crossing the bridge which leads over the river to the village and a farmhouse; the church-tower appears above trees. On the right, two men are sitting beside a fence and the path leads on past trees and farms. In the upper part of the tile is a hole for hanging. *Doorn, Huis Doorn foundation, former property of Kaiser Wilhelm II*

79   Large tableau of 14 by 8 blue and manganese tiles, with a tall ornamented vase standing on a marbled base; garlands on either side. Signed below: Anno 1697 J. van Oort à Amste. *At present in the bathroom of a private villa near St. Malo, Brittany.*

80a   Blue tile depicting a hilly landscape and a pair of Utrecht shepherds with their flock; spider motif in corners. *Rotterdam, Boymans van Beuningen Museum*

80b   Tableau of 16 blue landscape tiles with Utrecht shepherds, in some cases with the addition of mythological themes; spider motif in corners. *De Rijp, In 't Houten Huis Museum*

81a–c Three imitation marble tiles in mingled yellow, brown and white. *Rotterdam, Boymans-van Beuningen Museum, and Nieborów, Poland.*

81d,e Two pounces for tiles designed by Egbert Pietersz. of the Zoutsloot works; the first represents Christ's Entry into Jerusalem and the second is a decorative sketch for a set of four tiles in Louis XIV style. *Leeuwarden, Frisian Society*

82a   Blue tile depicting the administration of justice. The scroll below reads 'T(itula) 4.L(eges)29', referring to the relevant text in the Pandects. From a design by Sybrand Feijtema of the Zoutsloot tile-works, 1687. *Rotterdam, Boymans-van Beuningen Museum*

82b–e Four blue tiles with similar scenes from the same series. *Leeuwarden, Princessehof Museum*

83a,b Two tableaux, each of six blue tiles, with portraits of Prince William IV of Orange and his consort Anne of Hanover, each in a draped oval medallion; their arms are depicted below and their full titles are given in a cartouche. *Gouda, De Moriaen Museum*

84a,b   Two tableaux of 10 by 8 blue tiles with portraits of Louis XV of France and Marie Leszczyńska, on horseback in a hilly landscape with a town in the distance. Their names are given on the right and left-hand side of the picture respectively; the signature is 'I. Aalmis, Rotterdam'. The wall of the apartment containing these portraits is entirely covered with groups of four carnation tiles in manganese purple. *Ayeneux Castle near Soumagne, Belgium*

85a,b   Two large blue tiles, each with two portraits of artists from Houbraken's *De Groote Schouburgh*—Jacob Jordaens, Jan van Goyen, Frans van Mieris and Jan Steen—with drapery against a white background, oval or octagonal. Underneath are small sketches of their work, and their names are written along the edge. *Otterlo, Tegelmuseum*

85c,d   Two similar blue tiles with portraits of Anna Maria van Schurmann, Jacobus Bakker and Rembrandt van Rijn, Jacob van der Does and Paulus Potter, with details from their work. The names of Jacob van der Does and Anna Maria Schurmann are written above the picture; that of Paulus Potter, below. *Paris, Musée Carnavalet*

86a   Tableau of nine blue tiles showing cavalrymen at the gallop; spider motif in the corners. There is also a similar series in manganese. *Leeuwarden, Frisian Museum*

86b   Tableau of 16 blue tiles, each showing three riders in a diagonal composition: the so-called 'civilian riding-school'. *Leeuwarden, Princessehof Museum*

87a   Four blue and manganese tiles from a series of 16: each shows a rider in an eight-lobed scalloped medallion against a manganese background. The corner-designs join to form a four-leaf clover. *Amsterdam, Rijksmuseum*

87b   Four blue tiles each showing a horseman in a scalloped medallion with eight lobes, on a manganese background. Four corner-designs form a rosette with a star in the middle. *Enkhuizen, Zuider Zee Museum*

88a   Tableau of four blue tiles showing baskets filled with apples, pears, grapes and some flowers, in a roundel; in the foreground a spray of leaves and two pears; spider motif in the corners. *Enkhuizen, Zuider Zee Museum*

88b   Tableau of four blue and manganese tiles, with a basket of fruit and flowers in a lozenge frame; a sprig and more fruit are seen in the foreground; a white square is reserved on the manganese background. The corners of four tiles form a rosette of eight leaves with a star in the middle. *Enkhuizen, Zuider Zee Museum*

89a   Two blue tiles showing variegated bouquets in a vase and a basket, the vase standing in a coloured rectangular dish; corner-design of inverted flowers. *Enkhuizen, Zuider Zee Museum*

89b   Two blue tiles, each with a tulip and two marigolds in a Renaissance vase; corner-design of inverted fleurs-de-lis; baluster ornament at either side. *Enkhuizen, Zuider Zee Museum*

89c   Two blue tiles with tulips in a Renaissance vase, in a three-line roundel; debased meander design in corners. *Enkhuizen, Zuider Zee Museum*

90a,b   Detail of blue and manganese tile decorating the rib-vaulting in a cellar at Het Loo: a sequence of flower-vase designs in blue, in an octagonal frame, with a manganese border and small fleurs-de-lis reserved in the corners. *Apeldoorn, Het Loo palace*

314

90c   Fragment of a series of similar tiles decorating the wainscot and window, with blue landscapes in an octagon, a manganese border, and fleurs-de-lis in the corners. *Apeldoorn, Het Loo palace*

91a   Part of the panelling of a side-wall in the cellar, showing landscape, marbled and ornamental tiles. *Apeldoorn, Het Loo palace*

91b   Eight blue landscape tiles, showing fishermen by a river, views of a castle, skaters etc; corner-design of inverted sprigs. *Apeldoorn, Het Loo palace*

91c   Four blue and white tiles with large octagons in the centre and small paintings of a tent with two flags, a well, a tulip in flower and a sailing-ship. *Apeldoorn, Het Loo palace*

92a   Tableau of four blue tiles showing the city gates of Amsterdam, in a double roundel; corner-design of inverted carnations. *London, Victoria and Albert Museum*

92b   Tableau of 4 by 13 blue tiles showing cows and goats in a meadow; on the left is a farmhouse, on the right some trees behind a fence. *Makkum, Kingma Bank*

92c   Three blue tiles with river scenes: an angler in a rowing-boat, reflected in the water, a house and barn amid trees, and a village on the opposite bank; a rigged vessel moored at a landing-stage in the canal, a rowing-boat on the right; a rigged ship by the river-bank and a rowing-boat being made fast to a row of stakes and, in the right background, a house, with ships on the river in the distance. *Leeuwarden, Princessehof Museum*

93   Tile picture in an ornamental frame: 9 by 6 large blue tiles, showing the village of Molkwerum in Gaasterland. The church, on the left, is connected with the village by a bridge. In the foreground are cows in a meadow, with a path leading through it towards the church. *Leeuwarden, Frisian Museum*

94a   Group of four blue tiles with elaborate star ornamentation, known as *diaper* or *Alkmaar chintz*, from the Harlingen sample-book. *Gouda, De Moriaen Museum*

94b   Design for a star ornament: a sixteen-petalled flower surrounded by four blooms, linked with one another by a motif consisting of two leaves. Corner-design of a leaf pointing inwards. The complete pattern is formed by four tiles. Black and white watercolour from the Harlingen sample-book. *Harlingen, Hannema Huis Museum*

95a   Eight blue tiles from an ornamental tableau of twelve. A square formed by volutes encloses a stylized urn. The indentations and corners are symmetrically decorated with buds and blossoms. *Gouda, De Moriaen Museum*

95b   Eight blue tiles from a tableau of twenty, each with a dancing figure supported on a base with French sprigs. The medallions show a woman, a vase of flowers, the arms of a city (Gouda, Utrecht) etc. The corners of four tiles form an ornamental circle with an eight-petalled flower in the centre. *Gouda, De Moriaen Museum*

96a–c   Three blue tiles representing the Creation (Gen. 2 : 7), Moses burning the golden calf (Ex. 32 : 19), and the prodigal son engaged in riotous living (Luke 15 : 13). The scenes are framed in a design of four volutes. *Enkhuizen, Zuider Zee Museum*

96d–f   Three blue tiles representing Jacob's dream (Gen. 28 : 12), a messenger announcing Job's calamities (Job 1 : 14) and the Descent of the Holy Spirit (Acts 2 : 3); corner-design of inverted carnations. *Voorschoten, Mevr. E. M. Prins-Baronesse Schimmelpenninck van der Oye*

97   Tableau of 6 by 4 manganese tiles representing scenes from the Gospels and Acts of the Apostles. Each scene is in a two-line scalloped frame; the corner-designs of four tiles form small flowers. *Gouda, De Moriaen Museum*

98a   Blue picture in a yellow border, showing the outline of the town of Zutphen from across the IJssel. *Doetinchem, A. Vromen Jr. collection*

98b   Engraving with historical details concerning Zutphen, published by C. Bouttats at Antwerp. *Doetinchem, A. Vromen Jr. collection*

99a   Picture composed of 5 by 11 blue tiles showing several ships in the open sea, including an English warship and a galliot, the *Jonge Oranje 1748*. The outline of a town is seen on the horizon The picture is signed 'Dirck Danser' and was made at Harlingen for Kingma, the Makkum shipowner. *Makkum, Kingma Bank*

99b   Picture composed of 7 by 12 blue tiles, showing three ships: a koff with billowing sails, flanked by a State yacht and a merchant frigate, in an elaborate Louis XV frame. *Makkum, De Waag Museum*

100a,b Two of a series of twelve pictures, each composed of 6 by 4 blue tiles, showing various types of ship at sea: here a warship and a State yacht. *Makkum, De Prins inn*

100c   Fireplace decoration of 10 by 8 blue tiles. The lower part shows a tall bouquet of flowers in a basket resting on an ornamental base comprising a view of a city in a medallion enclosed between two volutes with a bird perching on each. The whole of this part is enclosed in a fireback border. On either side of this is depicted an orchard, with a man picking fruit and a woman carrying it in a basket on her head. Above, in the centre, is a second scene in a Régence border: a sea-fight with a merchant frigate, a warship and other vessels, and a town on the horizon to the left. To either side of this scene are vases with tall bouquets, resting on pedestals. *Dokkum, town hall, mayor's chamber*

101a   Tableau of 6 by 4 blue tiles showing a Greenland whaler in the open sea, with a border of flower-tiles. At present decorating the fireplace of the exhibition hall. *Harlingen, Hannema Huis Museum*

101b   Tableau of 4 by 4 tiles in a rococo border, showing the three-masted galliot *Victoria* at sea, flying a flag with a crowned double eagle. *Hooge (Germany), F. Boysen collection*

101c   Large picture of a whaling scene, on 8 by 6 manganese tiles in a twisted cable border with rosettes at the corners. *Gouda, De Moriaen Museum*

102a   Blue tile showing a lady and gentleman greeting each other; they are dressed in a fanciful style of the seventeenth to eighteenth century; spider motif in corners. *Harlingen, Hannema Huis Museum*

102b   Blue tile with symbolic representation of Autumn. It shows an open space in front of a corner house: wine-casks are being rolled away, while a gentleman with a long pipe converses with another holding a glass of wine. *Amsterdam, De Wildeman wine and spirit merchants, formerly Levert & Co.*

102c   Blue tile showing a bare landscape with a church tower. On the left is seen the corner of a wooden house and a flag inscribed MAGITO, the family name of the rope-dancer. Two members of his troupe stand in front of the house. The scene is framed in a double line, with stylized flowers as corner-decoration. *Rotterdam, Historical Museum*

102d   Manganese tile from a large tableau showing municipal arms: the canting

316

emblem of Hinloopen is seen supported by two angels. *Rotterdam, Historical Museum*

102e Group of four ornamental manganese tiles in Louis XIV style, the corners forming a flower with sixteen petals. *Delft, Huis Lambert van Meerten Museum*

102f Watercolour design for a blue tile with an octagonal border of volutes and flowers: a saddled horse is being shod while standing at a trough. *Rotterdam, Municipal Archives*

103a Picture composed of 3 by 2 large blue tiles: a woman in eighteenth-century chequered costume, wearing a hat, is dancing on a marble floor. Her right hand is raised and she holds a stick in her left. *Amsterdam, Rijksmuseum*

103b Picture composed of 3 by 2 very large blue tiles: a dancing man wearing a clown's cap, with long chequered breeches and a loose coat with bells attached to the hem. In his left hand he holds a drawn sword, and in his right a cartouche with the words: Hom, hom. *Leeuwarden, Frisian Museum*

103c A large picture composed of 7 by 6 blue tiles, with a border of volutes and blossoms. It is divided horizontally and shows, above, a coffin-maker's workshop, with various tools hung between the windows; below, part of a brewery, with a long pipe, vats and barrels. *Amsterdam, De Wildeman wine and spirit merchants, formerly Levert & Co.*

103d Tableau of 4 by 3 blue tiles representing *Het Ver(make)lijck Ganse Spel. Ian Loot 1710* ('The diverting game of the Goose'; Jan Loot is presumably the tile-maker). *Utrecht, Central Museum*

104 Blue tiled cellar of the Johan de Witt house, dating from 1647 and altered in 1726; restored in 1968 by the architect C. W. Royaards. *The Hague, Kneuterdijk 6*

105 Oval blue plaque showing a European lady in a rickshaw talking to a coolie. Round the edge are branches of dwarf fir, the mark of De Witte Starre and the initials IDB for Justus van den Bergh. After 1741. *Enschede, Twenthe Museum, M. G. van Heel collection*

106 Large picture composed of 4 by 3 blue tiles: within a narrow volute border, a decorated round vase with a tall bouquet of flowers stands on an oblong table. The signature is G:D:GRAAF 1785. *Amsterdam, D. F. W. Langelaan collection*

107a One of a pair of door-posts: between the capital and base of a twisted Ionic column, the arms of the Seven Provinces are suspended by a knotted cord amid foliage. The base shows a three-masted ship, with a distant landscape on the right. *Oudewater, Mevr. F. van der Lee-de Blécourt collection*

107b Two hearth pillars, each consisting of 13 blue tiles, with a grapevine and birds; plants growing at the foot; on each base a peacock, the one on the left spreading its tail. From a house at Edam. *The Hague, Johan de Witt house*

107c Two hearth pillars, each consisting of 10 blue tiles depicting a grapevine, with putti at the top and bottom holding a ribbon. Tulips are growing at the foot. Half-way up, a man on a ladder is picking grapes above a woman sitting with a basket on her lap. After the Harlingen sample-book. *Enkhuizen, Zuider Zee Museum*

108a Two hearth pillars, each consisting of 9 by 3 blue tiles placed diagonally. One shows trophies of the chase suspended from a garland, with a hunting-horn and dead game; the other, grapes and flowers with a cherub hovering amidst them. *Makkum, De Waag Museum*

108b Watercolour sketch by J. E. ter Gouw, 1876, of the original tiled fireplace in the Sommelsdijk Orphanage (12 by 8 blue tiles), with an urn of flowers enclosed in a border of tendrils. The tall bouquet is surrounded by birds and butterflies; the urn, large and ornamental with two handles, stands on a block of marble, with a parrot on a perch to the left and a cock to the right (cf. ill. 137a). *Amsterdam, Print Room of the Rijksmuseum*

109 Fireplace decoration of 13 by 6 blue tiles. A large bouquet, surrounded by birds and butterflies, in an ornamental urn on a marble pedestal; on the right is a parrot, on the left a blackbird in a hoop. On the front of the pedestal, in relief, is a garland of foliage with putti. From the architect's room adjoining the municipal carpenter's yard in Leiden. *Leiden, Lakenhal Museum*

110a Council chamber in Wormer town hall: the fireplace or *smuiger* of manganese tiles, with Biblical scenes in roundels; corner-design of carnations. The wall pictures represent cattle-breeding and whaling; inscriptions beneath, angels with laurel-wreaths above. Much restored. *Wormer, town hall*

110b Tiled fireplace from the kitchen of Petronella van Groenendijk-Dunois' dolls' house, 1677. *Amsterdam, Rijksmuseum*

110c Tile decoration of a nineteenth-century village fireplace in Drente; traditional Frisian pattern. *Anholt near Ruinen, Drente*

111 Original manganese tiled fireplace: *smuiger* of 1852 from the Zaan district, one of the last of this type to be made. *Obdam near Alkmaar*

112a One of three overdoors in a tiled room: 5 by 8 large manganese tiles with a rococo border, showing the port of Rotterdam with the Ooster-Nieuwe Hoofdpoort. Signed: Jan Aelmis à Rotterdam 1764. *Hamburg, Museum für Kunst und Gewerbe*

112b Panel from a tiled room (8 by 6 large manganese tiles) representing Sculpture, after an engraving by Amigoni. *Otterlo, Tegelmuseum*

113 Tiled room with fireplace consisting of 10 by 8 blue tiles. A koff in the open sea, within a hearthplate border; on either side an ornamental urn, with lid, on a pedestal. Above the koff, in an oval medallion, is the scene of Christ and Zacchaeus, surrounded by floral garlands. From a house at Workum, 1797. *Leeuwarden, Frisian Museum*

114 Part of a manganese-tiled barn at Bouwlust farm. In a square floral border, a picture of a farm with a hay-cart and cattle; in the distance are ships on a river. Smaller pictures to either side of the square represent a horse, cow, dog and cat. There are also birdcages and a clock marked v. d. WOLK TOT ROTTERDAM. Ascribed to J. v. d. Wolk, tile-maker at Rotterdam till 1841. *Bergambacht, South Holland*

115a,b Two pictures, each of 3 by 2 large blue tiles, showing rearing horses facing each other on a grassy bank beside a ditch. *Leeuwarden, Frisian Museum*

115c Picture of a bracket-clock; 3 by 2 large manganese tiles. The dial is inscribed UTRECHT A: TUREL 1775. Above is an hourglass with two snakes curved round it, a bone and a scythe, enclosed in four volutes. *Utrecht, Central Museum*

115d Picture composed of 6 by 5 blue tiles with a large, loose bouquet of flowers in an ornamental vase: the original house-sign of the Aelmis family's tile-works De Bloempot in Rotterdam (damaged on the left). *Rotterdam, Historical Museum*

116   Picture composed of 8 by 6 blue tiles with a symmetrical bouquet in an ornamental urn, standing on a pedestal with volutes. Between these is a medallion with a farm depicted on the right, windmills and other buildings in the background, and a plough with four horses in the front. The volutes and the upper edge of the pedestal are linked by two rearing horses. *Leeuwarden, Frisian Museum*

117   Blue tile, 62 cm. square, from the dairy at Hampton Court. Detail from one of the tiled walls with pilasters, showing William III on horseback. *Amsterdam, Rijksmuseum*

118   One of two blue tile pictures (11 by 14 tiles) showing harbour scenes by Cornelis Boumeester. Border of blue landscape tiles with manganese background and carnations in the corners. *Château de Rambouillet, near Paris*

119a   Interior of the octagonal 'Salettl', 1716–19. *Pagodenburg, in the grounds of Nymphenburg palace near Munich*

119b,c   Tiled staircase with Biblical scenes and two pictures, each 8 by 10 blue tiles, representing a mansion with statues on the façade and others in a park in front of it; the second picture shows the continuation of the park with avenues of trimmed trees. *Pagodenburg, in the grounds of Nymphenburg palace near Munich*

120   Detail of blue-tiled bathing pavilion with stairs, dressing-room and swimming-pool: 1718–21. *Bathing pavilion at Nymphenburg palace near Munich*

121   View of the suite of rooms: two antechambers, audience room, bed-chamber and bathroom, all decorated entirely with blue tiles in geometrical patterns with tulip and carnation motifs. *Brühl palace near Bonn*

122a   A wall in the summer dining-room with three blue tile pictures: two after paintings by Teniers, a large number of bouquets in vases and smaller dancing figures; ornamented dado. *Brühl palace near Bonn*

122b   Detail of ornamental tiles in bathroom. *Brühl palace near Bonn*

123   The bathroom, with ornamental blue tiling. *Brühl palace near Bonn*

124   Part of the staircase, with scenes of falconry. *Falkenlust hunting-lodge, Brühl near Bonn*

125a   Detail of one of the scenes: spectators on foot and on horseback. *Falkenlust hunting-lodge, Brühl near Bonn*

125b   Two pounces for the falconry scenes, from designs by François Cuvilliés. *Rotterdam, municipal archives*

126   Detail of a room with family portraits in a tiled border. *Falkenlust hunting-lodge, Brühl near Bonn*

127   Polychrome interior with a group of people; a Zealand cupboard against the wall, with Delftware standing on it. The signature G. Verhaast is on the window-frame. *Brussels, Musées Royaux d'Art et d'Histoire*

128   Large scene of 12 by 7 polychrome tiles. Version of a Chinese theme: the Bodhisattva Kwan-Yin scattering the dew of heavenly grace over the world. Tiles arranged incorrectly at the time of construction. *Amalienburg pavilion in the grounds of Nymphenburg palace near Munich*

129   The same picture shown in its correct arrangement by photographic

reconstruction (see also Plate VI). *Archives of the Bayerische Verwaltung der staatlichen Schlösser, Gärten und Seen, at Nymphenburg palace near Munich*

130a,b and 131a,b Two narrow polychrome pictures, each of 13 by 3 tiles, representing Chinese scenes: incorrect arrangement on the left, photographic reconstruction on the right (see also Plate VI). *Amalienburg pavilion; reconstructions in the archives of the Bayerische Verwaltung, Nymphenburg*

132   Large scene of 13 by 6 polychrome tiles showing a mountain landscape with a path leading down among pavilions, temples and some palm-trees. Small groups of Chinese are walking down it, also three Tapuya Indians. *Amsterdam, Rijksmuseum, Loudon collection*

133a   Picture composed of 11 by 10 polychrome tiles, showing a hilly landscape; grapes are being picked and loaded on to carts in sacks, while on the left a group of people are tasting the wine; muffle-kiln technique; signed I: Baen and M. van Kuyk, 1744. *Amsterdam, Rijksmuseum*

133b   Fragment of a polychrome column, of two tiles showing parrots among flowering branches; muffle-kiln technique. *Leeuwarden, Frisian Museum, Bisschop collection*

134a   Polychrome tile with the combined arms of the House of Orange and Great Britain–Brunswick, encircled by the Garter, 1752; corner-designs of inverted sprigs; muffle-kiln technique; ascribed to Hendrick Visseer. *Amsterdam, Rijksmuseum*

134b   Polychrome tile (1752) with the same arms and the Garter, enclosed in a laurel wreath, against a marbled background; muffle-kiln technique; ascribed to Hendrick Visseer. *Amsterdam, Rijksmuseum*

134c,d Two polychrome tiles, in imitation of porcelain, with different shaped flower-baskets in medallions; corner-design of hatched leaves, half-roses and leaves; muffle-kiln technique. *Woerden, G. de Goederen collection*

134e,f Two polychrome tiles showing ships in the open sea, in a double roundel; corner-design of flowers on a dark background; muffle-kiln technique. *Leeuwarden, Frisian Museum*

135   One of four polychrome tile pictures of a tall bouquet in an ornamental urn standing on a marble block, surrounded by birds and butterflies, with a peacock on the edge of the vase. To left and right of the base are a parrot on a perch and a cock. At the sides is a narrow border of tendrils and figures. *Château de Rambouillet near Paris*

136   Part of the reception-area and dining-room. Architectonic arrangement of panels with Ionic columns in manganese tiles, alternating with blue tiles depicting Biblical scenes in the panels. Design by François Cuvilliés. *Amalienburg pavilion in the grounds of Nymphenburg palace near Munich*

137a   Vase of flowers: originally a fireplace decoration of 12 by 8 blue tiles, showing a tall bouquet in an ornamental urn standing on a marble base and surrounded by birds and butterflies. To left and right of the base are a parrot on a perch and a cock. The border is of flower-tendrils and figures, at the top and sides. From the Sommelsdijk Orphanage. *Amsterdam, Rijksmuseum*

137b   Vase of flowers: 14 by 8 polychrome tiles, with a tall bouquet in an ornamental urn of blue Delftware with a panel on it depicting a woman sitting by a fountain. To left and right of the base are a parrot on a perch and a cock. *Copenhagen, National Museum*

138a   Vase of flowers: 13 by 7 polychrome tiles, with a tall bouquet in an orna-

320

mental urn of blue Delftware with a panel on which are depicted birds and plants. The urn stands on a marble base and is surrounded by birds and butterflies. To left and right of the base are a parrot on a perch and a cock. The border at the sides is half a tile broad, with a pattern of tendrils with, among them, nude figures: those at the top have baskets of fruit on their heads. *Amsterdam, Rijksmuseum, Isaac collection*

138b   Vase of flowers: 13 by 7 polychrome tiles, with a tall bouquet in an ornamental urn of blue Delftware with a scene of a park and fountain. Two smaller urns on square bases stand to either side. The border is composed of half-tiles, with a design of tendrils and birds. *Sèvres, Musée National de Céramique*

139a   Urn of flowers: 9 by 4 polychrome tiles, with a tall bouquet in an ornamental container on a pedestal, on either side of which are birds among tendrils. The base is flanked by exotic birds (English?). *London, Victoria and Albert Museum, Henry van den Bergh bequest*

139b   One of two flower-vase pictures of 8 by 4 polychrome tiles, with a tall bouquet in an ornamental vase with a decoration of birds and flowers, standing on a carved pedestal. Beside the pedestal and at the top of the picture are pairs of exotic birds (English?). *Veere, D. H. G. Bolten collection*

140a   Very large picture of 13 by 30 blue tiles, showing a couple dancing on a terrace to the music of a fiddler; onlookers to the right and left. *Lisbon, Cardoso collection*

140b   Very large picture of 13 by 33 blue tiles, showing a company at table on a similar terrace. The side of the house bears the date 1707. Ascribed to Willem van der Kloet. *Amsterdam, Rijksmuseum*

141   Very large picture of 13 by 8 blue tiles representing the Annunciation; four angels hovering in the clouds (see detail, ill. 142b). *Lisbon, M. Armando Coelho collection*

142a   Part of a tiled wall in the church showing scenes from the life of St. Teresa, after a South-Netherlands print of 1613. The dado shows putti disporting themselves with flowers. *Lisbon, church of Nossa Senhora da Conceiçao in the Carmelite convent*

142b   Signature: Willem van der Kloet fec. *Lisbon, M. Armando Coelho collection*

142c   Signature in a cartouche: J: van: Oort: A: Amst: fecit. *Lisbon, church of Nossa Senhora da Conceiçao in the Carmelite convent*

143   One of a series of eight pictures, each of 9 by 11 blue tiles; general view of the town and port of Middelburg; about 1715. From a print by Nicolaes Visscher or Hondius, 1609; ascribed to Cornelis Boumeester. *Saldanha palace at Junqueira, near Lisbon*

144a,b   Two polychrome blue tiles showing a vase of flowers, and a landscape in an octagon on a manganese background, with white fleurs-de-lis in the corners; probably manufactured by De Grieksche A. *San Fernando, private ownership*

144c   Set of 3 by 3 blue tiles with octagonal designs of flowers in a vase, landscapes and baskets of fruit on a manganese background, with white fleurs-de-lis in the corners; laid, with a border of tendrils, as part of an ordinary red-paved Andalusian floor. *San Fernando, originally Governor's house*

145   Detail of staircase, decorated with blue tiles as far as the domed roof; about 1765. *Nieborów palace near Warsaw*

146 Room next the staircase: the walls and ceiling are entirely covered in blue tiles. *Nieborów palace near Warsaw*

147a,b Part of the tiled room, covered with flower-vase pictures in medallions formed of plant tendrils. Between each row of these there are blue tiles representing in roundels a church, people greeting one another, riders, farms, windmills, signposts etc.; after 1750? *Wilanów palace near Warsaw*

148a,b The Bacchus and Diana rooms, restored and redecorated with tiles since the palace was burnt down in 1944. Those tiles that survived destruction are placed up near the ceiling; some have been retouched. *Lazienki palace, Warsaw*

149a–e Four blue tiles and a frieze, with examples of Dutch and non-Dutch tiles from the *Nieborów, Wilanów* and *Lazienki* palaces

150 Corner showing wall-decoration in a room of the palace: blue landscape tiles modelled on the original Dutch ones and manufactured by the Husarski tile-works at Cracow. *Lazienki palace*

151a Picture composed of 6 by 9 blue tiles: an incident at the battle of Waterloo with British cavalry in the foreground; after an engraving by F. A. Langendijk (1816?). *Dordrecht, Simon van Gijn Museum*

151b Fragment of a tiled wall showing the pattern of tendrils known as 'Jerusalem feathers' *(Jerusalemveeren)*, with a rosette formed by the corners of four tiles. White on a purple ground or blue on white, both with lustre glaze. *Utrecht, Central Museum*

151c Fragment of a tiled wall: three groups of four tiles in a foliage pattern with birds on the branches; white on purple. *Utrecht, Central Museum*

152 Tiled fireplace from a farm at Groede near IJzendijke in Dutch Flanders (see ill. 153a). The original tiled room has now been dismantled.

153a The tile decoration shown in ill. 152, relaid as a continuous scene in a blue marbled setting. The central picture shows British and Russian troops embarking for battle off Bergen-aan-Zee; on either side are military trophies and medallion portraits of the Duke of York and General Brune. The work is marked G.R. *Amsterdam, Willet-Holthuysen Museum*

153b Blue tile frieze from a series representing the wine harvest: a procession of ornamental cars with putti and children dancing and merry-making; signed Joost Thooft & Labouchere, Leon Senf, Auguste Le Comte, 1887. *Amsterdam, café-restaurant Die Poort van Cleve*

154a Picture composed of 2 by 3 large polychrome tiles: winter landscape. Young people are skating and curling at a bend in the frozen river leading past a farm. Beyond them a barge with hoisted sail is moored, and across the river is a windmill. *Utrecht, Westraven tile works*

154b Picture composed of 4 by 5 large polychrome tiles: *The Bend of the Heerengracht in Winter*; after the painting by C. Springer, 1882; made by H. Bottelier, painter at De Porceleyne Fles, 1883. *Amsterdam, W. J. Feltmann collection*

155a Large blue tile-picture (23 × 20 cm.) of the Chancery at Leeuwarden (1585), showing the Turfmarkt not yet filled in; about 1880. *Makkum, Tichelaar's Royal Porcelain and Tile Factory*

155b Large blue tile painting of Bolsward town hall (1615); about 1880. *Makkum, Tichelaar factory*

156a White tiled wall with *trompe-l'oeil* representation of a picture hanging by a cord from a rosette-headed nail: pastoral summer landscape with a treeless road in the centre and a distant view of Makkum; about 1845. *Makkum, Tichelaar factory*

156b Picture composed of 60 by 7 blue and manganese tiles: a seascape under a cloudy sky, with a key-pattern border (1776). The ship in the foreground is *De Snelle Jager*, after the engraving by A. van der Laan, while in the middle distance is one of the first paddle-steamers. The work is signed WJTZ (Willem Jan ten Zweege, tile-painter at Makkum); 1855. *Makkum, Tichelaar factory*

157a Indian-ink drawing of a peacock on a branch, with a border composed of lozenge shapes; signed below: *Jan R. Steensma 20/5 1914*. Copied from a wall painting in the home of the painter Christoffel Bisschop at Scheveningen. *Leeuwarden, Frisian Museum*

157b Painting composed of 13 by 5 blue tiles after a design by C. Bisshop, executed at Makkum by J. P. Tichelaar, 1914. *Leeuwarden, Frisian Museum*

158a,b Two tile paintings of trophies: fruit, floral garlands and game hang from ribbons; about 1965. *Makkum, Tichelaar factory*

158c One of a series of commissioned polychrome tiles with small Chinese figures and carefully copied ideographs; about 1965. *Makkum, Tichelaar factory*

158d Manganese tile representing a sea-horse, manufactured for the centenary of the Kingma Bank at Makkum, December 1969. *Makkum, Kingma Bank*

Sources of illustrations

Foto Abstede C.V., Utrecht 7b, 12a, 21a, 28e, 53a,b, 56, 64c – A.C.L., Brussel, 29b, 72a, 127 – Foto van den Berg, Amsterdam 16e, 17b, 21b, 28a,b,c, 32c,ds 43c,d, 44f, 46c, 51b,c,d, 53c, 55c, 60a,c, 70a,b – H. Boonstra, Amsterdam 66c, 102b, 103c – Jacques Buchholz, Paris 85c,d – Photo Clément Dessart, Angleur 84a,b – Foto A. Dingjan, The Hague 13a, 18b, 30, 32a, 73c – S. Everwijn, Amsterdam 106 – Bob Fleumer, Westzaan 110a – A. Frequin, The Hague 7c, 9b, 36, 47a,b,c, 51a, 82a, 115d, Pl. IV – M. Germann, Dordrecht 55b – W. v. d. Graaf, Alkmaar 46a – Fotobureau John Klaver, Rotterdam 2b,c, 3a,b, 5a, 8a,b,c, 9a, 11, 12c,d,e, 14b, 16f, 18a, 19a, 20b, 22e, 24a,b, 25, 26, 27, 29a, 31e, 33a,b, 35a, 39a,b,c,d, 40a, 42b, 44a,b,c, 46c,d, 54a, 58b,c, 61a,b, 62, 63, 67b, 70c, 83a,b, 94a, 95a,b, 97, 101c, 102c,d, 104, 107a,b, 114, 151a – Lepissier, Blois 75a,b,c,d,e,f – Lichtbeelden Instituut Amsterdam 111 – Photo Millet, Paris 79 – Oscar de Milliano, Suis 152, 153a – Franciszek Myszkowski, Warsaw 145 – Osinga Foto-ciné, Hoorn 21c, 38 – T. v. d. Reijken, Delft 77 – Fa Roosdorp, Deventer 14a - Schmölz & Huth Fotografen, Cologne 121 – Bozena Seredyńska, Warsaw 147a,b, 149a,b – A. Struiksma, Leeuwarden 3c,d, 23a, 81d,e, 93, 103b, 113, 115a,b, 116, 133b, 134e,f, 155a, 157b – P. J. Tichelaar, Makkum Pl. I, 92b, 99a,b, 100a,b,c, 101a, 108a, 155b, 156a,b, 158a,b,c,d, – Bob de Wit, Gouda Pl. II, Pl. III.

Fibula-van Dishoeck N.V. of Bussum provided blocks for the following: 122a, 123, 124, 125a,b, 130a,b, 131a,b.

List of museums and private collections

Achterberg collection	see Amstelveen
Alkmaar, H. B. J. Vlas	ill. 46a
Amalienburg pavilion	Plate vi; ills. 128, 130a, 131a, 136
Amstelveen, J. W. N. van Achterberg collection	ills. 8e,f, 9c, 10b,c, 13b,c,d, 16d, 17b, 21b, 22d, 28a,b,c, 32b,c,d, 58a, 70a,b
Amsterdam, W. J. Feltmann collection	ill. 154b
Amsterdam, D. W. F. Langelaan collection	ill. 106
Amsterdam, Die Poort van Cleve, café-restaurant	ill. 153b
Amsterdam, Rijksmuseum	Plate i; ills. 5b, 6a, 14c, 15, 20a, 41a,b, 42a, 59b, 69a,b,c, d,e,f, 73b,d, 76a, 87a, 103a, 110b, 117, 132, 133a, 134a,b, 137a, 138a, 140b
Amsterdam, Print Room of the Rijksmuseum	ill. 108b
Amsterdam, De Wildeman, wine and spirit merchants, formerly Levert & Co.	ills. 66c, 102b, 103c
Amsterdam, Willet Holthuysen Museum	ill. 153a
Anholt, near Ruinen (Drente)	ill. 110c
Apeldoorn, Jonkheer D. J. A. A. van Lawick van Pabst collection	ill. 49c
Apeldoorn, Het Loo palace	ills. 90a,b,c, 91a,b,c
Badenburg pavilion, Nymphenburg	ill. 120
Beauregard, castle near Cellettes, 5 miles from Blois	ills. 43a,b,e,f, 74, 75a,b,c,d,e,f
Bergambacht (South Holland), Bouwlust farm	ill. 114
De Bilt, Mejuffrouw M. A. H. van Es	ill. 51b
Bisschop collection	see Leeuwarden, Frisian Museum
Blois, Loir-et-Cher, France	see Beauregard

Index

Kloet, Willem Cornelisz. van der (Amsterdam) 62, 110, 111
Kocx of Delft, Adrianus 91, 124
Kocks, Pieter Adriaensz. (Delft) 91, 101
Kuyk, Michiel van (Delft) 102

Laen, Maeyke Jansdr. van der (Harlingen) 64
Leeuwen, Cornelis van (Delft and Harlingen) 63
Lier, Abraham Willemsz. van (Rotterdam) 56, 89 n.18
Loot, Ian (Utrecht) 81, 82
Lubbersz., Cornelis (Haarlem) 28

Noort, van *see* Oort
Nouts, Michiel (Antwerp and Delft) 30

Oort, Adriaen van (Amsterdam and Utrecht) 63, 120
Oort, Isaac van (Utrecht) 62, 123
Oort, Jan van (Amsterdam) 63, 111, 122
Overmeer, Jan Gerritsz. (Utrecht) 62
Oliviersz., Willem Jansz. *see* Verswaen

Peeters, Jan I 77
Piet, Simon Toenisz. van der (also Pijpe; Harlingen and Delft) 63
Pietersz., Egbert (Harlingen) 64, 76
Pietersz., Harmen (Haarlem and Delft) 25, 30
Pype, Simon Toenisz. van der, *see* Piet

Saen, Maria van der 32
Schut, Hendrick (Rotterdam) 56
Senf, Leon (Delft) 126
Smissen, Gijsbert van der (Rotterdam) 80
Sonneveldt, Cornelisz. Willemsz. (Rotterdam) 40
Spannenburg (Harlingen) 64

Swaen, Willem van der (Gouda) 19
Sybeda, Theunisz. Claes (Harlingen) 64

Thooft, Joost (Delft) 126
Tichelaar, P. J. (Makkum) 65, 66
Tjallingii, Frans (Harlingen) 64, 122
Traa, Willem van (Rotterdam) 121

Valckenhoff *see* Harmensz. Pieter
Verburgh, Jan (Delft) 101
Verhaast, Gijsbrecht Claesz. (Delft) 59, 99, 100
Verstraeten, Willem Jansz. (Haarlem) 37, 64
Verswaen, Willem Jansz. Oliviersz. (Gouda) 32
Verwer, Abraham 50
Verwijk, Laurens (Rotterdam) 121
Victorsz., Louwijs (Delft) 101
Vierleger, Hans Barnaert (Antwerp and Haarlem) 28
Visseer, Hendrick (Delft) 102
Vizeer, Pieter (Hendrick Visseer? *q.v.*) 59
Vogel, Jan Lourisz. de (Hoorn) 34
Vroom, Cornelis (Haarlem) 27
Vroom, Hendrick (Haarlem) 27

Waelpot, Pieter (Delft) 67 n.6
Weert, Nicolaes de (Delft) 91
Wolk, Johan van der (Rotterdam) 87
Wijtmans, Claes Jansz. (Rotterdam and Utrecht) 21, 25, 61-2, 63, 122
Wijtmans, Jacob Claesz. (Gorinchem) 21, 61

Zweege, Willem Jan van or Jacobus ten (Makkum) 80, 128

Locations, Tile factories and subjects

Amalienburg *see* Munich

334

336